AF540734

NEW HORIZON IN RURAL DEVELOPMENT

By

Dr. S.N. Tripathy

D.litt.

Professor of Economics
Mahatma Gandhi Labour Institute
Ahmedabad - 380 052
(India)

DISCOVERY PUBLISHING HOUSE PVT. LTD.
NEW DELHI-110 002

First Published-2008

ISBN 978-81-8356-328-4

© Author

Published by:

DISCOVERY PUBLISHING HOUSE PVT. LTD.

4831/24, Ansari Road, Prahlad Street,
Darya Ganj, New Delhi-110 002 (India)
Phone: 23279245 • Fax: 91-11-23253475
E-mail: dphbooks@radiffmail.com
dphtemp@indiatimes.com
Website: www.discoverypublishinghouse.com

Printed at:
Arora Enterprises
Laxmi Nagar, Delhi–110 092

Dedicated to

Late Deepak Bishoyi

economic conditions. Appropriate technologies with their enormous potentialities in enhancing the productivity of agriculture-based enterprises would help in creating employment opportunities. But over the years there has been decline in village industries on the wake of globalization and strong competitions at global level has made it a great problem for their survival and continuation. Given the predominance of the agricultural Sector in the national economy in terms of employment, a meaningful employment strategy for rural India should accord high priority to the development of agriculture and allied rural sectors. Rapid agricultural growth generally triggers a higher growth in output and employment in non-farm sectors. In India, the emergence of numerous growth poles, including corridors of development along highways, and above all, public expenditure on antipoverty and other rural development programmes and on rural infrastructure have been playing instrumental role in increasing output and employment in non-farm sectors.

However, agricultural growth ought to act as an important engine of growth for other sectors of the economy, especially in rural areas. Thus, for rural employment a policy packages should be aimed at: *(a)* Accelerating the rates of sectoral and national economic growth, *(b)* Reversing the trend of deceleration of agricultural growth and public investment in agriculture, *(c)* Promotional policies for labour intensive and higher income generating allied agriculture and non-agricultural activities in rural areas for domestic markets, and *(d)* Diversification of agriculture towards hitherto neglected dry land areas in central and eastern regions are highly imperatives in order to boosting up agricultural production and rural employment and finally, assaulting on rural poverty. The concept of National Rural Employment Guarantee Act (NREGA) is a major initiative of Government of India towards poverty reduction and income generation among rural poor families. In rural India, one major problem is of seasonal employment, i.e. a large number of people have to face lack of employment during certain times of the year.

Because of this, many communities in the dry and drought prone areas have to migrate seasonally to other parts of the country in search of work. This annual migration is a painful and disruptive process. Those who are left behind also do not have enough to eat or the barest money for other basic necessities and although there may be no famine. Thus, there has been definitely a slow malnutrition and starvation. Even when communities do not migrate they suffer a great amount of distress at such times. Their food intake is reduced, the children are withdrawn from schools, they go into debt and they are unable to attend to their health problems. At such times the need for a safety net is felt and NREGA is a very good protection for this problem. It is most necessary to promote organizing so that people can have a formal framework of accessing resources and schemes. Thus, they have a voice to decide where and how resources are to be allocated. NREGA, also by giving a right, helps people to organize themselves and to come together to represent a view.

Given the present set of provisions under the Bill and the implementation framework, it will be difficult to create sustainable and full employment. Full employment will be questionable because the Bill addresses unskilled labor only; and leaves behind skilled and semi-skilled operations in which a large number of rural poor are engaged. Sustainability will be difficult because the Bill considers unskilled operations that do not have year—round demand and the volume is dependent on activities that call for unskilled labour.

Unskilled work of earth digging does not generate enough work for 100 days. The Act sees employment only as unskilled labour, and that too digging, loading and unloading and carrying mud and stones. However, most of workers in the rural areas do have skills by which they earn their livelihoods. In our opinion, the Act should include the skilled work so that the employment generated is not only temporary for the 100 days but could become more long lasting.

The local vigilance group should be formed for one panchayat rather for each village. They should have a formal recognition by the panchayat body. The first step in this direction is to have a base line survey identifying the BPL families. It should not be a rigorous survey rather it should involve minimum information about the number of individuals, income from various sources and the property under his/her possession. Such information should be available to the vigilance groups. If the basic information can be displayed in local language in some common places of the village such as youth club or any other common places that would produce tremendous result. The role of community groups through vigilance is very much essential to the implementation of schemes under the NREGA, right from the beginning, to ensure that the provisions made under the Act are implemented in the right sense and equity and justice are ensured in every phase of its implementation. For example, apart from the role of PRIs and government monitoring mechanisms, it would be useful if local vigilance groups involved in livelihoods/employment (community organizations and NGOs) could survey wages, works done in their area etc. and build a compendium of sorts over a period of time. This could yield interesting information provided, wages actually received are checked out by the groups and reported. This is because while everyone knows full wages are not always paid and they differ immensely through seasons and regions. Moreover, there appears to be no systematic effort to document the difference or discrimination in wages and share the data.

The employment guarantee act, if effectively implemented would raise the purchasing power of the rural poor. This would lower the burden of food subsidies. It needs to be noted that the implementation of employment generation Programme in the part has suffered from many flaws including the high incidence of leakages. As there are many irregularities it has been suggested that the only meaningful employment guarantee scheme would be one, which is not targeted, but is universal and demand driven.

What the rural poor need is not merely a guarantee of 100 days of work in year but uninterrupted employment for most part of the year. Implementation is to be decentralized; control vested in local communities and Gram Sabhas. Transparency and accountability are to be ensured through in-built mechanisms for monitoring and social audit. The work projects should be entrusted to the panchayats. Studies show that panchayat control increases participation, transparency and accountability.

In the light of the above analysis the present work "New Dimension in Rural Development" is an attempt to through light on various dimensions in the sphere of economic development through the writings of 16 papers by eminent scholars in the field. The editor expresses his thanks to all the paper contributors whose papers have enriched the work. Certainly, the present work will be of immense benefit to the policy-makers, planners, researchers and general readers.

Dr. S.N. Tripathy

Contents

1

Panchayat Finance
A Study in Orissa

*Dr. S.N. Tripathy**
*Sri Premananda Pradhan***

Orissa is situated in the east coastal region of the country. Its geographical area is almost 4.74 per cent of India and its population is 36.7 million (2001 census), about 3.57 per cent of India's population. Orissa is one of the poorest states of the country. Compared to coastal region, the incidence of poverty is more acute in southern and northern regions of the state. It is higher among the scheduled tribes (about 23% of the total population), than scheduled castes and general castes. The rural families below the poverty line constitute 66.37 per cent (as per the estimates of Panchayati Raj Department, Government of Orissa, 1997).

In terms of development indicators, like literacy rate, infant mortality rate, per capita income etc. the living conditions of the people at the state are considerably lower than the national average. Dependence of population on primary sector occupations is significantly high. There has been little occupational diversification of population at the village level. Welfare programmes and minimum needs

* Professor, Mahatma Gandhi Labour Institute, Ahmedabad.
** Research Scholar, Lecturer in Economics Science College, Konkarada, Ganjam.

programme implemented by the state under social sector development to eradicate poverty and improve the living condition of poor people are far from satisfactory.

In the light of the aforesaid background, this paper examines the various aspects relating to Panchayat Finance in Orissa.

Orissa is one of the least unbanased states in India. According to 2001 census, around 87 per cent of the state's population live in 50,972 census/revenue villages. The highest incidence of poverty in Orissa is mainly because of the unequal distribution of the rural assets and under development of agricultural economy.

Development in order to be sustainable needs to be in tune with the felt needs and aspirations of the people. The ultimate aim is to remove rural poverty and ameliorate the socio-economic condition of the rural poor, through participatory development process. This can be possible only if the individual and the community become the focal point of development. No such development is possible without bestowing real decision-making power on the community. Such empowerment has to be an essential component in our planning and implementation of the programmes of the ministry, a predominant role for panchayati Raj Institutions has been envisaged.

Provisions made in the Panchayati Raj Act

There are 6234 Gram Panchayats, 314 Panchayat Samities and 30 Zila Parishads in Orissa. Constitution 73rd Amendment Act, 1992 was with a view to revitalizing the Panchayat Raj Institutions and enable people at the grass-roots level to effectively participate in the development process. Provisions for the panchayats (extension to scheduled area) Act, 1996 (PESA) came into force in the year 1996.

The important features of the Act are:

(i) A 3 tire system of Panchayati Raj for all states having population of 20 lakhs;

- *(ii)* Panchayat elections to be regularly held every 5 years;
- *(iii)* Reservation of seats for scheduled castes, scheduled tribes and women (not less than one-third of seats);
- *(iv)* Appointment of state Finance Commission to make recommendations as regards the financial powers of the Panchayats;
- *(v)* Constitution of district Planning Committees to prepare development plans for the district as a whole e and Gram Sabha at the village level.

The Panchayati Raj Institutions have been empowered and authorized to function as institutions of Self-Government. Powers have also been conferred on Panchayats with regard to *(i)* the preparation of plans for economic development and social justice and *(ii)* the implementation of such schemes as may be entrusted to them.

As per Article 243 H of the Constitution, state legislatures have been empowered to enact laws:

- *(i)* To authorize a Panchayats to levy, collect and appropriate some taxes, duties, tolls and fees;
- *(ii)* To assign the Panchayats, some taxes, duties, tolls levied and collected by the state Government;
- *(iii)* To provide for making grant-in-aid to the Panchayats from the consolidated funds of the state; and
- *(iv)* To provide for constitution of such funds for Panchayats for crediting all money received by or on behalf of Panchayats and also the withdrawal of such money there from.

The Institution of Gram Sabha is vital for the efficient functioning of Panchayati Raj Institutions. The Ministry of Panchayati Raj has exhorted the Sarpanchs to monitor and review the progress of the different schemes.

A four-pronged strategy has been adopted to make the rural community. This includes:

(i) Enhancing the level of awareness about the schemes;

(ii) Promoting transparency in the implementation of the programmes;

(iii) Encouraging people's participation; and

(iv) Ensuring accountability through social audit.

It is obvious from the analysis that in order to ensure that Panchayati Raj Institutions (PRIs) function as instruments of local government, it is significant that their functional and financial autonomy is guaranted.

Panchayats being closer to the people, their right to information and accessibility to the panchayats must be ensured.

Finance of the Panchayats in Orissa

In Orissa, the Panchayat Samities and Zila Parishads do not have any taxation power. It is the Gram Panchayats, which are empowered to levy taxes. The resource base in panchayats in Orissa is extremely poor. At present, the Panchayats are levying tax on vehicle, latrine, street light and drainage. Gram Panchayats also derive income from lease of properties like tanks, markets and ferry ghats. The collection of tax revenue is of the order of Rs. 3.00 crore to Rs. 5.00 crore per annum and that of non-tax revenue is of the order of Rs. 7.00 crore. The break up of Gram Panchayats income range-wise is depicted in Table 1.1.

Table 1.1: Income-Range Wise Distribution of Gram Panchayats in Orissa

Income Range	*Number of GPs in the income range*
Below Rs. 10,000/-	3661
Above Rs. 10,000/-, but less than Rs. 20,000	757
Rs. 20,000/- and above	1816
Total	6234

Source: Memorandum to 12th Fin[illegible] Commission, Government of Orissa.

The assigned revenue varies form Rs. 30 crore to Rs. 35 crore. In addition, State Government bears the establishment cost to the tune of Rs. 100 crore per annum on the average.

The financial position of the Gram Panchayats is so precarious that none of the GPs is able to provide matching share for the purpose of utilizing of tenth finance commission award. In fact, State Government had to bear matching contribution to the detente of Rs. 167.50 crore for the period from 1995-96 to 1999-2000 in order to utilize the, total Local Body Grant of Rs. 200.99 crore recommended by 10th Finance Commission in favour of the PRIs for Orissa. The Eleventh Finance Commissions have recommended Rs. 346.60 crore towards maintenance of civic service. Matching contribution at the rate of 25 per cent of the grant recommended by the Eleventh Finance Commission comes to Rs. 86.40 crore. The state government is required to provide the amount in favor of the Rural Local Bodies. Out of this Rs. 46.82 crore (2001-02 Rs. 8.50 crore. and 2002-03 Rs. 38.32 crore.) have so far been distributed among the rural local bodies.

In view of the deplorable financial position of the panchayats the following submissions were made.

Matching Share not to be Insisted

An obligation has been imposed by the earlier Finance Commissions on the State Government to meet a share in the grant given by the Central Government to the Local Bodies. Firstly, the obligation of the Finance Commission is to recommend measures to augment the Consolidated Fund of the States in supporting their local bodies. Thus, whatever support is given by the Central Government as per the recommendation should primarily come to the States and should become a part of the support that they give to their Panchayati Raj.

Secondly, the State's matching contribution should be viewed vis-a-vis the overall fiscal situation of the States. In the context it may be pointed out that the debt over hang is the greatest problem for Orissa. The debt servicing liabilities is nearly 120 per cent of the State's own revenue and about 52 per cent of the State's total revenue. In most of the days, the State Government account is in overdraft. In 2001-02 out of 365 days. The State Government account was in ways and means limit for 107 days and overdraft for 257 days. In 2002-03, the State Government account was in ways and means for 169 days and in overdraft for 189 days. Because of unsustainable debt burden and rising expenditure on pension and salary, the gap in Non-Plan account is of the order of Rs. 3300.00 crore. In order to have a plan size of Rs. 3200.00 crore, the State Government is required to raise resources to the extent of Rs. 65.000 crore and out of this Rs. 6500.00 crore; the loan component is more than Rs. 4500.00 crore. Under such precarious financial condition, it is not possible to make any substantial release in favour of the Panchayats and Municipalities. The recommendation of the 10th and 11th Finance Commissions providing matching share by the Local Bodies have cast an additional burden on the State exchequer. It is, therefore, suggested that there should be no utilization of the grant to be recommended by the 12th Finance Commission.

Maintenance of Capital Assets

A large number of buildings, roads, water bodies and other community assets are being created with the fund released under different rural development and anti-poverty programme.. But there is no money either with State Government or Panchayats for maintenance of these important assets.

For maintenance of these assets the requirement of fund is quite essential. Eleventh Finance Commission did not grant any fund for maintenance of assets. It is necessary to maintain Panchayat Samiti roads and Grama Panchayat roads. There are 20373.19 kms of approved Panchayat Samiti road and 139973.19 kms of approved G.P. roads in the State. Break of road is given in Table 1.2.

Table 1.2: Panchayat Samiti and Gram Panchayat road in Orissa

Sl.No.	*Panchayat Samiti*	*Gram Panchayat*	
1.	Black Top Road	3,000 kms	Nil
2.	Metal Road	4,000 kms	14,000 kms
3.	Moorum Base Road	6,000 kms	42,000 kms
4.	Earthern Road	7,373 kms	83,973 kms

To begin with, the 12th Finance Commission is to provide Rs. 1000.00 crore towards maintenance of the buildings, roads and other works or capital nature.

Grama Panchayat Office Buildings

Out of 6234 Grama Panchayats in the State, 1114 Gram Panchayats have no buildings. Break up of existing buildings is given in Table 1.3.

Table 1.3: Room-wise Distribution of Gram Panchayat Office Building in Orissa

One room building	2500
Two room building	2000
Three room building	620
No building	1114

Capacity Building

Election to the PRIs was held during February-March 2002. All total 1,00,862 representatives have been elected out of which 23,748 belong to ST and 14,354 belong to SC, the details of which given in Table 1.4.

Among the newly elected representatives quite large number of them belong to ST, SC, OBC and women category. They need training to make them aware of their responsibilities and powers.

Special Provision for PESA

While releasing grants to PRIs, Eleventh Finance Commission have allotted funds to Gram Panchayats for

Table 1.4: Elected Representatives in PRIs

		Total	*Out of which ST*	*Out of which ST*
Zela	President	30	-	-
parishad	Vice-president	30	-	-
	ZP Members	794	205	152
Panchayat	Chairman	314	1672	1009
Samiti	Vice-chairman	314		
	PS members	5599		
Grama	Sarpanch	6234	21871	14354
Panchayat	Naib-sarpanches	6234		
	Ward Members	81313		
Total		100862	23748	14354

Source: As shown in Table 1.1.

providing basic services viz. primary Health, Primary Education, Safe drinking water, Street light and sanitation including maintenance of other common properties resources.

Eleventh Finance Commission have not taken into consideration implementation of provisions Panchayats (Extension to Scheduled Areas) Act, 1996. PESA has got greater implication for implication for Orissa because 22 per cent of total population belongs to Scheduled Tribe. Out of 314 Panchayat Samitis, 118 (intermediate level of panchayat) Samitis are situated in scheduled areas. 1931 Gram Panchayats out of 6234 Gram Panchayats are situated in Scheduled Areas.

PESA envisages that PRIs will strive to improve the quality of lives of the Scheduled Tribe people in scheduled areas. Therefore, special Grant-in-Aid should be provided to Panchayat Raj Institutions in the Scheduled areas of Orissa taking into consideration the constitution of Panchayat Raj Institutions as per PESA.

Considering the disparity in standard of living of tribal people living in scheduled areas priority should be given to provide them the basic requirement of life.

Strengthening the Accounting of Panchayats

States have been making continuous efforts to empower their local bodies in raising their own resources and improving the tax effort. However, there is need for legislation of Local Fund Fiscal Responsibility Act that makes it, mandatory for the Local Fund Authorities to have a Medium Term Financial Programme, Budget, Account Statement and Audit.

It is noteworthy that the 11th Finance Commission had provided Rs. 4.33 crore for maintenance of accounts of village level panchayats. Further Eleventh Finance Commission had also provided Rs. 4.47 crore for creation of database relating to finance of Rural Local Bodies.

Basic Services

11th Finance Commission had provided Rs. 345.59 crore to Orissa State for Rural Local Bodies for providing basic

Table 1.5: Requirement of Funds by Rural Local Bodies in Orissa

Rs. in crore

Sl.No.	*Description*	*Amount*
1.	Maintenance of Capital Asset	1000.00
2.	Gram Panchayat Office Buildings	33.42
3.	E-Governance in Panchayati Raj Institutions	70.94
4.	Capacity Building	9.00
5.	Special provision for PESA	590.00
6.	Strengthening the Accounting Staff	10.00
7.	Basic Service	1000.00
	Total	2713.36

Sources: As shown in Table 1.5.

services viz. Primary Health, Primary Education, Safe drinking water, Streetlight and sanitation including maintenance of common properties.

A memorandum to 12th Finance Commission was submitted in which Rs. 2713.36 crore has been sought for the developing of rural local bodies.

Urban Local Bodies (ULBs)

The Eleventh Finance Commission (EFC) has recommended grants amounting to Rs. 39.96 crore payable during the period from 2000 to 2005 in favour of Urban Local Bodies of the State. The main objectives of utilization of the above grants are that, they should be utilized towards maintenance of Civic Services which include provision of Primary Education, Primary Health Care; Safe Drinking Water, Street lighting, Sanitation including drainage and scavenging facilities, maintenance of cremation and burial grounds, public conveniences and other common property resources. Out of Rs. 39.96 crore, Rs. 8.14 lakh was earmarked for development of Database relating to the finances of the Urban Local Bodies.

Solid Waste Management in Urban Local Bodies

Around 54,96,318 people out of total population of 3,67,06,920 live in 103 ULBs of the state and this constitutes 14.97 per cent compared to All India Average of 27.78 per cent. Absences of Solid Waste Management System and drainage system in the urban areas have led to pollution of major river systems and cities of the State. The problem may aggravate in coming days, unless timely actions are mounted in providing Solid Waste Management System and Comprehensive Drainage System in each ULB.

Solid Waste Management, though an obligatory function of Urban Local Bodies, the service is poorly performed resulting in problems of health, sanitation and environmental degradation. With the growth in urban population and the rapid pace in urbanizations the situation is becoming more and more critical. Thus there is need to formulate environment management strategies for cities in well adequate institutional arrangements.

The urban areas do not have the system of primary collection of waste from the source of waste generation. The weast is therefore discharged/thrown on the streets/open spaces/water bodies etc. the waste collected by the sweepers in varying degrees is then to the waste storage depot, popularly known as dustbins, where the waste is deposited in open spaces or in unscientifically designed/constructed dustbins posing a serious threat to health to health and environment. Trucks to open dump yards where it is disposed off most unscientifically and unhygenically. This result in environmental degradation and contamination of land and subsoil water resources.

The entire system of solid waste management, therefore needs to be designed scientifically in terms of the recommendations the Supreme Court Committee and Municipal Solid Waste (Management and Handling) Rules, 2000.

All these requirements cause acute financial pressure and hence, there is a need to evolve viable policy for mitigating financial crisis. The leakages of investible funds, their misappropriation and corruption must be controlled to reduce the pressure for rural finance. Government can only function as a facilitator and catalyst for sustainable development in rural areas and therefore, through literacy and education, development of skill and income generating activities people should co-operate themselves for their progress and prosperity.

REFERENCES

1. Annual Report, 2001-02, Government of India, Ministry of Rural Development.
2. Orissa Development Report, Planning Commission, Government of India, New Delhi, 2002.
3. Memorandum to 12th Finance Commission, Government of Orissa, 2004.

2

Forest

Forest Resources and Environment

*Dr. Prafulla Chandra Mohanty**

Forests are the important resources of a country. It is counted as the one of the valuables of the nation. Forest creates environment and environment creates climate. So both are interdependent. Forest boosts the economy in many respects. It directly effects the environment, the climate and observes lot of wastes and allows the living species in good and comfortable health. Forests produce a lot of products which add to our economical status, It habitats wildlife, medicinal plants etc. In some countries, forests became the backbone of their economies. "Forests are close formation of trees growing together at one place". It is very important for the national economy of any country of the world. Like the farms it provides raw materials to some specific industries dealing with the manufacturing of rubber, paper, artificial textiles, medicines, etc. It is marked that the economy of some countries like Norway, Sweden, Canada, Finland, USSR etc. largely depends on their forest resources. So, forestry has started to develop as a special branch in almost all the countries of the world and the countries having deficiency in forests are trying to develop it artificially. A total of 7485

* Dr. Prafulla Chandra Mohanty is Working as a Sr. Faculty Member in College at Aska Science College, Aska-761111, Ganjam, Orissa.

million acres of land are covered by forests in the world, out of this 2090 million acres are in Asia, 774 millions acres are in Europe, 797 million acres are in Africa, 2092 million acres are in South America, 1449 million acres are in North America and 283 million acres are in Australia. Thus 28 per cent of the total forest area of the world is in Asia 10 per cent is in Europe, 111 is in Africa, 28 per cent is in South America, 19 per cent is in North America only a 4 per cent is in Australia.

India has a vast forest area. Out of its total area of 32.80 lakh square kilometres, 7.53 lakh sq metre of land is covered by forests. Thus the total forest area is about 23 per cent of the total area. Now it is reduced to 22.1 per cent by 2000 AD) of the country. This forest area is classified as of 83 per cent accessible and 17 per cent as of inaccessible, The forests of Assam, Karnataka, Orissa, West Bengal, Bihar, UP, Madhya Pradesh and Andhra Pradesh etc. are of accessible nature and of Himachal Pradesh, Arunachal Pradesh and Jammu and Kashmir have been still remaining in inaccessible for the human beings. On the basis of ownership, 96 per cent of the total forest area belongs to State Governments and the rest 4 per cent belong to corporated bodies and private individuals.

Forest is not merely an ancillary activity to agriculture. Forests occupy an important position in the economy of a country. In India, where forestry is a less important primary activity, its contribution to net national product is around 1.0 per cent. It provides direct employment to more than 1 lakh persons and another 3 lakh persons are of in partly employment, forest is the source of fodder for about 3 crore cattle. Industrial and fuel wood is the main forest product. Fuel wood still remains the main source of energy for consumption in rural areas. Apart from providing industrial wood for wood based industries, forests are also a source of a number of minor products like bamboo, canes, grasses, kendu leaves, lac, resins, medicinal plants, gums, tanning materials, dyes, essential oils, fatty oils and fat etc. The demand for some of these minor forest products exists in foreign markets and if their output is stepped up, they can prove to be valuable foreign exchange earners. Forests also confer a variety of ecological benefits. They moderate the climate of the region and reduce the extremes of the temperature, presence of forest in a region increases humidity in air, and reduces the uncertainty element in rainfall. Trees such a lot of water during rains which raises the underground water level. Forests also prevent soil erosion because they check flow of water. Forests reduce the intensity of floods, as they regulate the supply of water in steeams and reservoirs. Again water flowing through forests carries with it highly fertile soil, which is left behind in agricultural fields raises their fertility. In substance, forests have an immense environmental value. Their indiscriminate destruction in any country can disturb the ecological balance and play havoc with the economic life of the country, in this context a paper is made to study the importance of forests and the sizes of forests in the nation as well as in the State of Orissa, its different uses and abuses (deforestation). The paper also tries to highlight on the Statewise distribution of forests in India, Geographical Distributions, Different Forest products, it's effect on bio-diversity and on some of the deforestation statistics. Towards the end it narrates different problems and comments with a conclusion.

Forests have a many faced ecological role to play which affects human life directly. They create the dangers of cloud drifting, soil erosion, floods, wind erosion, and groundwater evaporation. They also protect a wide variety of flora and fauna, provide recreation, and can effectively control air pollution of moderate magnitude. Thus importance of forests for the benefit of mankind as well as for other forms of life cannot be overemphasized.

India's population has risen from 370 million in 1947 to 1100 million in 2006, constituting more than 18 per cent of the world population. India also has 15 per cent of World's livestock, but only 2 per cent of the geographical area, 1 per cent of forest area, and 0.5 per cent of pasture lands. Per capita availability of forest in India is 0.07 hactres by the year 2000 A.D. as per Government of India Survey, which is much lower than the world average of 0.8 ha. India has a forest area of 64 million ha, which constitutes only 19.5 per cent of the total land area at present as against 33 per cent of National Forest Policy of 1988. Closed type of forest having forest cover density of 40 per cent or more is approximately only 11 per cent of the country's total land area. The average annual production of wood per hactre is 0.7 m^3 (cubic metre) as compared to the world average of 2.1 m^3. It has been estimated that about 157 million tones of firewood are required for fuel every year by the rural population, whereas production is only 58 million tones (Government of India 1993). The remaining demand is met by illegal cutting and encroachment of the forest. Though there are some trends in the area of an improvement in the quality of forest, there is still need have massive reforestation programmes, control over hacking and grazing and provision of cheap fuel through alternative tocologies such as Solar Power or biogas plants, more kerosene and LPGs should be made available to save the forest from deforestation.

Soil is the non-renewable natural resource which supports practically all terrestrial plant life and consequently human life. About 130 million hactare of land (45 per cent of the geographical area) is affected by serious soil erosion through ravine and gully, shifting, cultivation, cultivated waste lands, sandy areas, deserts and waterlogging. This results in soil degradation. Under favourable conditions in India, it takes almost a thousand years to form only 2.3 cm of soil layer from wheathered rocks. It is reported that the loss of one mm of cultivated soil could cost 10 kg of nitrogen and 2 kg of phosphorus.

India has a rich heritage of species and genetic strains of flora and fauna. Overall 8 per cent of world species are found in India, it is estimated that India is tenth among the plant rich countries of the world, eleventh in terms of number of endemic species of higher vertebrates and sixth among the centres of diversity and origin of agribiodiversity. The total number of living species identified in India so far as 2,00,000. Out of the total twelve biodiversity hot spots in the world, India has two one in the north east region and other is the Western Ghat Region.

But as the forests are becoming hare, many of these are fast becoming extinct or coming to the verge of extinction. These species and varieties provide a challenge to geneticists, animal behaviourists, botanists, zoologists, economists and many others who have a lot to learn about and from them, About 1143 animals comprising 71 species of mamals, 88 species of birds and 5 species of reptiles as rare and endangered wild animals. Similarly, many plant species, which have forests as their sustaining source, are also disappearing rapidly. To preserve them, special bioreserves should be created.

India's environment is drastically attacked and destroyed in the past 50 years of time by the process of deforestation. According to FAO, India was supposed to have last 3.4 million hac. of forest land between 1950 to 1972 alone. During the period over 70 per cent of forest area was last due to agriculture and other 17 per cent was last to river valley projects, industries, roads and communications. Till today the process of deforestation has continued at the current annual rate of 1.3 to 1.5 million hac. A recent report (International Union for the Conservation of Nature and Natural Resources, IUCN) mentions that India has last 2.5 million hactare of mangrove forests in this century alone. It has been estimated that inorder to maintain the balance at least 10 million hactare of degraded land need to be brought under forest for per annum,

The forest ecosystem in Orissa is depleting at a much faster rate than it being remedied by taking of plantation. The impact of various sectors of denudation have brought in a change in the traditional system of management of the forests as well as other natural resources like land, water, etc. This is happening at a time when the whole social fabric is under severe strain because of ignorant, poverty, unemployment, underemployment and unproductive employment, particularly of the rural poor in forest areas. The recorded of forest area of Orissa has and around undergone following changes with the passages of time.

Table 2.1: Forest Area of Orissa

Year	Area in Sq.km
1970-71	72,800 sq.km.
1977-78	67,675 sq.km.
1980-81	59,693 sq.km.
1984-85	59,555 sq.km.
1988-89	57, 183,57 sq.km.
1995-96	56,059,52 sq.km.
2005-06	50,000 sq.km. (Projectd)

Forest Problems

The biggest problem of the Indian forests is the inadequate and fast dwindling forest cover. It has already been mentioned that forests cover only 23.43 per cent of the area against the required coverage of 33 per cent. Even this small percentage of forest cover is seriously threatened by the increasing demand for major and minor forest products. These products are badly needed for fuel, building and to feed a large number of forest based industries. Vast forest tracts have been cleared for agriculture. Shifting agriculture in different parts of the country has played havoc with forests. Overgrazing is a big factor which is responsible or serious damage to forests. India possesses a livestock population of over 412 million of which 270 million are bovine animals, about one-tenth of which graze in the forests. Whenever forests are easily accessible, the livestock entirely depends on grazing in them.

The forests are thick, inaccessible, slow growing and lack in gregarious stands in many parts of the country. Some of them are very thin and comprise only of thorny bushes. These factors make their utilization uneconomical because there is good deal of wastage and it makes very expensive in spite of the cheap labour available in India.

One of the biggest problems faced by the Indian forests is the lack of proper transport facilities. About 16 per cent of the forest land in India is inaccessible and does not have proper transport facilities. It must be remembered that the major product of the forests is timber which is a cheap and bulky commodity. As such it cannot afford high freight charged by the railways and roadways. Therefore, they cannot be economically exploited without the availability of cheap and efficient transport facilities. Unfortunately, in India, the railways serve thickly populated areas only and are not of much use to forests. All weather roads in the forest areas are badly lacking. Water transport has only limited scope. Considering these facts we can easily say that transport with reference to forests is inadequate in India. Large tracts of vegetal cover are destroyed every year by forest fires. Forest fires in India are most destructive in dry season. Insufficiency of properly trained personnel is also a big handicap,

Conclusion

Forests give life to leaving beings. In order to carry on a leaving society in the leaving world, it is required to stay with plants, If this rate of dangerous deforestation. Global warning etc. will continue the living society will in no time collapse. So it is highly essential to protect forests:

ANNEXURES

Table 2.2: Estimates of Wastelands in India (Lakh Hectares)*
Forest and Non-Forest Degraded Areas

States	*Non-Forest degraded Area*	*Rank*	*Forest degraded Area*	*Rank*	*Total*	*Rank*
Andhra Pradesh	76.8	5	37.3	2	114.2	4
Assam	9.3		7.9		17.3	
Bihar	39.0	8	15.6	8	54.6	8
Gujarat	78.4	4	6.8		78.4	6
Haryana	24.0		0.7		24.8	
Himachal Pradesh	14.2		5.3		19.6	
Jammu & Kashmir	5.3		10.3		15.7	
Karnataka	71.2	6	20,4	6	91.6	
Kerala	10.5		2.3		12.8	
Madhya Pradesh	129.5	2	72.0	1	201.4	1
Maharashtra	115.6	3	28.4	4	144.0	3
Manipur	0.1		14.2	10	14.4	
Meghalaya	8.1		11.0		19.2	
Nagaland	5.1		8.8		13.9	
Orissa	31.6	10	32.3	3	63.9	7
Punjab	11.5		0.8		12.3	
Rajasthan	180.0	1	19.3	7	199.3	2
Sikkim	1.3		1.5		2.8	
Tamil Nadu	34.0	9	10,1		44.0	9
Tripura	1.1		8.6		9.7	
Uttar Pradesh	66.3	7	14.3	9	80.6	5
West Bengal	22.0		3.6		25.4	
Union Territory	8.9		27.1	5	36.0	10
Total	937.0		358.9		1295.7	

* Includes wasteland due to natural causes and desert areas of Rajasthan.

Source: Government of India (1989), Developing India's Wastelands, Ministry of Environment and Forests, New Delhi.

Table 2.3: Forest Area Lost (Between 1951 and 1972)

Purpose	*Area in thousand hectares*
River Valley Projects	401
Agricultural Purposes	2,433
Roads and communications	55
Establishment of Industries	125
Miscellaneous	388
Total Forest Area last	3,402

Source: Forest Resources of Tropical Asia FAO, 1981.

Table 2.4: Deforestation and Problems of Soil Erosion and Land Degradation

Sl.No.	*Problems*	*Million Hectares*
1.	Total Geographical Area	329
2.	Area in Water and wind erosion	144
3.	Area in special problems ravines salinity, waterlogging etc.	30
4.	Shifting, cultivation	5
5.	Avg. Area Annual Floods	8
6.	Cropped Areas on floods	4
7.	Total Drought prone area	260

Source: Indian Agricultural in brief, 27th ed., 2000.

Table 2.5: Type of Forest and its Effect on Rainfall

Sl.No.	*Type of Forest*	*Rainfall*
1.	Ever Green Forests (Tropical)	200-300 cm
2.	Deciduous Forests (Monsoon forest)	150-200 cm
3.	Dry forests (Rajasthan, Punjab)	75-100 cm
4.	Hill forests (Hill Area)	
5.	Tidal forests (Mangrove), Ganga, Mahanadi, Godavari and in Coastal planes.	

Source: The Pearson General Knowledge Manual, 2004, pp. 3, 138-39.

Table 2.6: Forests in India's Land Classifications (%)

Sl.No.	*Land Area*	*Percentage*
1.	Net Area sown	46.1
2.	Covered by forests	22 .1
3.	Not available for cultivation	13.4
4.	Follow land	8.3
5.	Other uncultivated land	10.2

Source: The Pearson General Knowledge Mannual, 2004, pp. 3, 138-39.

Table 2.7: Distribution of Forests in India

Sl. No.	*State/UTs*	*Recorded forest area (sq. km.)*	*% of forest area to geographical area*	*Per Capita forest area in hectares*
1	*2*	*3*	*4*	*5*
1.	Andhra Pradesh	63,726	23.2	0·10
2.	Arunachal Pradesh	51,540	61.5	6.00
3.	Assam	30,708	39·1	0.14
4.	Bihar	29,226	16.3	0.03
5.	Goa (Including Daman & Diu)	1,256	32·9	0·10
6.	Gujarat	19,388	9.9	0.05
7.	Haryana	1,687	3.9	0.01
8.	Himachal Pradesh	37,591	67.7	0·74
9.	Jammu & Kashmir	20,174	9.1	0.26
10.	Karnataka	38,646	20.2	0.09
11.	Kerala	11,222	28.9	0.04
12.	Madhya Pradesh	1,55,414	35.0	0.23
13.	Maharashtra	63,861	203	008
14.	Manipur	15,154	67.9	0.03
15.	Meghalaya	9,496	42.3	0.54

(Contd....)

Table 2.7: (Contd....)

1	*2*	*3*	*4*	*5*
16.	Mizoram	15,935	75.6	2.32
17.	Nagaland	8,625	52.0	0·71
18.	Orissa	59,555	38.2	0·19
19.	Punjab	2,842	5.5	0·01
20.	Rajasthan	31,539	9.2	0.07
21.	Sikkim	2,650	37.3	0 66
22.	Tamil Nadu	22,599	17.5	0.04
23.	Tripura	6,292	60·0	0.23
24.	Uttar Pradesh	51,502	17.5	0.04
25.	West Bengal	11,379	13.4	0.02
26.	Andaman & Nicobar Isands	7,171	86.9	2.58
27.	Chandigarh	31	27.2	0005
28.	Dadra & Nagar Haveli	207	42.2	0·15
29.	Delhi	42	2.8	
30.	Lakshadweep		-	
31.	Pondicherry		-	
	Total	7,70,078	23.4	0·09

Note: Recorded forest area pertains to period 1989.

Source: India-a Comprehensive Geography, Natural Vegetation Forest Resources, p. 15.

REFERENCES

1. *Reference Orissa:* An Indian State of Eastern Region, Enterprising Publishers.
2. *District at a Glance,* 2005, Orissa Government of Orissa Directorate of Economics and Statistics.
3. *Indian Economy,* S.K. Mishra & V.K. Puri, 2003 Edn., p. 103. Himalaya Publishing House, Bombay.

4. *Indian Economy:* Rudra Dutta. 2006 ed. & BKPM Sundaram.

5. India Development Report, 1997, K. Parekha, Indira Gandhi Institute of Development Research.

6. *Fundamentals of Environmental Studies:* S.N. Tripathy, and Surnakar Panda, 2005, Vrinda Publications Pvt. Ltd.

7. *Environmental Studies:* B.R. Satapathy & Amiya Prasad Das.

8. *Statesman* of 21-3-2006, p. 6.

9. *The Pearson General Knowledge Manual*, 2004.

10. *World Resources:* M.S. Kar, Books and Books, Cuttack.

3

Access to Agricultural Credit, its Gap and Delivery to Farmers

*Dr. Jogasankar Mahaprashasta**
*Prakash Chandra Pradhan***

The existence of imperfection in the capital market in rural areas of developing countries has been an important feature which has drawn the attention of a number of scholars. An important character of the credit market in rural areas is that access to credit is far easier for some groups than for others. Following technological change in agriculture and a greater need of credit to small farmers to facilitate the adoption of technology, the question of small farmers' and poorer groups' effective access to the formal credit institution is of a crucial significance. It has been argued that increased productive credit is essential for the generation of adequate growth of production and for changing its composition and distribution in favour of deficit producers (Lipton, 1976). Additional formal credit is supposed to shift rural borrowing from informal moneylenders to formal institutions, to encourage borrowing for the use of new technology, in- proved inputs etc., to provide modern mechanism for increase in production and income for rural poor (Donald, 1976; Sinha, 1976).

* Dr. Mahaprashasta, Lecturer in Economics, Christ College, Cuttack (Orissa).

** Mr. Pradhan is a Research Scholar, Berhampur University (Orissa).

The existence of capital market imperfections in the rural areas of developing countries has engaged the attention of a member of economists and other social scientists (Griffin, 1979; Ladman and Adams, 1978; Lipton. 1976; Rutton, 1986; Braveman and Guasch, 1986; Eswaran and Kotwal, 1986; Mallick and Sohai, 1991). An important feature of this market is that access to credit is easier for some groups than others. Of late, institutional agricultural credit has been assigned a leading role in rural development efforts in most developing countries, including India. Additional formal credit is supposed to shift rural borrowing from informal moneylenders to formal institutions, and it encourages increased borrowing for the exploitation of new technology, improved inputs etc. The growth of agricultural output and productivity will increase per capita real income which will reduce the risk premium and thereby reduce the rural rates of interest which are generally high (Ghatak, 1975, 1977-1983; Bottomley and Nudds, 1969; Bottornley, 1975). Consequently, it will weaken the position of the rural moneylenders (Iqbal, 1988).

The policy-makers evolved various institutions and regulating mechanisms to ensure the flow of cheap credit to the desired sections of rural society i.e. to the small farmers and rural poor for displacing or at least reducing the influence of informal lenders on these sections. Despite enormous expansion of institutional credit infrastructure and consequent flow of formal credit to the rural areas, there are increasing evidences indicating that the primary advantage has accrued to large farmers (Gonzalez, 1981; Lele, 1981; Lipton, 1976; Braverman and Guasch, 1986; Egger, 1986 Rangarajan, 1990). Again the flow of credit is confined to developed regions as well as to the better off sections of rural society, leaving the backward regions as well as the small farmer and rural poor continuously dependent on informal agencies (Shivamaggi, 1993; Rao, 1970; Rao, 1980; Panda, 1988; Sarap, 1990; Bhende, 1986; Desai, Haque and Sunita, 1988; Haque and Verma, 1988; Throat, 1990). Evidence from these studies suggests that a small proportion of the total number of farmers in rural areas receive loans from institutional sources. Among them who access to formal credit, a very small group has monopolies a major share of the total volume of credit disbursed.

In India during the last four decades or so substantial funds have been channelised into rural capital market to strengthen the formal financial sector and to increase the rural farmer's access to credit, particularly the small and marginal farmers and other poorer groups. The proportion of formal credit in total credit in rural areas has increased from about 8.9 per cent In 1951-52 to 62.20 per cent in 1981. The share of the commercial banks, which was about one per cent in 1951-52, went up by 28.00 per cent in 1981-82, catching up with the share of cooperative credit institutions.

Thus given the supply of credit, a number of factors operate in such a way that small and marginal fanners are discriminated from getting adequate loans from these institutions which are *(i)* asset-based lending policies *(ii)* higher transaction cost in case of small farmers *(iii)* delay in sanctioning of loan *(iv)* lower social status due to caste *(v)* lack of education *(vi)* tenancy structure and *(vii)* political clout of large farmers. The situation is more precarious in backward region.

In the present study an attempt has been made to anayse the actual access of different categories of sample farmers (sub-marginal, marginal, small, medium and large) to the formal and informal credit, credit delivery system, credit gap, defaulters and over dues in both developed as well as in backward areas.

The study is organized into four sections. Section 1 is the introduction with a brief review of studies in the area of access to agricultural credit. Section 2 deals with the objectives, database and sample design, hypothesis formulated in the study. The descriptive and empirical analysis of the study is represented in Section 3. Finally, Section 4 is the conclusion.

Objectives of the Study

With the above background this paper is developed with the following broad objectives.

(i) To study the role of formal and informal credit agencies in terms of the supply or availability of rural credit in the developed and backward areas;

(ii) To study about the delivery of formal credit in terms of time taken in the developed as well as backward areas;

(iii) To analyse the credit gap for formal as well as informal credit in the developed as also in backward areas;

(iv) To analyse about defaulters and overdues in formal as well as informal credit in the developed as well as backward areas.

Database and Sample Design

The present study is based on primary data collected from a random sample of 277 farm households selected from ten sample villages-five sample villages of Salipur and five sample villages of Narasingpur block in Cuttack district, a developed district of Orissa. Out of 277 households, 137 households were selected from the Salipur block and the rest 140 households from Narasingpur block. The household level relevant data were collected using structured questionnaire during November 2004. Salipur is a developed block situated in the eastern part of the district getting the highest irrigation with around agriculture development whereas Narasingpur is an undeveloped block situated in the extreme west part of the district having mostly unirrigated and hilly areas.

The five villages were purposively selected from each block on the basis of flow of credit, distribution of various categories of farmers belonging to different social community in such a way that, in terms of agricultural development and credit availability the villages broadly represent two development scenario. From each village, samples of 25-30 cultivating households are selected from each size categories of farmers.

The different size-categories of farmers are: *(i)* landless labourers having no land for cultivation *(ii)* sub-marginal farmers cultivating upto 1.25 acres *(iii)* Marginal farmers having land for cultivation from 1.26 to 2.50 acres *(iv)* small farmers cultivating from 2.51 acres to 5.00 acres *(v)* medium farmers cultivating from 5.00 acres to 10.00 acres and *(vi)* large farmers cultivating 10.01 acres and above. For selection of sample households a list of total cultivating households along with the land operated has been prepared on the basis of the village land record. The cultivating households are then arranged in six size-categories in order to give due weightage to cultivating households of various size categories. The allocation of 25-30 cultivating households to each of the farm-size group is made in proportion to their share in total cultivating households in the village, thus, making the total sample representative in nature.

Hypothesis

(i) Access to credit has positive relationship with farm-size in case of both formal and informal credit;

(ii) Small and marginal farmers are discriminated for accessing to formal and informal credit;

(iii) The access to formal and informal credit is more for the farmers of developed area than the farmers of backward area;

(iv) Time taken for obtaining formal short from loans is inversely related to the size of holding both in developed as well as backward area;

(v) The credit gap is more in case of backward area in comparison to developed area;

(vi) The proportion of defaulters is diminishing with the increase in the size of farm both in developed and backward area;

(vii) Average overdues the increase in the decreasing with the increase in the size of the firm both in developed as well as in backward area.

Access and Distribution of Different Types of Credits

On the basis of past studies certain emerging issues of rural credit can be carried out which will give focus of the present study. A review of the earlier studies on the access to formal credit indicates that despite enormous expansion of institutional finance the consequent flow of credit in the rural areas has been largely confined to better off sections of rural society, leaving the small farmers and rural poor continuously dependent on informal agencies. The positive relationship between farm-size and proportion of borrowing from co-operatives and government sources observed in 1951-52 continued even after the entry of commercial bank in seventies and eighties. The second factor mentioned by several studies relates to the institutional bottlenecks of the formal agencies in terms of their assets based lending policies, complex formalities and procedures and the lower economic and social status of poor rural households, reflected through qualitative factors such as education and caste background as the major cause of lower accessibility to formal loans. Others give an explanation which focuses on limited credit demand among the rural poor. They argue that most poor do not seek formal credit because they lack profitable investment opportunities, some are either not aware of the availability of formal credit, do not know-how to use formal credit, or are too timid to request formal loans. The present study seeks to fill up the gap by including the above-mentioned aspects. It will be more comprehensive in another sense that it tries to examine access to the formal credit as well as the informal credits agencies across the various size categories of farmers.

The cooperatives are the dominant sources of formal finance followed by commercial banks in the district of Cuttack. However, the development of institutional finance across the districts varies significantly. It also appears that agricultural development and the development of institutional finance go hand in hand. In order to bring out the regional variations of accessing to institutional finance, we decided to form the homogeneous regions on the basis of agricultural development and development of credit in the districts of Orissa. So far as agricultural development is concerned different indicators are used such as percentage of gross irrigated area to gross cropped area, per hectare consumption of fertilizer (in kgs), yield rate of rice per acre (in kgs), cropping intensity etc. In the case of institutional credit yield rate of rice per hectare of gross cropped area is taken as indicator of agricultural development for formal credit.

Access to Formal Credit

This empirical verification is based on our sample survey of both developed and backward area. Out of 277 land-holding households, 104 households (37.54 per cent) borrowed from the formal sources. Out of the five categories of farmers, the medium and large farmers obtained credit maximum of about 50 per cent. The submarginal and the marginal farmer borrowers constituted about 31 per cent each. Amount of formal loan in the developed area is Rs. 8,09,000/- in the backward area it is Rs. 2,42,050/- in total it is Rs. 10,51,050/-. In the developed area, out of 137 households, 69 households, i.e. 50.36 per cent availed formal credit, on the contrary only 35 households i.e. 25 per cent received formal credit in backward village during, the reference year this is represented in the Table 3.1.

Further the formal credit formed 55.45 per cent of the total credit in the developed village, while it formed only 37.93 per cent of total credit in backward village. It clearly shows the bias of formal credit in favour of developed village, while the backward village largely depends on informal sources for its production credit requirements.

The inequality in the share of total formal credit among size groups is more pronounced in developed village. The medium and large farmers who constitute only 8.75 per cent of the total sample households accounted for a total of 18.41 per cent of the total formal credit received in developed village. On the other hand submarginal and marginal farmers

Table 3.1: Borrowing of Farm Households from the Formal Institutions According to Size of Holding (2002-03)

Developed

(in Rs.)

Size of holding (in acres)	*% of households in the group*	*No. of household borrowed*	*% of households borrowed*	*Amount of formal loan in (Rs.)*	*Proportion of formal loan to total loan*	*% of formal credit to total formal credit*	*% of area owned to total area*
1	*2*	*3*	*4*	*5*	*6*	*7*	*8*
Upto 1.25	33.58	18	39.13	162000	49.62	20.02	11.29
1.26-2.50	32.12	21	47.72	194000	47.62	23.98	26.61
2.51-5.00	25.55	22	62.86	304000	60.2	37.58	38
5.01-10.00	8.02	7	63.64	137000	72.87	16.93	20.95
10.01 and above	0.73	1	100	12000	54.55	1.48	3.15
Total	100	69	50.36	809000	55.84	100.00	100

(Contd...)

Table 3.1: (Contd...)

1	2	3	4	5	6	7	8
Backward							
Upto 1.25	32.86	11	23.91	42500	29.95	17.56	9.56
1.26-2.50	37.86	10	18.86	82050	34.64	33.90	27.42
2.51-5.00	17.14	8	33.33	69500	46.00	28.71	22.37
5.01-10.00	10	5	35.71	38000	53.90	15.70	24.28
10.01 and above	2.14	1	33.33	10000	25.64	4.13	16.37
Total	100	35	25	242050	37.86	100.00	100
Aggregate							
Upto 1.25	33.21	29	31.52	204500	43.66	19.46	10.36
1.26-2.50	35.02	31	31.95	276050	42.85	26.26	27.05
2.51-5.00	21.3	30	50.85	373500	56.93	35.54	29.62
5.01-10.00	9.03	12	48	175000	67.7	16.65	22.74
10.01 and above	1.44	2	50	22000	36.07	2.09	10.23
Total	100	104	37.54	1051050	50.33	100.00	100

Note: Compiled from field survey data.

who constitute 65.7 per cent of the total households received only 44 per cent of the formal credit received in developed village. But it is interesting to note that small farmers' position is good in the developed village as they receives 37.58 per cent of the formal credit though they constitute only 25.65 per cent of the households. The inequality in the distribution of formal credit is more than that of the inequality in the ownership of land. However it is found that even the medium and large farmers are receiving less percentage of formal loan in comparison to the percentage of area owned by them. It is perhaps because of their self-sufficiency, and less dependence on formal loan or easy access to informal loan. The same trend continues in the backward area. The submarginal and marginal farmers constitute 70.72 per cent of the households where as they received 51.26 per cent of the formal credit. The small farmers who constitute 17.14 per cent of the households received 28.03 per cent of the formal credit. The medium and large farmers constituting 12.14 per cent of the households received 19.91 per cent of formal credit received in backward village.

It is also seer, in both areas that the percentage of households borrowing from formal sources has increased with the increase in the size of the holdings with marginal deviation in case of medium and large farmers.

This indicates that submarginal and marginal farmers have less access to formal credit institutions than did the small, medium and large farmers in the survey area. A positive point is noted here that small farmers position has improved.

Access to informal Credit

Access to informal credit in the developed area, backward area and in aggregate by different farm size groups is represented in the Table 3.2.

Informal sources have provided Rs. 10,37,200 towards loan in aggregate out of which the share of developed village is Rs. 6,39.900 and the share of backward village comes to Rs. 3,97,300.

Table 3.2: Borrowing of Farm Households from the Informal Sources According to Size of Holding (2002-03)

Developed

Size of holding (in acres)	*% of households in the group*	*No. of household borrowed*	*% of households borrowed*	*Amount of formal loan in (Rs.)*	*Proportion of formal loan to total loan*	*% of formal credit to total formal credit*	*% of area owned to total area*
1	*2*	*3*	*4*	*5*	*6*	*7*	*8*
Upto 1.25	33.58	33	71.74	164500	50.38	25.71	11.29
1.26-2.50	32.12	33	75.00	213400	52.38	33.35	26.61
2.51-5.00	25.55	23	65.71	201000	39.8	31.41	38
5.01-10.00	8.02	4	36.36	51000	27.13	7.97	20.95
10.01 and above	0.73	1	100.00	10000	45.45	1.56	3.15
Total	100	94	68.61	639900	44.16	100.00	100

(Contd...)

Table 3.2: (Contd...)

Developed

1	*2*	*3*	*4*	*5*	*6*	*7*	*8*
Underdeveloped							
Upto 1.25	32.86	31	67.39	99400	70.05	25.02	9.56
1.26-2.50	37.86	33	62.26	154800	65.36	38.96	27.42
2.51-5.00	17.14	12	50.00	81600	54	20.54	22.37
5.01-10.00	10	11	78.57	32500	46.1	8.18	24.28
10.01 and above	2.14	2	66.67	29000	74.36	7.30	16.37
Total	100	89	63.57	397300	62.14	100.00	100
Aggregate							
Upto 1.25	33.21	64	69.57	263900	56.34	25.44	10.36
1.26-2.50	35.02	66	68.04	368200	57.15	35.50	27.05
2.51-5.00	21.3	25	42.37	282600	43.07	27.25	29.62
5.01-10.00	9.03	15	60.00	83500	32.3	8.05	22.74
10.01 and above	1.44	3	75.00	39000	63.93	3.76	10.23
Total	100	183	66.06	1037200	49.67	100.00	100

Notes:(i) Compiled from field survey data.

(ii) Prop-Proportion, Amt-Amount.

It is found that a total of 49.67 per cent of the total loan is provided by the informal sources. Out of the sanction, contribution in developed area is 44.16 per cent and in backward area is 62.14 per cent. This trend shows that the access to formal credit is less in backward area it comparison to developed area. The formal agencies are expanding more in developed area. It is again found that as the farm size increases the percentage of households borrowed decreases in case of informal credit both in developed and backward areas as well as in aggregate with marginal variation. This variation is found in case of large farmers both in developed and backward area. This is because of their financial stability, the moneylenders are providing loans at less rate of interest to them. They compete with the formal sources of credit. Again submarginal and marginal farmers category together get the major percentage of informal credit i.e. 59.68 per cent in developed area, 63.71 per cent in backward area, 61.21 per cent as a whole. As the amount of informal credit is provided by the moneylender basing on production, it has very less significance with the land owned by the farmers.

Average Formal and Informal Credit

The average formal and informal credit received per farmer per borrower and per acre are depicted it the Table 3.3. It is seen that average formal loan per farmer in aggregate is Rs. 3,790.79, in developed area it is Rs. 5,905.11 and in backward area it is Rs. 1,721.79. In case of informal loan, average informal loan per farmer in aggregate is Rs. 3,770.04, in developed area it is Rs. 4,743.80 and in backward area it is Rs. 2,817.14.

It is seen that the average formal as well as informal credit received per farmer, in the developed area samples is much higher than that of backward area samples. It increases with increase of the farm size in aggregate and in both the areas except the medium farmers. The table shows that average formal loan per borrower in aggregate is Rs. 10,106.25 in developed area it is Rs. 11,724.64 and in backward area it is Rs. 6,915.71. In case of informal loan, average informal loan per borrower in aggregate is Rs. 5,834.07 (almost half of that in case of Rs. 6938.17 and in backward area it is Rs. 4,586.05. As far as the average borrowings are concerned the formal sector provided higher per borrower funds to the borrower in both the developed area and backward area. On the other hand in both formal as well as informal loan, the backward area has lower average figures in comparison to developed area. The average borrowing per borrower is Rs. 6,915.71 and Rs. 4,586.05 in the formal and informal loan respectively in backward area while in case of developed area the figures area Rs. 11,724.64 and Rs. 6,988.17 respectively in formal and informal loan. In the developed area, the medium farmers in the formal as well as in informal loan avail highest average loan whereas in backward area, the large farmers avail highest average loan in both formal as well as informal credit market. The average formal as well as informal credit per borrower in the farmers of developed area is much higher (almost double) than that of backward area samples and it increases with increase of the farm size in aggregate and in bath the areas except the larger farmers in developed area, medium farmers in backward area and large farmers in aggregate. However, comparing the developed area and backward area it is found that the difference of average formal loan is more visible in developed area than backward area. Further the informal credit per farmer and per borrower has increased significantly with farm size in the backward area samples.

Credit used per acre of landholding is another measurement of the access to credit and efficient utilization of credit in the agricultural operations. Generally, higher the landholding higher is the credit requirement, but of course the large landholders with higher annual income may not resort to borrowings for their agricultural operations.

As the Table 3.3 shows amount of average formal credit per acre as a whole is Rs. 1,536.71 for developed area it is Rs. 2,548.43 and in backward area it is Rs. 660.42. The average informal credit per acre as a whole is Rs. 1,526.84, for developed area it is 2,047.25 and in backward area it is Rs. 1,076.10. In the developed area, the submarginal farmers avail maximum loan from both formal and informal source of the amount Rs. 4,521.35 and Rs. 4,591.12 respectively. The same result is found in backward area and as a whole also. The average formal as well as informal credit per acre is decreasing with increase in the size of the farm in developed areas backward area and in aggregate with marginal variation. The average formal loan per acre in total in the developed area as well as in aggregate is slightly higher than that of informal sources. But it is significant that even in developed region the average informal loan per acre in total is higher than average formal loan per acre in case of submarginal and marginal farmers category. This speaks of marginal farmers less access to formal credit which forces them to opt for informal credit whatever may be the effective rate of interest. The condition in backward area is more precarious. The average informal loan per acre in those area is higher than the average formal loan per acre in case of submarginal farmers, marginal farmers, small farmers, large farmers and in total.

Distribution of Estimated Production Credit According to Agency

The distribution of production credit among the size groups provided by various credit agencies is depicted in the Table 3.4.

Institutional credit is supplied to the farmers by three financial institutions: (1) Cooperatives (2) Commercial banks (3) Regional Rural Banks (RRBs) or the Gramya banks. About 50.33 per cent of the total credit is supplied by the formal agencies of which cooperatives top with 24.06 per cent share followed by the commercial banks with 22.70 per cent share and the Gramya bank role is very negligible in this regard which shares about 3.57 per cent of the total formal loan.

Out of the total formal credit, developed area avails 55.84 per cent of it. Here the commercial banks top with a credit

Table 3.3: Average Formal and Informal Credit Received by Size Groups (Amount in Rs.)

Developed

Size of holding	*Per farmer*		*Per borrower*		*Per acre*	
(in acres)	*Formal*	*Informal*	*Formal*	*Informal*	*Formal*	*Informal*
Upto 1.25	3521.4	3576.09	9000	4984.85	4521.35	4591.12
1.26-2.50	4409.09	5077.27	9238.09	681.25	229.64	2644.41
2.51-5	8685.71	5742.86	13818.18	8739.13	2519.89	1666.11
5.01-10.00	2454.55	4636.36	19571.43	12750	2060.15	766.92
10.01 and above	12000	10000	12000	10000	1200	1000
Total	5905.11	4743.8	11724.64	6988.17	2548.43	2047.25

(Contd...)

Table 3.3: (Contd...)

1	*2*	*3*	*4*	*5*	*6*	*7*
Backward						
Upto 1.25	902.17	2160.87	3863.63	3427.59	1213.25	2837.57
1.26-2.50	1548.11	2866.04	8205	4746.88	816.42	1511.44
2.51-5.00	2895.83	3400	8687.5	6800	847.77	995.36
5.01-10.00	2714.29	2321.43	7600	2954.54	426.97	365.17
10.01 and above	3333.33	9666.67	10000	14500	166.67	483.33
Total	1721.79	2817.14	6915.71	4586.05	660.42	1076.1
Aggregate						
Upto 1.25	2211.96	2868.48	7017.24	4256.45	2885.97	3724.24
1.26-2.50	2845.88	3869.07	8904.84	5864.06	1492.32	2028.87
2.51-5.00	5822.03	4789.83	12450	8074.28	1843.35	1394.73
5.01-10.00	7000	3340	14583.33	5566.67	1125.40	536.98
10.01 and above	5500	9750	11000	13000	314.29	557.14
Total	3790.79	3770.04	10106.25	5834.07	1536.71	1526.84

Note: Compiled from field survey data.

Table 3.4: Distribution of Estimated Firm Credit According to Agency Among Size Groups

(in '000 Rupees)

	Developed						Backward						
	Upto 1.25	*1.26-2.50*	*2.51-5.00*	*5.01-10.00*	*10.01 above*	*Total*	*Upto 1.25*	*1.26-2.50*	*2.51-5.00*	*5.01-10.00*	*10.01 above*	*Total*	*Grand Total*
1	*2*	*3*	*4*	*5*	*6*	*7*	*8*	*9*	*10*	*11*	*12*	*13*	*14*
Govt.	0	0	0	0	0	0	0	0	0	0	0	0	0
%	0	0	0	0	0	0	0	0	0	0	0	0	0
Co-op	80	101	110	51	12	354	18.8	51.2	35.5	36	10	148.5	502.5
%	24.50	24.79	21.78	27.13	54.55	24.43	13.25	21.62	21.51	51.06	25.64	23.23	24.06
Gramya Bank	21	21	14	10	0	66	6.6	1.85	0	0	0	8.45	74.45
%	6.43	5.15	2.77	5.32	0	4.56	4.65	0.78	0	0	0	1.32	3.57
Com. Bank	61	72	180	76	0	389	17.1	29	37	2	0	85.1	474.1
%	18.68	17.67	35.64	40.43	0	26.85	12.05	12.24	24.49	2.84	0	13.31	22.70
Other	0	0	0	0	0	0	0	0	0	0	0	0	0
%	0	0	0	0	0	0	0	0	0	0	0	0	0

(Contd...)

Table 3.4: (Contd...)

1	2	3	4	5	6	7	8	9	10	11	12	13	14
(A) Total FC	162	194	304	137	12	809	42.5	82.50	69.5	38	10	242.05	1051.05
%	49.62	47.62	60.20	72.87	54.55	55.84	29.95	34.64	46.00	53.90	25.64	37.86	50.33
Moneylender	164.5	187.4	176	36	10	573.9	53.5	146.4	68.6	32	29	329.5	903.4
%	50.38	46.00	34.85	19.15	45.45	39.61	37.17	61.81	45.40	45.39	74.36	51.54	43.26
Trader	0	14	0	0	0	14	0	2.5	6	0	0	8.5	22.5
%	0	3.44	0	0	0	0.97	0	1.06	3.97	0	0	1.33	1.08
Landlord	0	0	0	0	0	0	3.4	0	7	0	0	10.4	10.4
%	0	0	0	0	0	0	2.40	0	4.63	0	0	1.63	0.50
Any other	0	12	25	15	0	52	42.5	5.9	0	5	0	53.4	105.4
%	0	2.95	4.95	7.98	0	3.59	29.95	2.49	0.00	7.09	0	8.35	5.05
(B) Total 1FC	164.5	213.4	201	51	10	639.9	99.4	154.8	81.6	32.5	29	397.3	1037.2
%	50.38	52.38	39.80	27.13	45.45	4.16	70.05	65.36	54.00	46.10	74.36	62.14	49.67
Total (A+B)	326.5	407.4	505	188	22	1448.9	141.9	236.85	151.1	70.5	39	639.35	2088.25
%	100.00	100.00	100.00	100.00	100.00	100.00	100.00	100.00	100.00	100.00	100.00	100.00	100.00

Notes: *(i)* Complied from field survey data.

(ii) FC-Formal Credit, IFC-Informal Credit.

share of 26.85 per cent followed by cooperative with 24.43 per cent and Gramya Bank with 4.56 per cent. Backward area receives 44.16 per cent of the total formal credit. Out of which cooperatives provide maximum credit to the tune of 23.23 per cent followed by commercial banks with 13.31 per cent and Gramya bank with 1.32 per cent of it. Out of the total loan availed in backward area, the share of formal credit is 37.86 per cent which is far less than institutional credit availed by the developed area.

Informal credit is mainly supplied by the moneylender, traders and marginally by landlords and relatives etc. About 49.67 per cent of the total credit is provided by the informal sources of which moneylenders top with 43.26 per cent share. Other sources only provide negligible amount of loan. In developed area moneylenders provides credit up to 39.61 per cent of their total credit and in backward area it provides 51.54 per cent of their total credit.

It reveals that the moneylenders are the major source for landless labourers, submarginal, marginal farmers both in developed as well as in backward area. In backward areas, the moneylenders remain as the major source in all categories of farmers including the large farmers. It is because of the easy access to informal credit and fear of loosing land in case of default in formal loan. Even if there is no linkage, the moneylenders dominate in backward area in spite of the presence of cooperatives, commercial bank and Gramya bank. Out of total credit obtained in both developed and backward areas, a total of 43.26 per cent of total loan is provided by the moneylenders. It is found that the cooperatives and commercial banks are the major sources for medium and large farmers in developed area. Cooperatives are working with equal force both in developed as well as backward area.

It is evident from the fact that out of the total loan in developed area, it provides 24.43 per cent of loan and out of the total loan in backward area it 21 provides 23.23 per cent of formal loan, second to moneylenders. But commercial banks comes rent providing 22.70 per cent of the total loan. It is noted that the commercial bank provides 26.85 per cent of the total loan in developed area, which is ahead of cooperatives, but it provides only 8.45 per cent of the total loan in backward area. The commercial banks are unable to reach at backward area. Gramya Bank is providing only 3.57 per cent of the total loan, that to 4.56 per cent in developed area and 1.32 per cent in backward area. Thus Cooperatives remain as the ultimate alternative e to moneylenders.

From the above observations, it is clear that the formal credit is confined to only the medium and large farmers in the developed villages leaving the marginal and landless farmers in the developed area and almost all the households in the backward area entirely dependent on informal sources.

Delivery of Formal Credit

The time taken for getting agricultural loan from formal agencies from the date of applying to date of receiving the last instalment of loan according to the size of holding is shown in Table 3.5. In the case of submarginal and marginal farmers, it takes only one and half month to obtain total amount of loan, whereas in the case of large farmers it takes less than half of that time. Even after the loan has been sanctioned, the small farmers have to wait for some days to collect the amount. Thus, it is clear that the time taken for obtaining formal short-term loans is inversely related to the size of holding. In other words, less and less time required for obtaining formal short-term loans as the size of the farm increases. It also explains the easy access of large farmers to formal credit in comparison to small and marginal farmers

It may be noted that in the case of long-term loans, the time taken may be expected to be even more (George et al., 1985) because of the numerous formalities and procedures. Long-term loans have not been considered here because of the extremely small number of cases.

Table 3.5: Delivery of Formal Credit According to Average Time Taken and Size of Holding in Orissa

Size of holding (in acres)	*Days taken from day of applying to day of sanction*	*Date of sanction to date of receiving*	*Days taken from the date of apply to date of receiving*
Developed			
Upto 1.25	48.44	8.39	56.83
1.26-2.50	33.65	7.91	41.57
2.51-5.00	34.82	11.82	4664
5.01-10.00	46.14	5.29	51.43
10.01 and above	25	5	30
Backward			
Upto 1.25	23.67	7	30.67
1.26-2.50	29.46	8.62	38.08
2.51-5.00	34.67	3.33	38
5.01-10.00	11	7.8	18.8
10.01 and above	10	3	13
Aggregate			
Upto 1.25	38.53	7.83	46.37
1.26-2.50	32.14	8.17	40.31
2.51-5.00	34.77	5.35	44.13
5.01-10.00	31.5	6.33	37.83
10.01 and above	17.5	4	21.5

Source: Compiled by the author from field survey.

Credit Gap for Formal Loan

Credit gap implies the difference between the potential demand for production, credit and the actual credit provided by the formal agencies. Credit gap for different categories of farmers in developed area, backward area as well as taking all sample farmers in aggregate is depicted in Table 3.6(a) and in Table 3.6(b).

It is seen that in aggregate the credit gap is found to be 36.01 per cent. It implies that total sample farmers are receiving only 63.99 per cent of their potential demand for production credit. This credit gap is 31.90 per cent in case of developed area farmers, whereas it is 46.77 per cent in case of backward area farmers. This again points out that the flow of credit is much more in developed area than backward area. Out of the total amount of credit gap in aggregate term, the submarginal and marginal farmers category together account for 42.20 per cent credit gap. This gap for them is 25.86 per cent in developed area and 71.44 per cent in backward area which clearly explains that the credit gap is glaring for submarginal and marginal farmers in the backward areas. For this reason, the submarginal and marginal farmers in backward region depends heavily on informal sources irrespective of higher rate of interest. Table 3.6(b) depicts credit gap in case of informal credit which reveals that in the developed area the credit gap is 5.73 per cent, it is much lower at 3.17 per cent in underdeveloped area. Aggregate percentage of informal credit gap is found to be 4.78 which indicates that around 95 per cent requirement informal credit is fulfilled. One important feature of the informal credit is that the credit gap is nil for medium and large farmers is developed area and small, medium and large farmers in underdeveloped area. Submarginal and marginal farmers together are worst sufferer in both the areas. Anyway in term of informal credit compared to the formal credit the gap is much lower.

Defaulters and Overdues of Formal Loan

The issues of overdues in case of formal loan is depicted in the below Table 3.7. This indicates that the proportion of defaulters is diminishing with the increase in the size of farm in aggregate. However, paradoxically the proportion of defaulters is increasing with the increase in size of the farm in case of developed area farmers (with the exception of large

Table 3.6(a): Credit Gap of Formal Sources

(In Rupees)

	Loan required				Loan sanctioned						
Size of holdings (in acres)	Co-op. Bank	Gram. Bank	Comm. Bank	Total	Co-op. Bank	Gram. Bank	Comm. Bank	Total	Credit Gap	% of Credit Gap	% of credit gap to total credit gap of each size
1	2	3	4	5	6	7	8	9	10	11	12
Upto 1.25	116000	30000	72000	218000	80000	21000	61000	162000	56000	25.69	14.78
1.26-2.50	127000	26000	83000	236000	101000	21000	72000	194000	42000	17.80	11.08
2.51-5.00	211000	35000	26000	506000	110000	14000	180000	304000	202000	39.92	53.30
5.01-10.00	83000	30000	85000	198000	51000	10000	76000	137000	61000	30.81	16.09
10.01 and above	30000	0	0	30000	12000	0	0	12000	18000	60.00	4.75
Total	567000	121000	266000	1188000	354000	66000	389000	809000	379000	31.90	100

(Contd...)

Table 3.6(a): (Contd...)

	1	*2*	*3*	*4*	*5*	*6*	*7*	*8*	*9*	*10*	*11*
Backward Area											
Upto 1.25	24800	6600	55100	86500	18800	6600	16100	41500	45000	52.02	21.25
1.26-2.50	93500	1850	93000	188350	51200	1850	29000	82050	106300	56.44	50.19
2.51-5.00	51000	0	45000	96000	32500	0	37000	69500	26500	27.60	12.51
5.01-10.00	60000	0	2000	62000	36000	0	2000	38000	24000	38.71	11.33
10.01 and above	20000	0	0	20000	10000	0	0	10000	10000	50.00	4.72
Total	249300	8450	195100	452850	148500	8450	84100	241050	211800	46.77	100.00

(Contd...)

Table 3.6(a): (Contd...)

	1	2	3	4	5	6	7	8	9	10	11
Aggregate											
Upto 1.25	140800	36600	127100	304500	98800	27600	77100	203500	101000	33.17	17.10
1.26-2.50	220500	27850	176000	424350	152200	22850	101000	276050	148300	34.95	25.10
2.51-5.00	262000	35000	71000	602000	142500	14000	217000	373500	228500	37.96	38.68
5.01-10.00	143000	30000	87000	260000	87000	10000	78000	175000	85000	32.69	14.39
10.01 and above	50000	0	0	50000	22000	0	0	22000	28000	56.00	4.74
Total	816300	129450	461100	1640850	502500	74450	473100	1050050	590800	36.01	100.00

Source: Compiled by the author from field survey.

Table 3.6(b): Credit Gap of Informal Source

(in Rupees)

Size of holdings (in acres)	Total loan required					Total loan sanctioned							
	Money-lender	Trader	Landlord	Any other	Total	Money-other	Trader	Landlord	Any	Total	Credit	% of credit gap Gap	% of credit gap to total credit gap of each size
1	2	3	4	5	6	7	8	9	10	11	12	13	14
Upto 1.25	176000	0	0	0	176000	164500	0	0	0	164500	11500	6.53	29.11
1.26-2.50	207400	19000	0	12000	238400	197400	14000	0	12000	223400	15000	6.29	37.97
2.51-5.00	189000	0	600	25000	214000	176000	0	0	25000	201000	13000	6.07	32.91
5.01-10.00	36000	0	0	15000	51000	36000	0	0	15000	51000	0	0	0
10.01 and above	10000	0	0	0	10000	10000	0	0	0	10000	0	0	0
Total	618400	19000	0	52000	689400	583900	14000	0	52000	649900	39500	5.73	100.00

(Contd...)

Table 3.6(b): (Contd...)

1	2	3	4	5	6	7	8	9	10	11	12	13	14
Underdeveloped													
Upto 1.25	53500	0	3400	52500	109400	53500	0	3400	42500	99400	10000	9.14	77.52
1.26-2.50	146400	2500	0	5900	154800	146400	2500	0	3000	151900	2900	1.87	22.48
2.51-5.00	68600	6000	7000	0	81600	68600	6000	7000	0	81600	0	0	0
5.01-10.00	32000	0	0	500	32500	32000	0	0	500	32500	0	0	0
10.01 and above	29000	0	0	0	29000	29000	0	0	0	29000	0	0	0
Total	329500	8500	10400	58900	407300	329500	8500	10400	46000	394400	12900	3.17	100.00

(Contd...)

Table 3.6(b): (Contd...)

1	2	3	4	5	6	7	8	9	10	11	12	13	14
Aggregate													
Upto 1.25	229500	0	3400	52500	285400	218000	0	3400	42500	263900	21500	7.53	41.03
1.26-2.50	353800	21500	0	17900	393200	343800	16500	0	15000	375300	17900	4.55	34.16
2.51-5.00	257600	6000	7600	25000	295600	244600	6000	7000	25000	282600	13000	4.40	24.81
5.01-10.00	68000	0	0	15500	83500	68000	0	0	15500	83500	0	0	0
10.01 and above	39000	0	0	0	39000	39000	0	0	0	39000	0	0	0
Total	947900	27500	10400	110900	1096700	913400	22500	10400	98000	1044300	52400	4.78	100.00

Source: Compiled by the author from field survey.

Table 3.7: Percentage of Defaults and Overdues of Formal Loan (2002-03)

Size of household (in acres)	*No. of household borrowed*	*No. of defaults*	*Defaults as % borrowers*	*Total amount of loan*	*Total amount of overdues*	*Avg. overdues per defaulters*	*Overdues as as % of total loan outstanding*	*% of loan defaulted by the group to total loan defaulted*
1	2	3	*4*	*5*	*6*	*7*	*8*	*9*
Developed area								
Upto 1.26	18	12	66.67	162000	112000	9333.33	69.14	21.36
1.26-2.50	21	15	71.43	194000	106300	8858.33	54.79	20.27
2.51-6.00	22	17	77.27	304000	214500	12611.65	70.56	40.91
5.01-10.00	7	6	85.71	137000	91500	15250	65.79	17.45
10.01 and above	1	0	0	12000	0	0	0	0
Total	69	50	72.46	809000	524300	10486	64.81	100.00

(Contd...)

Table 3.7: (Contd...)

1	*2*	*3*	*4*	*5*	*6*	*7*	*8*	*9*
Backward area								
Upto 1.25	11	11	100	42500	38400	3490.91	90.35	25.51
1.26-2.50	10	9	90.00	82050	60850	6761.11	74.16	40.42
2.51-5.00	8	6	75.00	69500	29300	4883.33	42 16	19.46
5.01-10.00	5	1	20	38000	22000	22000	57.89	14.61
10.01 and above	1	0	0	10000	0	0	0	0
Total	35	27	77.14	242050	150550	5376.79	62.20	100.00
Aggregate								
Upto 1.25	29	23	79.31	204500	150400	6539.13	73.55	22.29
1.26-2.50	31	24	77.42	276050	167150	6964.58	60.55	24.77
2.51-5.00	30	23	76.67	373500	243800	10600.00	65. 27	36.13
6.01-10.00	12	7	58.33	175000	113500	16214.29	64.86	16.82
10.01 and above	2	0	0	22000	0	0	0	0
Total	104	77	74.04	1051050	674850	8764.29	64.21	100.00

Source: Compiled by the author from field survey.

farmer as the number of household in the sample is one) and this proportion is decreasing with the increase in size of the farm in case of backward area farmers.

Total amount of loan and total amount of overdues and overdues as percentage of total outstanding loan, have the same trend in both developed and backward area farmers.

Average overdues per defaulters in aggregate is increasing with the increase in the size of the farm. The same result is found in case of developed farmers with the exception of marginal farmers. In case of backward farmers the only exception to this finding is the small farmers category.

The percentage of loan defaulted by the group to total loan defaulted depicts a typical trend. It increases with the increase in the size of the farm upto small farmers, then it starts falling,

In general it is found that with the increase in the size of the farm, the amount of overdues, fall because of their self-sufficiency.

Defaulters and Overdues of informal Loan

The issue of overdues in case of informal loan is depicted in the below Table 3.8.

It shows that in aggregate the proportion of defaulters is increasing with the increase in the size of the farm upto small farmers category, but then it starts falling. However, the proportion of defaulters is increasing with the increase in size of the farm in case of developed area farmers (with the exception of large farmer as the number of household in the sample is one) and decreasing with the increase in size of the farm in case of backward area Farmers with only deviation in case of small farmers category.

Total amount of overdues (in aggregate) is almost 70 per cent for submarginal and marginal farmers category. This explains their less access to formal credit and their poverty and vulnerability. As the farm size increases, the amount of

Table 3.8: Percentage of Defaults and Overdues of Informal Loan (2002-03)

(In Rupees)

Size of household (in acres)	*No. of borrowers*	*No. of defaults*	*Defaults as % to total borrowers*	*Amount informal loan*	*Total amount of overdues*	*Per defaulter Avg. amount of overdues*	*Overdues as % to total loan out outstanding by the group*	*Percent of loan defaulted by the group to total defaulted*
1	2	3	4	5	6	7	8	9
Developed area								
Upto 1.25	33	15	45.45	164500	47500	3166.67	28.88	24.75
1.26-2.50	33	17	51.52	223400	95500	5617.65	42.75	49.77
2.51-5.00	23	14	60.87	201000	10900	778.57	5.42	5.68
5.01-10.00	4	4	100.00	51000	38000	9500	74.51	19.80
10.01 and above	1	0	0	10000	0	0	0	0
Total	94	50	53.19	649900	191900	3838	29.53	100.00

(Contd...)

Table 3.8: (Contd...)

1	*2*	*3*	*4*	*5*	*6*	*7*	*8*	*9*
Backward area								
Upto 1.25	31	21	67.74	99400	71700	3414.29	72.13	26.30
1.26-2.50	33	22	66.67	151900	107800	4900	70.97	39.55
2.51-5.00	12	9	75.00	81600	69100	6877.78	84.68	25.35
5.01-10.00	11	1	9.09	32500	5000	5000	15.38	1.83
10.01 and above	2	1	50.00	29000	19000	19000	65.52	6.97
Total	89	54	60.67	394400	272600	5048.148	69.12	100.00
Aggregate								
Upto 1.25	64	36	56.25	263900	119200	3311.11	45.17	25.66
1.26-2.50	66	39	59.09	375300	203300	5212.82	54.17	43.77
2.51-5.00	35	23	65.71	282600	80000	3478.26	28.31	17.22
5.01-10.00	15	5	33.33	83500	43000	8600.00	51.50	9.26
10.01 and above	3	1	33.33	39000	19000	19000.00	48.72	4.09
Total	183	104	56.83	1044300	464500	4466.35	44.48	100.00

Source: Compiled by the author from field survey.

Note: Avg-Average, Amt-Amount.

overdues and the percentage of loan defaulted by the different categories of farmers to total overdues decreases.

However, the average amount of overdues (in aggregate) is increasing with the increase in the size of the farm. This is quit; similar to the trend found in case of formal loan. However, in case of developed area farmers, the exception is small farmers and in case of backward area farmers, the exception is medium farmers.

The percentage of loan defaulted by the group to total loan depicts no clear-cut trend. It first increases, then falls, then rises, then again falls.

In general it is found that with the increase in the size of the farm, the amount of overdues is falling. But the percentage of overdues to total loan is found to be much higher in case of backward area farmers than developed area farmers.

Defaults and Overdues

It is seen that the proportion of defaulters is diminishing with the increase in the size of the farm.

Total amount of overdues, overdues as percentage of total outstanding loan shows the same trend i.e. falling with the increase in the size of the farm.

Average amount of overdues is increasing with the increase in the size of the farm in case of developed, backward as well as in case of all farmers in aggregate.

The percentage of loan defaulted by the different categories to total defaulted clearly shows that it is negatively related to the size of the farm. In aggregate, the submarginal and marginal farmers constitute 56.17 per cent of the total loan defaulted. In developed area it is 50.45 per cent and in backward area it is 65.88 per cent. This again explains the lower economic status of submarginal and marginal farmers. They depend too much en informal credit due to lack of access to formal credit.

Summary of Findings

Agricultural credit is the basic factor of development in rural India. The submarginal, marginal and small farmers are the worst sufferers. They are deprived and neglected classes in the agricultural sector with regard to their access to credit which subsequently affects the input use by them and their production. So all sections of people right from the researcher down to the planner take keen interest in studying the rural credit market along with the lifestyle, their demographic features, the level of development made in their areas and the problems faced by them, their solutions etc. It helps them to reorient or recast the development policy in desired directions.

It is observed that the percentage of formal credit to total formal credit and the average formal credit are increasing with the increase in the size of the firm from submarginal to marginal and from marginal to small but after that it starts falling. Thus it signifies that, even though the large farmers have access to formal credit, they are opting for less amount of loan because of their self-sufficiency or they are able to arrange the loans among themselves without interest or with marginal interest. The informal credit shows almost the same trend, but little bit erratic. It is observed that the average amount of formal loan is higher than that of informal loan in developed area and the average amount of informal loan is higher than that of formal loan in backward area. The average formal as well as informal credit per acre is decreasing with increase in the size of the farm. The average formal loan per acre for the developed area as whole and for all samples is slightly higher than that of informal loan. But it is remarkable that even in developed region, the rural informal loan per acre is higher than that of informal loan in case of submarginal and marginal farmers categories. This indicates the marginal farmer's less access to formal credit. It is interesting to observe that out of the total loans obtained by all the households, in all categories moneylender's contribution is the highest. This speaks that even in developed area, informal credit exists with a strong foothold.

The parabolic trend indicates that the demand for loan initially increases with the increase in the size of the firm and it starts decreasing further with increase in the size of firms. This is because the large farmers have less demand for loan which may be due to availability of own resources for agricultural finance. It is also noticed that the elasticity of demand for formal and informal loans is higher in developed areas than undeveloped areas. It may be due to the fact that the farm households in developed areas use more fertilizer, pesticides and other agricultural inputs as most of their holdings are irrigated. Hence, require more formal and informal loans to meet the cost of inputs. On the other hand, the farm households in undeveloped areas may or may not use such inputs as most of their holding are rainfed.

Apart from the above findings, it is found that the required credit is not being provided by the formal agencies. The credit gap is 31.90 per cent in developed area, 46.77 per cent in backward area, in aggregate is and 36.01 per cent term. This speaks of the lower access to formal credit by all farmers as per their requirement. This indicates the area where the formal agencies can make effort.

It is also seen that more than 70 per cent of the formal credit borrowers are defaulters in paying the loan. Total overdue more than 60 per cent in the year 2002-03 in formal credit market. The overdue as well as percentage of defaulters are less in case of informal market compared to the formal market.

Suggestions for Rural Credit Policy

Keeping in view the above findings of this study a suggested rural credit policy-frame for the future is built with the following objectives.

1. Indiscriminate of improvement the access of formal credit by enabling submarginal, marginal an small farmers to get required formal credit.
2. To minimize the effective cost of borrowing by way of decreasing the transaction cost and opportunity cost of formal loan.

3. To bring about technological change in agriculture through effective use of modern input with the help of cheap agricultural credit.

4. To enhance repayment of loan by increasing returns on capital investment in agriculture.

5. Marginalisation of role of moneylender by minimizing formal credit gap.

The nationalization of commercial banks opened a new vista to bring these banks in a big way in the area of agricultural finance. Since then, there has been a shift in the government policy by practicing the Multi-Agency Approach (MAA) in rural credit. Consequently a number of institutions started functioning to serve the financial needs of the Indian peasantry. Among these institutions mention may made specifically of cooperative societies, commercial banks, regional rural banks and farmers' service societies, which operate at grass roots level and are supported by Central Cooperative Banks, RRBs at district level with RBI and NABARD at the national level.

REFERENCES

1. Bhende, M.J. 1986, "Credit Markets in Rural South India", *Economic and Political Weekly,* Vol. 21, Nos. 38 and 39, pp. A119-24.

2. Bottomley, A. and D. Nudds, 1969, "A Widow's Course Theory of Capital Supply in Underdeveloped Rural Areas", *The Manchester School of Economics and Social Studies,* Vol. 24, No. 3, pp. 364-78.

3. Bottomley, A., 1975, "Interest Rates Determination of Underdeveloped Rural Areas", *American Journal of Agricultural Economics,* Vol. 87, No. 2, pp. 279-91.

4. Braverman, A. and J.L. Guasch 1984, "Capital Requirements. Screening and Interlinked Sharecropping and Credit Contracts", *Journal of Development Economics,* Vol. 14, No. 3, pp. 359- 74.

5. Braverman, A. and J.L. Guash, 1986, "Rural Credit Markets and Institutions in Developing Countries: Lessons for Policy

Analysis from Practice and Modern Theory", *World Development*, Vol. 14, No. 10, pp. 1253-67.

6. Desai, D.K., 1988, "International Credit Requirement for Agricultural Production—2000 A.D.", *IJAE*, Vol. 43, No. 3, 1988.

7. Desai, Haque and Sunita, 1988, "Regional and Class Disparities in the Flow of Agricultural Credit in India, *IJAE*, Vol. 43, No. 3, 1988.

8. Donald, G., 1976, Credit for Small Farmers in Developing Countries (Boulder, Colorado Westview Press).

9. Egger, P., 1986, "Banking for the Rural Poor: Lessons from Some Innovative Savings & Credit Scheme", *International Labour Review*, Vol. 125, No. 4, pp. 447-62.

10. Eswaran, M. and A. Kotwal, 1986, "Access to Capital and Agrarian Production Organisation", *The Economic Journal*, Vol. 96, No. 382, pp. 482-98.

11. George, P.T., D. Namsivayam and G. Ramachandraiah, 1985, "Rural credit and Farmer's Borrowing Costs: A Case Study", *Prajnan*, Vol. 14, No. 2, pp. 21-34.

12. Ghatak, S., 1975, "Rural Interest Rates in the Indian Economy", *Journal of Development Studies*, Vol. 11, No. 3, pp. 190-201.

13. Ghatak, S., 1977, "Rural Credit and the Cost of Borrowing: Interstates Variations in India", *Journal of Developing Areas*, Vol. 18, No. 1, pp. 21-34.

14. Ghatak, S., 1983, "On Interregional Variations in Rural Interest Rates in India", *Journal of Developing Areas*, 18(1): 21-34.

15. Gonzalez Vega, C., 1981, "Interest Rate Policies, Agricultural Credits and Income Distribution in Latin America", Paper Presented at the 2nd International Conference on the Financial Development of Latin America & Caribbeans, Carabolleda, Venezuela.

16. Griffin, K., 1979, *The Political Economy of Agrarian Change*, London: Macmillan.

17. Haque and Verma, 1988, "Regional and Class Disparities in the Flow of Agricultural Credit in India", *Indian Journal of Agricultural Economics,* Vol. 43, No. 3, July-Sept. 1988.

18. Iqbal, F., 1983, "The Demand for Funds by Agricultural Households: Evidence from Rural India", *The Journal of Development Studies,* Vol. 20, pp. 68-86.

19. Iqbal, F., 1988, "The Determinants of Moneylender Interest Rates: Evidence from Rural India", *The Journal of Development Studies,* Vol. 24, No. 3, pp. 364-78.

20. Ladman, J.R., and D.W. Adams, 1978, "The Rural Poor and Recent Performance of Formal Rural Financial Markets in the Dominican Republic", *Canadian Journal of Agricultural Economics,* Vol. 26. No. 1, pp. 43-50.

21. Ladman, J.R., 1984, "Loan Transactions Costs. Credit Rationing and Marketing Structure: The Case of Bolivia", in D.W. Adams, D.H. Graham and J.D. Vonpischke (Edn.) *Undermining Rural Development with Cheap Credit* (Boulder Co.: Westview Press, 1984).

22. Lele, U., 1981, "Cooperative and the Poor: A Comparative Perspective", *World Development,* Vol. 9, No. 1, pp. 55-72.

23. Lipton, M., 1976, "Agricultural Finance and Rural Credit in Poor Countries", *World Development,* Vol. 4, No. 7, pp. 543-53.

24. Mallick, S.C. and J. Sohail, "Role of Institutional Credit in the Agricultural Development of Pakistan", *Pakistan Development Review,* 30(4) Winter 1991; pp. 1039-50.

25. Panda, R., 1988, "Credit Financing of Primary Agricultural Cooperative Societies Among Farm Households in Orissa", *Indian Journal of Agricultural Economics,* Vol. 43, No. 3.

26. Rangarajan, V., "Rural Credit System for Agriculture and Rural Poor in Tamil Nadu", Bulletin: *Madras Development Seminar Series,* 20(12); Dec. 90; pp. 562-88 (ISN=12120).

27. Rao, C.H. Hamanumanth, "Farm Size and Credit Policy", *Economic and Political Weekly, Review of Agriculture,* December 1970, p. 157.

28. Rao, J.M., 1980, "Interest Rates in Backward Agriculture", *Cambridge Journal of Economics,* Vol. 4, No. 2, pp. 159-67.

29. Rudra, A., 1982, *Indian Agriculture: Myth and Reality*, Allied Publishers New Delhi.

30. Ruttan, V.W., 1986, "Assistance to Expand Agricultural Production", *World Development*, Vol. 46, pp. 39-63.

31. Sarap, K., "Factors Affecting Small Farmers' Access to Institutional Credit in Rural Orissa India", *Development and Change*, 21(2): Apr. 1990, pp. 281-308.

32. Sarap K., 1990, "Factors Affecting Small Farmer's Access to Institutional Credit in Rural Orissa, India", *Development and Change*, Vol. 21, No. 2, pp. 281-307.

33. Sarap K., 1991 (Unpublished), "Small Farmers Demand for Credit with Special Reference to Sambalpur District. Western Orissa", Ph.D. Thesis, University of Delhi.

34. Shivamaggi, H.B., "Problem of Rural Credit in India", *EPW*, 28(26): 26 June 1993, pp. 1361-68.

35. Shivamaggir, H.B., "Problem of Rural Credit in India", *EPW*, 28(26): 26 June 1993, pp. 1361-68.

36. Sinha, R., 1976, *'Food and Poverty: The Political Economy of Confrontation'*, (New Delhi Ambika Publication).

37. Throat, S.K., 1990, Farm Size, *Credit Policy and Access to Institutional Finance in Developing Agriculture.*

38. Throat, S.K., 1991, *'Regional Dimensions of Rural Credit in India'*, Criterion Publisher, New Delhi.

4

Socio-economic and Environmental Impacts of JFMS
A Case Study of VSSS Under Digapahandi Range in Orissa

R.K. Panda[*] *& Dr. K.C. Patnaik*[**]

Introduction

In recent years, there has been an interesting intervention in the governance of forest resources through Joint Forest Management (JFM). Significant progress of this type of governance is reported in terms of area under JFM and the number of associated Forest Protection Committees. As per the recent information available, 27 State Governments have issued resolutions in favour of JFM for the protection and conservation of forest resources. By December 2002 there were 64,000 JFM committees managing 14.26 million hectares of forest land in different states (MOEF, 2003).

The development of Joint Forest Management owes much to the National Forest Policy, 1988, which emphasises the involvement of village committees living close to the forest

* Mr. Panda is a Lecturer in Economics, P.G. Department of Economics, Khallikote (Auto) College, Berhampur, Orissa.

** Dr. Patnaik is Senior Lecture in Economics, University College, Berhampur. Orissa.

in protection and development of forests. The subsequent notification in 1990 by the Government of India to State Governments makes an instruction to involve local communities in the management, protection and development of forests. In the year 1995, the Resolution was slightly modified to involve women and landless households as well as usufruct sharing by the communities. To provide legal backup to JFM committees, it was further revised on February 21, 2000. The main provisions of JFMs, as per, Forest Policy 1988 includes: *(i)* Maintenance of Environmental stability through preservation and restoration of ecological balance *(ii)* conservation of natural heritage *iii)* check on soil erosion *(iv)* sustainable increase in forest coverage through massive afforestation *(v)* increase in forest productivity and encouragement for massive utilisation of forest resources.

Functioning of JFMs

The Joint Forest Management needs a Village Level Organisation (VLO) of people for the purpose of their participation in the management. Such organisations may be the existing village Panchayat itself, or may be a newly formed organisation such as a cooperative society or a development society or a Forest Protection Committee. Actually, most of the VLOs involved in JFM are in the form of Village Forest Protection Committees. The primary objective of village Forest Protection Committee is to provide a visible role to the local communities in planning, management and protection of forests and to give them a share in the benefits from these forests. Thus, the basic thrust of JFM is to establish grassroots community based institutions for the protection and management of forests.

The present paper seeks to analyse the socio-economic and environmental and ecological impacts of VSSs promoted under the JFM Scheme implemented by the Forest Development Agencies in Orissa. The outcome of the present study is based on the data collected using PRA and RRA methods.

The Study Area

There are fourteen Vana Surakshya Samittees (VSSs) and created under Digapahandi Range which are located at Digapahandi, Patapur, Nuapada and Chikiti Sections of the Concerned forest Range. Out of the total treated area of 250 hectares, 90 hectares (36.0%) under ANR, 105 hectares under AR (42.0%) 35 hectares under Bamboo (14.0%), 15 hectares (6.0%) under silvipasture and 5 hectares (2.0%) under medicinal plantation have been treated (Details shown in Annexure-1).

The project period is between 2005-06 to 2009-10 and 2006-07 to 2010-11 for the VSSs created in Digapahandi range. By July 2006 fund of Rs. 1800033 have been released to carry out the different components of the VSS programme. VSS wise break-up of the funds released is shown in Annexure-1. Of the total funds released, an amount of Rs. 1286131 have been utilised (Details shown in Annexure 1).

Following are different types of SMC works observed during our field visit.

- Waterhole
- Check-dam
- V-ditch
- Contour bunding

Project Benefits

	Name of the VSS	*Project Benefits*
1.	Kishorechandrapur	• Forest loss prevented • Increased availability of fuel and timber in future • Increase in income of forest dependent households • More employment • Increased no. of goats and sheep • More plantation consciousness

	Name of the VSS	*Project Benefits*
2.	Raipur	• Profuse regeneration of Bamboo trees • More no. of barking deer reported • Complete prevention of forest fire
3.	Kamalpur	• Place is fast becoming a tourist place • More inflow of tourists • Frequent picnic parties in the VSS area • Profuse regeneration of bamboo trees • In-migration of elephants • Non-interference of wild animals in croplands
4.	Gaida	• Reduction in illicit transportation of timber • Reduction in forest fire • Profuse regeneration of trees due to ANR and AR plantations • Increased fodder availability • Increased concentration of wild animals • In-migration and settlement of elephants
5.	Harina	• Increased stall feeding practices by the villagers • In-migration of wild animals • Flow of streams from forest • Reduction in top soil erosion • Reduction in illicit stone transportation

	Name of the VSS	*Project Benefits*
		• Reduction in the incidence of forest dependent households • Massive regeneration of trees • Once extinct, reap pearance of Gunduri at the village forest
6.	Boripadar	• More interest for plantation • Restricted open grazing • Introducing crossbred cows • Preventing forest fire • Additional income
7.	Podabadi	• Any type of benefit not reported
8.	Moreibadi	• Sufficient availability of firewood • More awareness for observing the forest • Better quality of life due to the convergence of programmes like WATSAN and Swajaladhara with JFM works
9.	Bagada	• Massive regeneration of bamboo trees • Multiple regeneration of plants • More MFPs • Reduction in illicit stone transportation
10.	Kandhakhududi	• Plenty availability of fuel and timber against the future benefits
11.	Balipadar	• More availability of fuel wood, timber and fodder as future benefits
12.	Patrachudi	• Increased stall feeding practices • Indigenous cows being replaced by she-buffaloes increased milk production

	Name of the VSS	*Project Benefits*
		• Increased plantation consciousness • Plenty availability of firewood and bamboo as future benefits
13.	Narsinghagad	• Future availability of fuel and timber • Sustainability of forest resources • Scenic beauty of the forest
14.	Pipiliguda	• Future availability of firewood and timber • More availability of other MFPs are expected

Suggestions for Improvement

- Early finalisation of micro plan and PRA is to be ensured for all the VSS.
- For the better social impacts of the programme Entry Pont Works (EPWs) are to be completed on priority basis.
- Village Development Funds are to be created for the sustainability of the project.
- There should be smooth flow of funds to ensure plantation and maintenance works.
- The concerned secretary at Chikiti Section is to be proactive for the effective Implementation of JFM programme at Kandhakhududi and Balipadar VSS.
- The Secretary of Harina VSS should be involved for the better involvement of the villages in connection with conducting meetings and maintaining records and registers.
- Women members of the VSSs are to be encouraged for attending VSS meetings.

Concluding Remarks

Despite many of the project constraints and limitations, JMFs have been hailed as the promoters of rural development in terms of improving the quality of life of the rural masses both through direct and indirect ways. Indirectly, it has influenced a sustainable and integrated development of plants, animals, human beings thereby proving itself as an effective instrument of biodiversity.

ANNEXURE-1

Table 4.1: Physical and Financial Achievement of the VSSS in Digapahandi Range

		Physical Achievement under different components including spill-over (Creation only) in hectare						*Financial Achievements up to July under different components including (Creation only)*						*Financial Achievements (in Lakh)*	
Sl. No.	*Name of the VSS*	*ANR*	*AR*	*Bamboo*	*Pasture*	*Mixed*	*Total*	*ANR*	*AR*	*Bamboo*	*Pasture*	*Mixed*	*Total*	*Total funds released July' 06*	*Funds utilised up to July' 06*
1.	Kishorechandrapur	10.00	10.00	5.00	-	-	25.00	30750	85,603	31135	-	-	137488	1.77	1.55
2.	Raipur	10.00	5.00	-	-	-	15.00	39253	53384	-	-	-	93087	1.03	1.00
3.	Kamalapur	10.00	20.00	-	-	5.00	35.00	39218	147698	-	-	45780	332696	2.92	2.65
4.	Gaida	10.00	10.00	-	5.00	-	25.00	36713	66883	-	24672	-	128268	1.80	1.38
5.	Hanna	10.00	-	5.00	5.00	-	20.00	39244	-	23105	18294	-	80643	1.12	1.03
6.	Boripadar	10.00	5.00	5.00	-	-	20.00	16528	29040	118765	-	-	64333	1.25	0.64
7.	Podabadi	-	10.00	5.00	-	-	15.00		53244	199960	-	-	73204	1.19	0.73
8.	Moraibadi	-	15.00	-	-	-	15.00	-	76634	-	-	-	76634	1.40	0.76
9.	Bagada	10.00	-	-	-	-	10.00	21114	-	-	-	-	21114	0.53	0.21
10.	K. Khududi	-	15.00	5.0	-	-	20.00	-	89754	11073	-	-	100847	1.65	1.01
11.	Balipadar	10.00	-	-	-	-	10.00	12095	-	-	-	-	12095	0.54	0.12
12.	Patrachudi	10.00	-	-	-	-	10.00	16279	-	-	-	-	16279	0.53	0.16
13.	Narsinghagada	-	10.00	5.00	5.00	-	20.00	-	62341	21011	19540	-	102891	1.49	1.02
14.	Pipliguda	-	5.00	5.00	-	-	10.00	-	32.786	22091	-	-	34877	0.72	0.54

Source: Data collected from the Forest Range Office, Digapahandi.

5

Special Employment and Poverty Alleviation Programmes in India

*Ananta Basudev Sahu**

Poverty in India is a complex socio-economic phenomenon. It is neither a new nor it is suddenly appeared, but there has been much awareness of the poroblem with in and out side the country (Ahulwalia, 1974). According to Lewis, "We come closer to describing what poverty is when we define it as the inability to satisfy one's material wants or needs". Poverty can also defined as a social phenomenon in which a section of the society is unable to fulfill even its basic necessities of life. When a substantial segment of the society is deprived of the minimum level of living and continues at a bare substantial level, that society is said to be plagued with mass poverty. Mass poverty exists in third world countries, but the pockets of exist in the developed countries of Europe and America. It has two attributes i.e. the absolute and the relative. In the absolute standard, minimum physical quantities of cereals, pulses, milk, etc., i.e. those are deprived of these; they are remaining in poverty line. According to the relative standard, income distribution of the population in different fractile groups is estimated and a comparison of the levels of living of the top to 10 per cent with the bottom

* Research Officer, International Institute for Population Sciences, Mumbai-88.

5 to 10 per cent of the relative standard. According to 2001 Census, 26 per cent of people living in below poverty line in India. As regards to states of India, Orissa, Bihar, Madhya Pradesh etc. are the major poverty stricken states. In this paper researcher highlighted major poverty eradication and gainful employment generation programme since independence.

The problem of poverty and unemployment is considered as the biggest challenge to development planning in India. High poverty levels are synonymous with poor quality of life, deprivation, malnutrition, illiteracy and low human resource development. The slogan of poverty eradication has been adopted by all political parties in one form another and there is a national agreement for the global poverty alleviation. The national consensus on poverty alleviation provided the necessary condition for launching various schemes and programmes aimed at achieving the objectives. But the persistence of poverty during all these years suggests that national consensus on objectives did not provide sufficient conditions for poverty alleviation.

Table 5.1: Estimate of Poverty (Ratio)

Year	*All India*	*Rural*	*Urban*
1973-74	54.9	56.4	49.0
1977-78	51.5	53.14	45.2
1983-86	44.5	45.7	40.8
1987-88	38.9	39.1	38.2
1993-94	36.0	37.3	32.4
1999-2000	26.1	27.1	23.6

Source: Ministry of Finance, Government of India, Economic Survey, 2000-01.

Special Employment and Poverty Alleviation Programmes

1. **Integrated Rural Development Programme (IRDP):** This programme is operated in our country since 1980.

Table 5.2: Comparative Study of Population in Top Ten States in India

States	*1973-74*	*1993-94*	*1999-2000*	*Rank*
Orissa	66.18	48.56	47.15	1
Bihar	61.91	54.96	42.60	2
Madhya Pradesh	61.78	42.52	37.43	3
Sikkim	50.86	41.43	36.55	4
Assam	51.21	40.86	36.09	5
Tripura	51.00	39.01	34.44	6
Meghalaya	50.20	37.92	33.87	7
Arunachal Pradesh	51.93	39.35	33.47	8
Nagaland	50.81	37.92	32.67	9
Uttar Pradesh	57.07	40.85	31.15	10

Source: Ministry of Finance, Government of India, Economic Survey, 2000-01.

This programme aims at providing self-employment to the rural poor. Assistance is provided in the form of subsidy and bank credit. The target group consists of small and marginal farmers, agricultural labourers and rural artesian living below the poverty line. The 25 per cent of subsidy are provided to the small farmers, 33 per cent are provided to the marginal farmers, agricultural labourers and 50 per cent subsidy are provided to the Scheduled Castes and Tribes. (Kapila, 1933).

2. **Training of Rural Youth for Self-Employment (TRYSEM):** Training of Rural Youth for Self-employment (TRYSEM) aims at providing basic technical and entrepreneurial skills to the rural poor in the age group of 18 to 35 years to enable them to the take up income generating activities. This Plan had announced in nineties. During the Eighth plan, 15.28 lakh youth were trained under TRYSEM, of self employment and remaining unemployed (Kapila, 2003).

3. **National Food for Work Programme:** National Food for Work Programme was launched on November 14, 2004 in 150 most backward districts of the country with the objective to intensify the generation of suplementary wage employment. The programme is open to all rural poor who are in need of wage employment and desire to do manual unskilled work (Economic Survey, 2001).

4. **Development of Women and Children in Rural Areas (DWCRA):** The special scheme for development of women and children in rural areas (DWCRA) was started in 1982-83 on a pilot basis, in 50 districts and has now been extended to all the districts of the country. It aims at improving the living conditions of women and thereby children though the provisions of opportunities for self employment. DWCRA also providing more income generating activities for supplementing their incomes. It also encourages the habit of thrift and credit among the poor rural women to make them self-reliant. This programme also takes care family welfare, health care, nutrition, education, childcare, safe drinking water, sanitation and shelter to improve the quality of life of the family and community. This programme was successfully implemented in Andhra Pradesh, Kerala, Tripura and Gujarat. But in other states the performance was not so well (Kapila, 2003).

5. **Swaranjayanti Gram Swarozgar Yozana (SSGY):** SSGY, launched in April 1999, aims at bringing the assisted poor families (Swarozaris) above the poverty line by organizing them into Self Help Groups (SHGs) through a mix of bank credit and Government subsidy (Economic Survey, 2005).

6. **Sampoorna Grameen Rozgar Yojana (SGRY):** SGRY launched in 2001, aims at providing additional wage employment in all rural areas and thereby food security and improve nutritional levels. The SGRY is open to all rural poor who are need of wage employment and desire to dimanual and unskilled work around the village. The programme is implemented through Panchyat Raj institutions (Economic Survey, 2001).

7. **Rural Housing Indira Awaas Yojana (IAY):** The Indira Awaas Yojana (IAY) operationalised from 1999-2000 is the major scheme or construction of houses for the poor, free of cost. The Ministry of Rural Development (MORD) provides equity support to the Housing Urban Development Corporation (HUDCO) for this purpose (Economic Survey, 2005).

8. **Prime Minister's Rozgar Yojana (PMRY):** PMRY started in 1993 with the objective of creating self-employment opportunities to the educated unemployed youth by assisting them in setting up any economically viable activity. So far about 20 lakh units have been set up under the PMRY, creating 30.4 lakh. The targets for additional employment opportunities under the tenth plan and 2004-05 are 16.50 lakh and 3.75 lakh are respectively (Economic Survey, 2005).

9. **Pradhan Mantri Gramodaya Yojana (PMGY):** The PMGY launched in 2000-01 envisages allocation of Additional Central Assistance (ACA) to the States and Union Territories for selected basic services such as primary health, primary education, rural shelter, rural drinking water, nutrition and rural electrification. For 2003-04 as well as 2004-05, the annual allocation of ACA for PMGY was 2,800 crore (Economic Survey, 2005).

10. **Drought Prone Area Programme (DPAP):** The DPAP was launched in 1973 in arid and semiarid areas with poor natural resource endowments. The objective was to promote more by better soil and moisture conservation, more scientific use of water resources, afforstation and live stock development through development of fodder and pasture resource, and in the long run to restore the ecological balance. The DPAP covers 615 blocks of 91 districts in 13 states. Now it was converted to Drought Prone Areas Programme (DPAP), Desert Development Programme and integrated Wastelands Development Programme (IAWP). During 2004-05 allocation of Rs. 300 crore, Rs. 215 crore and

Rs. 368 crore provided for DPAP, DDP and IAWP respectively (Kaplia, 1993).

11. **Rural Employment Generation Programme (REGP):** The REGP, launched in 1995 with the objective of creating employment opportunities in rural areas and small towns, is being implemented by the Khadi and Village Industries Commission (KVIC). Entrepreneurs can establish village industries by availing of margin money assistance from the KVIC and bank loans for the projects with a maximum cost of Rs. 25 lakh. For 2004-05, a target of creating 5.25 lakhs job opportunities has been set up during the tenth plan period (Economic Survey, 2005).

12. **Antvodaya Anna Yoiana (AAY):** The AAY launched in December 2000 provides food grains at a highly subsidized rate of Rs. 2.00 per kg, wheat and rice Rs. 3.00 per kg to the poor families under the Targeted Public Distribution System (TPDS). (Economic Survey, 2005).

13. **Swarna Jayanti Sahari Rojagar Yojana (SJSRY):** The SJSRY programme launched in December 1997. The Urban Self-Employment Programme and the Urban Wage Employment Programme are the two social component of SJSRY. This programme implemented for alleviation of urban poverty (Economic Survey, 2005).

14. **Valmik Ambedkar Awas Yojana (VAMAY):** To the construction and up gradation of dwelling units for the slum dwellers and provides healthy and enabling urban environment through community toilets under Nrimal Bharat Abhiyan, VAMBAY yojana launched in December 2001. For the year 2004-05, out of the tentative Central Fund Allocation of Rs. 280.58 crore, up to December 31, 2004 an amount of Rs. 223.66 crore has been released covering 1,06,146 dwelling units and 20,139 toilet seats (Economic Survey, 2005).

15. **Pradhan Mantri Gram Sadak Yojana (PMGCY):** This programme was launched December 2000, is a

programme to provide road connectivity through good roads of 500 persons or more in the rural areas by the end of the tenth plan period (Sowni, 2005).

16. **Annapura Yojana (AY):** This scheme was launched on April 2002 as a totally Central Govt. sponsored. It aims to providing food security to meet the requirement of those senior citizens who though eligible for pension under the National Old Age Pension Scheme, 10 kgs of foodgrains per person per month are supplied free of cost (Sowni, 2005).

17. **Indira Awas Yojana (IAY):** IAY aims to providing dwelling units free of cost to the poor families of the Scheduled Caste and Scheduled Tribes, free bonded labourers and the non-SC/ST persons below the poverty line (Sowni, 2005).

18. **National Social Assistance Programme (NSSAP):** The NSSAP launched in 1995 with the objectives of providing social assistance benefit to poor household affected by old age, death of primary bread earner and maternity care. The programme has here components National Old Age Pension Scheme (NOAPS), National Family Benefit Scheme (NFBS) and National Maternity Benefit Scheme (NMBS) (Sowni, 2005).

19. **Employment Assurance Scheme (EAS):** EAS stated October 1993. The primary objective of the EAS was creation of additional was employment i.e. the lean agricultural scheme (Sowni, 2005).

20. **Jai Prakash Rozgar Guarantee Yojana (JPRGY):** The scheme seeks to provide guaranteed employment to the unemployed in the most distressed districts of the country (Sowni, 2005).

Goals for Tenth Plan (2002-07): The goals are finalized for 10th Plan under the post reform era where market forces are catalysts for economic activity. India is all set to emerge as an Economic Superpower in the world economy. Assuming these things the goals is set as Tenth Five-Year Plan are:

- Doubling the per capita income in a decade.
- Growth rate of Gross Domestic Product (GDP) to be 8 per cent per annum.
- Harness the benefits to growth to improve the quality of live through reduction in poverty ratio by 5 per cent point by 2007.
- Growth in gainful employment to keep pace with addition to labour force.
- Stress is on rural development, agriculture, irrigation, agro-forestry, small and medium enterprises, communication, technology, tourism etc. It is a crucial spur to employment and alleviation poverty.

Conclusion

Poverty is the pivotal factor of economic backwardness. To reducing rural poverty, agricultural growth is important. Secondly, in rural areas there is need for rural industrialization, for employment generation agrobased industry may set up locally so that people can be employed. To eradicate mass poverty regional disparities should be reduced. The Government of India should increase the development expenditure particularly social sector expenditure in poorer states like Bihar, Orissa, Madhya Pradesh, Uttar Pradesh, etc. so that poverty may be eradicated. There is also need to implementation of the anti-poverty programme with the involvement of Panchayats and Non-Government Organization (NGOs). Self-Help Groups (SHGs) and local people participation etc. But lack of consensus, will and hard effect poverty alleviation is in slow progress.

REFERENCES

1. Ahluwalia, M.S. (1974), *"Inequality: Some Dimensions of the Problem in Chennery"*, H.B. et al. (ed) *Redistribution with*

Growth, Oxford University Press, London, Government of India (2002), Planning Commission, *"Tenth Five-Year Plan"*, New Delhi.

2. Ministry of Finance, Governement of India, Economic Survey, 2000-01, *Poverty Alleviation Programmes.*

3. Ministry of Finance, Governement of India, Economic Survey, 2004-05, *Poverty Alleviation Programmes.*

4. Sowam S.V. (2005), *Strargries of Poverty Alleviation in India*, edited by Dr. Sita Ram Singh, Poverty Alleviation in the Third World.

5. Uma Kaplia (2002), *India's Economy in the 21st Century.*

6. Uma Kaplia *(2003), India's Economy Since Independence, 1993.*

6

Employment Planning in India
Approaches and Experiences

Deepak Bishoyi & Anadi Charan Sethi***

The unemployment problem in India today has becoming explosive which may threaten our political entity if some suitable effective measures are not taken well in time. In its true perspective it appears to be the root cause of various problems facing our country at present. It has created economic disparities and social imbalances. On an average we see today that every fifty man of our working employable forces in cities, towns and rural areas is unemployed or idle. When psychologically analyzed this idle man of the working force is carrying a load of worries and uncertainties about his future economic life. Temperamently he is not only frustrated but also impatient. His nonutilization for a long time in the constructive channel of nation building poses a problem and remains always a potential danger to our country. The state, thus, shall have to think of ways and means to employ its both skilled and unskilled idle manpower to its optimum use for nation-building tasks with a sense of urgency (Forum of Education, 1972). In this paper makes an attempt to analysis the historical prospective of employment planning in India. Here it is made some brief

* Ph.D. Scholar, Institute for Social and Economic Change, Bangalore.
** Researcher, International Institute of Population Science. Mumbai.

review of all the five years plans till today and finally analyses some approaches and experiences of employment planning in India.

Although the problem of unemployment has been with us in an acute form since the end of World War I, Government policy until the First Five-Year Plan was drafted in 1950-51. It is true that the Royal Commission on Labour discussed the subject in 1931, but all that they said was that "the setting tin of public employment agencies would not be itself be an effective remedy for general unemployment agencies for general unemployment arising out of economic depression". They ended by making the obvious statement that "while these agencies might help in increasing the mobility of labour, they could not augment the quantum of employment, which depended on measures such as greater industrialization".

Towards the end of World War II, however the Central Government felt that something ought to be done. A Directorate General of Resettlement and Employment was according set up at New Delhi (with regional offices in every major Province) to plan the orderly absorption on civil life of ex-servicemen and discharged war workings. Although the objective was strictly limited to these specified categories, the hope was entertained in at least some quarters that this Directorate would ultimately develop into a permanent origination to tackle the entire problem of unemployment. In the years immediately after the partition of the subcontinent, this Directorate took upon itself a considerable portion of the responsibility for the rehabilitation, in suitable employment, of displaced persons from both wings of Pakistan (Das, 1968).

Then came the Five-Year Plans. It was inevitable that eradication of unemployment would from a major plank of Government policy both in the formulation and execution of these plans. Government took note of the fact that the problem of unemployment and under employment had been aggravated by such factors as

(a) the rapid growth of population,

(b) the disappearance of the old rural industries which provided part-time employment to a large number of persons in the rural areas,

(c) inadequate development of the non-agricultural sector from the point of view of employment,

(d) the large displacement of population as a result partition.

Employment planning as thus concerned with three basic issues—demographic, educational and economic. As such, any employment planning must aim at examining, and suggesting solutions to the demographic, educational and economic aspects of the employment problem. In an under developed country like India, employment policy must aim at three objectives.

1. *Demographic Objective:* A reduction in the birth rate in the coming decades and/or an expansion in the employment opportunities to absorb the available workforce;
2. *Educational Objective:* Diversification and change of educational facilities in accordance with economic requirements of the country (Employment-education coordination);
3. *Economic Objective:* Diversification and growth of employment opportunities. The central objective of economic planning, in India, was to initiate a process of development which would raise living standards and create new opportunities for a richer and more varied life. (Government of India, 1952). Poverty and unemployment and adopted various strategies for its solution.

First Plan Strategies

For tackling the problem of unemployment, foremost consideration was given in the first plan to the rural sector, mainly because of the magnitude and seriousness of it problem. Expansion in rural employment opportunities, it was held would also relieve the pressure on urban employment. The plan was, however, unable to estimate precisely the magnitude of rural unemployment. The first plan document stated that some authorities had put the figure at 30 per cent; but in addition to this, there is chronic under-employment (Government of India, 1952). However, its quantitative assessment was left as an open question. As for the growth of population and the consequent increase in the labour force, the plan projected that population would grow by 1.25 per cent pre annum.

The main thrust of the rural works programmes lay in the extension of minor and major irrigation works, covering approximate 19 million acres, land reclamation and revival and development of rural industries. These projects being labour-intensive in chapter, the same amount of capital would generate more work opportunities then in the large-scale industries. The plan had also provided Rs. 150 million for the development of twelve rural industries. On a general plane, the plan has suggested: *(a)* the extension of mixed farming, *(b)* undertaking public works programmes during the slack agricultural season. The possibilities of these majors were not known.

The employment potential of major irrigation and power projects was calculated to be 250,000. It was assured that Rs. 1000 millions would be spend annually on this account and that be spent annually on this account and that 20 per cent of this account and that 20 per cent of this would be spent on wages (direct and indirect). It was further on assumed that 250,000 workers would be employed annually on these projects, on the assumed wage rate of Rs. 2.5 per day for an average working year of 300 days. Thus, it would create job opportunities for 1.25 million people over the plan period (Government of India, 1952).

Second Plan Strategies

The expected growth of labour by 10 million within the second plan period had been based on the assumption that the population would increase by 1.25 per cent per annum.

The census of 1961 had however, revealed that the population of India had growth by 78 million between 1951 and 1961. The actual rate of growth was thus found to be 1.97 per cent annum. On this basis, the actual increase in population, within the second plan was of the order of 39 million. Taking the labour force to be 39.1 per cent of the total population, its natural increase within the plan period must have been about 16 million. The plan had projected it to be 10 million.

Even if we accepted the contention of the second plan that the backlog of unemployment at the beginning of the plan was no more than 5.3 million, the total requirement of additional job by the end of the plan period would have been of the order of 21.3 million. The plan document had estimated that public outlays would generate about 8 million additional jobs during the plan period.

Even if we suppose that the various targets of growth in employment had been achieved, there still remained a shortfall of 13.26 million jobs by the end of the second plan. Thus does not take account of educated unemployment. But as compared to the expenditure target of Rs. 46, 000 million. The shortfall in expenditure of Rs. 2000 millions must have lowered the employment given by the plan. A confrontation of this comes from the third plan document which said, "....in terms of unemployment the economy suffered significant deterioration in last five years" Government of India, 1961).

Third Plan Strategies

Growth of population between 1961 and 1966 was reckoned at 54 million. On this basis, the increase of the labour force was calculated to be 17 million during the third plan; it was assumed that the labour force was 31.4 per cent of the total population. But later census figures have shown that population grew during the decade 1961 to 1971 by an annual rate of 2.23 per cent and that 43 per cent of the population now constituted the labour force. That implies that the population by 1966 was to be 490.4 million, an increase of 51.2 million between 1961 and 1966. The new entrants to the labour force were likely, to be 22 million rather than the 17 million projected by the plan document. The total requirement of employment opportunities within the plan period was thus of the order of 35 million from the backlog of unemployment and 22 million for the new entrants. The third plan document, on the other hand, planned the creation of about 14 million additional jobs, about 10.5 million outside agriculture and about 3.5 million in agriculture. Even if the plan target of employment was archived there would still be shortfall of 21 million jobs by the end of the third plan.

The total employment required in rural sector had been estimated to be 9 million in the second plan document. We have already seen about that the additional rural employment created within the second plan was only 1.5 million, leaving a backlog of employment at the beginning of the third plan of 7.5 million. The third plan document estimated that out of the 17 million new entrants, about a third plan would be in urban areas. It decided that two-third of the additional labour force of 17 million would have to be absorbed in non-agricultural occupations, that is that another one third of the 17 million should be encouraged to move to urban areas. Even then the balance of 5.57 million would swell the numbers of the rural workforce. If the backlog of 7.5 million were added to it, the rural employment workforce seeking employment would be 13 million. In these circumstances, the relief given to underemployment in rural areas simply did not exist.

Annual Plan Strategies

The end of the Third Five Year Plan may be regarded as a watershed in the process of planning in India. In the process of planning began with what was euphemistically called a "plan holiday" for three successive years, 1966-67 to 1968-69. Annual plans for these years were, however, drawn up and implemented. Naturally little could be achieved in employment certain during these years of annual plans. Nevertheless, it is worthwhile to examine the strategies originally planned form the first draft outline of the fourth plan, published in August 1966 (Government of India, 1966), because it covers the period of the annual plans.

Fourth Plan Strategies

The fourth plan out emphasis on labour-intensive programmes, These included development of agriculture, rural infrastructure, including communication and transport links, rural electrification, water management, rural industries, decentralization and dispersal of industrial investment, and rural urban housing. The improvement plan would, as a consequence, give performance to small scale over large scale projects. The emphasize on generation of employment were not, however, to compromise with the principal productive employment with high degree of efficiency. Capital intensive projects would be limited to those were technological considerations and economics of scale made labour intensive techniques economically unrealistic (Government of India, 1969).

The national plan also listed various scheme expected to generate additional employment in the organized sector. But in consonance with the recommendations of the Expert Committee no attempt was made to quantify the employment potential of the various projects of the plan. The plan accepted the estimate the Register General that the growth of population would be 2.5 per cent per annum during the fourth plan period,

Fifth Plan Strategies

The programmes included in the fifth plan were to have labour intensive basis, to maximize the generation of employment opportunities, Major efforts would have to be made to expand opportunities for self-employment to the maximum level possible, especially in sectors like agriculture, small industries, services, comers and trade. Consistent with the overall policy of the fifth plan, emphasizes was to be laid on the creation of job opportunities for poorer sections of the population and to improve the earnings of those were only partially employed (Government of India, 1974).

The fifth plan also envisaged consolidation, diversification and improvement in the quality of vocational training and its closer relation to employment potential and needs. Funds were provided for gradual modernization of the equipment of Industrial Training Institutes. Stress was also laid on training and research to meet the requirements of the plan, In institute for Electronics and Instrumentation was to be set up within the plan period and several other training institutes were envisaged, The plan also considers outing turn and requirement for technically qualified personnel. It recommended restructuring the educational and training programmes, so as to remove the imbalance between supply and demands educated and technically qualified persons.

Sixth Plan Strategies

During this period, new additions to the labour force were expected to be of the order of 34.3 million. The Sixth Plan projects estimated on employment generation of the order of 39.3 million during 1980-85. Thus at the end of the Sixth Plan, 12 million persons would account for the backlog of employed. The growth employment generation during the Sixth Plan works out of 4.32 per cent per annum.

To sum of it may be stated that by end large, the employment targets of the Sixth Plan have been fulfilled. The Seventh Plan, according to the 32nd round of NSS is to stated with a backlog of 13.9 million persons, but on the basis of a more recent 38th round NSS information the Seventh Plan is to stated with a backlog of 9.2 million in March 1985.

Seventh Plan Strategies

The Seventh Plan (1985-90) has given two estimates of employment usual status the most comprehensive concept following the methodology given in the Sixth Plan. Given the scenario has obtaining on the eve of the Seventh Plan,

"The backlog employment at the outset of the Seventh Plan has been estimated 9.2 million for the age group 5-plus. It has also been seen that net additions to the labour force in this age group would be 39.38 million." Thus the overall magnitude of employment requirement for the Seventh Plan works out to be 47.58 million. Working on the envisaged growth rate of 5 per cent in GDP and the impact of poverty eradication programmes aimed at providing self-employment and wage employment for the poorer sections of the community, the Seventh Plan mentioned: "it is expected that additional employment of the order of 40.36 million standard person years would be generated during the Seventh Plan within implied growth rate of 3.99 per cent per annum.

Since during the eighties, the growth of labour force has been taking place at the rate of 2.2 per cent per annum, but the growth rate of employment has been 1.55 per cent per annum, the situation would naturally result in an increase in the magnitude of unemployment.

Taking 28 million as the backlog of unemployed in 1990, net additions to the labour force during 1990-95 are expected to be 3 7 million. Thus the total number of persons requiring employment during Eighth Plan would be around 65 million. It is expected that during 1995-2000, labour force would increase by 41 million. Thus by the year 2000 AD, the total number of job seekers would be around 106 million. The Planning Commissions, therefore, concludes, "Employment growth in the aggregated over the estimated employment of 300 million in 1990 would have to be about 4 per cent compound per annum if the goal providing employment to all is to be achieved by the end of the Eighth Plan, and over 3 per cent per annum if it is to be attained by 2000 AD". The Approach paper of the Eighth Plan has accepted 3 per cent growth of employment as its goal for 1990-95. This appears to be realizable goal if a proper employment oriented strategy is developed.

Ninth Plan Strategies

The backlog of employment in Ninth Plan (1997-2002)

has been reckoned has 7.5 million on the basis of usual status concept. There would be net addition of 53 million to the labour force during the Ninth Plan. Thus, the Ninth Plan has to provide for the total employment of 60.5 million on the basis of the employment elasticities of the various sectors and the expected growth rate, additional employment likely to be generated with 7 per cent overall growth is likely to be 53.9 million. At the end of the Ninth Plan, the backlog of the employment is expected to be reduced to 6.6 million in 2002 indicating usual status employment of the order 1.5 per cent. From the data, it evident that agriculture is likely to contribute about 32 per cent of additional employment (27.93 million). Trade and Transport are expected to contribute 9.9 million or 8.3 per cent of additional employment. Manufacturing is expected to contribute 5.55 million additional employment opportunities the contribution is small industry. This service sector is another major area of the employment generation. An additional 5.45 million job opportunities (10 per cent) are expected in the service sector. This is a scenario of near full employment.

The Planning Commission has visualized the backlog of employment at 7.5 million in the beginning of the Ninth Five-Year Plan (1997) on the basis of usual status concept. There would net addition of 53 million to the labour force during the Ninth Plan. Thus the Ninth Plan has provided for the total employment of 60.5 million.

Tenth Plan Strategies

The Approach Paper to the Tenth Plan, approved by the NDC in September 2001, prescribed provision of gainful high-quality employment to the addition to the labour force over the Tenth Plan period. A subsequent assessment of unemployment situation in the base year of the Tenth Plan 2002 showed that to clear the backlog of unemployment, 35 million employment opportunities are required to be created. The Tenth Five-Year Plan, however aims at provision of gainful employment in excess of the addition to the labour force.

The Planning Commission Social Group on creation of 10 million Employment Opportunities a Year in Tenth Plan noted that the causes underlying this sharp fall need to be investigated further. According, the Group has adopted a 1.8 per cent growth rate of labour force in the Tenth Plan period (2002-07), i.e. a much slower decline in the period beyond (2007-12). With suitable programmes and policy changes, the same 8 per cent growth rate can generate an additional 19.32 million person years of employment opportunities over the Tenth Plan. The recommended scenario will not only absorb all additional to labour force generated over the Tenth Plan. This recommended scenario will not only absorb all additions to labour force generate over the Tenth Plan in gainful manner, but also reduce the level of unemployment by nearly half and will eliminate it completely by the end of the Eleventh Plan. To summarize, nearly 20 million person years of employment opportunities have to be created by selective innovative programmes and policies leading to a changed pattern of growth in favour of labour intensive sector; the remaining 39 million will come from the normal buoyancy of growth as perceived over from the recent past (1993-94 to 1999-2000), giving a total of 50 million person years over the Tenth Plan.

Employment Strategies of UPA Government

The UPA Government's employment principles are to ensure economic growth of at least 7-8 per cent annually generating employment.

- A National Employment Guarantee Act to be enacted to provide at least 100 days of employment every year at minimum wages to at least one person in every poor household. A massive food-for-work programme to be started as an interim measure.
- A National Commission to be established to examine the problems facing enterprises in unorganized and credit support for which a National Fund is to be created.

- Khadi and Village Industries Commission to be revamped and new programmes launched for modernization.
- Top priority to investment, credit and technology for continued growth of agriculture, aquaculture, afforestation, during etc. to create new jobs.
- Credit facilities for small scale industry and self-employment to be expanded all support for services industry including software, IT, transport, telecommunications and tourism.
- Enabling the textile industry to meet new challenges posed by the adoption quotas in January 2005; fresh impetus to jute industry.

It has already been pointed cut that economic planning in India can be divided into two district phases. The period covering up to fifth year can be regarded as an era of various planning. The second phase starts with the plan to till now. In the first phase of planning, the failure of the plans to make a real dent in the problem of unemployment can be explained as a gap between the need for and the availability of jobs, even if we ignore the comments of the expert Committee. In other world, it was a case of imbalance between supply and demand of employment opportunities. The most important reason account for the failure of the first three plans was their inability to make anything like a dependable estimate of the actual dimensions of the problem of unemployment, for lake of data, and to design appropriate strategies on a commensurate scale.

Plan, in the second phase, were executive in a haphazard fashion. The experience gained in planning techniques could not be used to advantage, mainly because of political and administrative indecision. They were executed under adverse conditions which prevented the achievement of the growth and employment targets. The Expert Committee's recommendations gave a good excuse jobs outside the organized sector of the economy. Beyond that everything was vague, and the strategies suffered from lack of quantification. Without any target, the drawing up of employment strategies is like groping one's way in the dark. The writer feels strongly that slightly imperfect data are better than no data.

After studying all the various plan documents, one is left with the inevitable conclusion that, apart from the appropriateness or otherwise of plan strategies, employment targets could not be achieved in full because of shortfalls in performance in part, because of weaknesses and inadequacies in the implementing machinery. There have been significant failures in putting the available capacity to full use and in securing the degree of coordination of complementary projects which might have maximized their output. The implementation apparatus has been honeycombed with corruption and inefficiency, leading probably to considerable wastage of resources, and resulting in non-fulfillment of targets of development and therefore of employment.

In conclusion, it can be said that wrong strategies and weak implementation have been solely responsible for the non-fulfillment of one of the principle objectives of the plans-the removal of poverty and unemployment. Lesion should be drawn from this past experience for the future of planning.

REFERENCES

1. Das, N. (1968), Unemployment and Employment Planning, Orient Longmans, New Delhi.

2. Government of India (1952), Planning Commission, The First Five-Year Plan, New Delhi.

3. Government of India (1956), Planning Commission, The Second Five-Year Plan, New Delhi.

4. Government of India (1952), Planning Commission, Review of the First Five-Year Plan, New Delhi.

5. Government of India (1961), Planning Commission, The Third Five-Year Plan, New Delhi.

6. Government of India (1969), Planning Commission, The Fourth Five-Year Plan, New Delhi.

7. Government of India (1976), Planning Commission, The Fifth Five-Year Plan, New Delhi.

8. Government of India (1980), Planning Commission, The Sixth Five-Year Plan, New Delhi.

9. Government of India (1985), Planning Commission, The Seventh Five-Year Plan, New Delhi.

10. Government of India (1991), Planning Commission, The Eight Five-Year Plan, New Delhi.

11. Government of India (1997), Planning Commission, The Ninth Five-Year Plan, New Delhi.

12. Government of India (2002), Planning Commission, The Tenth Five-Year Plan, New Delhi.

13. Robinson, A., Brahamananda, P.R. and Deshpande, L.K. (1983), "Employment Policy in a Developing Country," Vol. 2, International Economic Association, The Macmillan Press Ltd., London.

14. Study Report of the Committee on Education and Total Employment, "Educated Unemployment in India," Hindustan Publishing Corporation (India), Delhi 7.

7

Development of Infrastructure in the Era of Globalisation

*Deepak Bishoyi**

The development of rural infrastructure is crucial for the growth of rural economy as well as welfare. It contributes directly to the improvement of living conditions of the people. Poverty assessment studies emphasize the close relationship between isolation and rural poverty. Infrastructure facilities and improvement in delivery of services can reduce the costs and time of the various economic and social activities taken up by rural people.

The present paper focuses the development of infrastructure in the context of globalisation. It highlights the importance of infrastructure in the economic, the extent of growth of important components of developing like roads, railways and electricity during 1995 to 2001 and finally analysis the impact of development during globalisation era.

Importance of Infrastructure

Infrastructure is an integral part of the development of any country. Infrastructure is not simply about the construction of large projects. It is about providing and delivering basic services that people need for everyday life-

* Ph.D. Scholar, Institute for Social and Economic Change, Bangalore-32.

water, sanitation, modern energy, roads and other aspects of transport and access to modern information communication technology. Infrastructure acts as the foundation of any economy. It plays a complex role in fostering economic growth. Entrepreneurial activity in any economy is being stimulated with the provision of infrastructure through certain of numerous opportunities and reduction in social cost. It is started that the rate of growth of infrastructure should be higher then the rate of growth of Gross National Product (GDP) to achieve steady economic growth.

The index if infrastructure growth determines the relative achievement of a state in provision of economic, social and institutional infrastructure to its people. With the help of infrastructure a country could convert its raw materials into final products and this is likely to influence the export performance of an economy. Establishment of a major industrial project in any region attracts ancillary industries due to availability of basic infrastructure services. It transforms an agrarian rural economy into a modernized industrial economy. The rural character of the region undergoes a change leading to the development of an urbanized culture. A phenomenal change in attitude appears with in pursuance of gainful economic activities replacing the traditional indifferent attitude of the people.

The developed as well as developing countries of the world are characterized by unbalances in their regional development. While a part of the economy is more advanced and scientifically developed some other parts are highly backward adhering to traditional way of living. To transform such region, it is necessary to create the requirement infrastructure, so that economic activities will follow in subsequent periods. It is also necessary to develop a proper coordination between different socioeconomic services. Many of these services are interdependent, for example, construction of roads, construction of distribution network is necessary before power generation, etc. Development of micro-enterprises, be it an individual firm, a partnership concern or a joint stock company heavily depends on the availability of basic infrastructure like power, roads; transport; water supply, etc. All these arguments reinforce the importance of infrastructure in any country.

Adequate quantity, quality and reliability of infrastructure are important preconditions to determine a country's success or failure in diversifying production, expanding trade, coping with population growth and reducing poverty. Availability of adequate infrastructure raises productivity and Lower cost of production (Kuldip Kaur, 1997).

Infrastructure is a multi faceted phenomenon of provisioning socio-economic inputs. It is not the "engine" but the "us heels" of economic activity (Budhadet Ghosh and Kunal Chattopadhyay, 1997).

Infrastructure and World Development Report

Due to its increasing importance for both developed and developing the World Bank selected infrastructure as the focal theme for World Development Report in 1994. The report stated that the role of infrastructure in economic growth is substantial, significant and frequently greater than that of investment in other forms of capital. From regional economic point of view development infrastructure sector of a union is an important precondition for it development as the nature and scale of development depends upon the level of infrastructure (Biswajit Gaha, 1997). Provision and maintenance of adequate infrastructure services at reasonable cost are absolutely necessary if rapid economic growth is to be achieved and sustained (Economic Survey, 1996-97). Wide divergence in the demand for and supply of infrastructure services is not conducive for steady growth of an economy.

In India too, particularly since the liberalisation and globalisation of the economy, considerable development has been made in the field of telecommunications and electronic media provides prominent examples. However, the corporate India does not seen to beyond the obvious (L. Shridharam, 2002).

Inputs for Infrastructural Development

Resource availability is a must for providing infrastructure. The recent India Infrastructure Report, 2001 dealt with various issues and names of reforms in different infrastractural sectors, but did not deal with the resource aspects. The India infrastructure investment rising from Rs. 600 billion (in 1996-97) to Rs. 1100 billion (in 2000-01) and to Rs. 1800 billion (in 2005-06), excluding investments needed by railways, airports and civil aviation. These estimates need to be constructed against the fact that the public sector outlay under the ninth plan is just of the order of Rs. 8.6 million (for 5 years). It is anybody's guess where the government is going to find resources of this order. It is paradigm shift in our thinking process that has to be brought about to tackle problems of the kind and any kind, in a capital scare country like India.

The Indian experiment of creating rural infrastructure by pursuing deliberate policy in of recent origin. However, several specific programmes of rural economy to achieve sustained economic development. In view of this any discussion on development of rural infrastructure invests examining the strategies for rural development in India due to their close interdependence.

In the high of the aforesaid backdrop we will focus the development of infrastructure during 1995 to 2001 on the basis of secondary published sources of date.

Development of Infrastructure (1995 to 20001)

It is now well recognized that specialisation and "gain from trade" are the key sources of improved resource utilisation, and thus India's growth strategy. In order to harness these gains from trade, the transactions costs involved in trading need to be law, for trading with in the country and for international trade. Hence, the problems of transportation and communications, roads, railways, airports, telecom, ports, the postal system, electricity transmission and distribution have been a prominent focus of economic policy in the 1990s. In the era of globalisation the thrust of infrastructure policy has been to create a sound regulatory framework, in areas like rural infrastructure where cost recovery is innately difficult there is a greater role for government to foster infrastructure provision even if it is not directly profitable.

The ultimate goal of infrastructure policy is to effectively deliver infrastructure service of high quality and at low prices to households and firms in the country. The success of policies in infrastructure must be judged by the quality, quantity and prices that end users are charged for these services, and comparisons with global standards.

1. *Roads and Road Transport*

In the last 30 years, roads have grown in prominence as a mechanism for moving goods and people in the country. India has an extensive road network of more than 3.3 million kms making it one of the largest in the world. The road network comprises of national highways, state highways, district roads and special purpose roads (for military, ports, etc.) out of total roads network of all types in India, Panchayat Roads constitute 42.6 per cent, while PWD roads account for 38.0 per cent, urban roads from 9.4 per cent and projected roads account for 10.0 per cent. The surfaced roads account for only 56.5 per cent of all types of roads in India. The majority of Panchayat Roads remain unsurfaced which constitute about 63 per cent of total Panchayati Road length. The national highway, state highway and other PWD roads had almost surfaced (83%) in India (K.N. Raju, 2000).

It is informed from the Table 7.1 that these have been a remarkable progress in the construction; of roads in terms of kilometres as a crucial infrastructure from 1995-96 to 1998-99. The increase has been impressive so far as national highway road construction is concerned during 1995-96 to 2000-01.

The total length of roads increases 2302.5 thousand kilometres to 2526.0 thousand kilometres in the year 1995-

96 to 1998-99. Out of these the surfaced road has increased 1263.4 thousand kilometres to 1448.6 thousand kilometres during the same period. Similarly the length of national highway in the year 1995-96 was 34.3 thousand kilometres and on March 3l, 2002 it is 58.112 kilometres.

Table 7.1: Operations of Road Transport

Sl.No.		1995-96	1997-98	1998-99	1999-2000	2000-01
1.	Length of roads (Thousand kms)					
	Total	2302.5	2457.7	2526.0	NA	NA
	Surface	1263.4	1401.7	1448.6	NA	NA
2.	Length in NH (Thousand kms)	34.3	38.4	49.4	—	58.112*
3.	Length of SH (Thousand kms)	132.9	134.3	135.7	NA	NA

NH - National Highways

SH - State Highways

NA - Not Available

*National Highways are surfaced and the total length is 58.112 km (as on March 31, 2002)

Source: Economic Survey, 2002-03, Government of India.

The share of roads in the total public sector outlay/ expenditure has declined over the plan periods. There was a decline of 2.5 percentage points, from 5.5 per cent during the forth plan period to 3 per cent in the eight plan period. Out of the total expenditure of Rs. 15,611.92 crore incurred under JRY from 1989-90 to 1995-96, an amount of Rs. 3260.91 crore was spent on rural roads, which constitute about 21 per cent (Table 7.2). About 6.7 lakh kms of rural roads were laid under JRY during 1989-90 to 1995-96.

At the existing level of availability of funds, it may take several decades to establish road connectivity in all the villages in the country. Once the roads are built, they must be maintained at least to a minimum level of reasonable standard. The funds available for maintenance are only about 20 to 30 per cent of the actual requirements. During the ninth plan the estimated requirement of funds for

Table 7.2: Expenditure on Construction of Rural Roads under Jawahar Rojgar Yojana Programme

Sl. No.	*Year*	*Total Expenditure under JRY*	*Expenditure on rural roads*	*Percentage of expenditure on rural roads to total expenditure*
1.	1989-1990	1939.51	576:24	29.70
2.	1993-1994	2938.91	610.29	20.80
3.	1994-1995	2488.96	382.14	15.40
4.	1995-1996	1523.98	126.21	8.28
	Total	15611.92	3260.91	20.90

Source: Annual Report 1995-96, Ministry of rural Areas and Employment.

maintenance was about Rs. 5000 crore per annum for the rural road development with the present level of funding, serious constraints on the availability of funds could be discerned.

Railways

The Indian Railways is one of the largest railway system in the world. It has an extensive network which is spread over 63,140 route kilometres in 2000-01, comprising Broad Gauge (45,099 Rkm), Metre Gauge (14,776 Rkm) and Narrow Gauge (3,265 Rkm). Approximately 25 per cent of the network is electrified. Yet, railways are yet to reach most parts of rural India. India had 62,666 route kilometres in 1995, there is slow increase in railway network in the during the period 1995-96 to 2000-01.

Railways offer largest employment opportunity directly and immense other avenues to millions of people indirectly. And railways are undoubtedly the backbone or lifeline of India as it can bring people closer to each other.

Rural Energy/Power

Energy is the hub of socio-economic development without which life becomes miserable while trade, industry and

Table 7.3: Operations of Indian Railways

Year	*Route kilometres (thousand)*	
	Electrified	*Total*
1995-1996	12.3	62.6
1998-1999	13.8	62.8
1999-2000	14.3	62.8
2000-2001	14.9	63.1

Source: Economic Survey, 2002-03, Government of India.

agriculture suffer setbacks. Over the year, use of electric energy has grown pervasively in commercial, domestic and agricultural sectors. Electricity generation in India which was 379.9 billion kWh units in 1995-96 increased to over 499.5 billion kWh units by 2000-01 registering an annual compounded growth of 7.5 per cent.

Table 7.4: Energy Generated (Gross) (Billion kWh)

Year	*Hydro*	*Thermal*	*Utilities nuclear*	*Total*	*Net increase*
1995-1996	72.6	299.3	8.0	379.9	29.5
1996-1997	68.9	317.9	9.1	395.9	16.0
1997-1998	74.6	337.0	10.1	421.7	25.8
1998-1999	82.9	353.7	11.9	448.5	23.8
1999-2000	80.6	386.8	13.3	480.7	32.2
2000-2001	74.5	408.1	16.9	499.5	8.8 1

Source: Economic Survey 2002-03, Government of India.

The shortage of power in March 1995 was estimated to be 16.5 per cent. The rural areas will be the first culprit to absorb shocks of power cut for long hours. The policy of supplying uninterrupted power to industries and urban areas causes erosion of supply in rural areas. The rural lighting and irrigation pump sets suffer severely due to paucity of power supply. The commercial power losses in 1994-95 were

Rs. 63 billion. The target of power generation have not been achieved in any of the plan period, the shortfall between target and achievement ranged from 30 to 50 per cent. Thus, addition to instrlled capacity and power generation are inadequate. Investment into power also, continues to be insufficient. The demand for power during 1996-2006 is estimated to be 111,500 MW requiring an investment of about Rs. 6244 billion. Power theft and transmission and distribution losses have averaged to 22 per cent, which is alarmingly high. Despite opening the power sector for private and foreign investment, the response is not encouraging. As power is a basic necessity to rural India, the Governments (both Union and State) must allocate sufficient funds and set up monitoring committees to enable judicious use of these precious funds. Indian economy is sustained by agro and allied sectors contributions (over 27 per cent of GNP). Had these sectors and all villages were provided with continuous power supply, the economy would have been much stronger than what it is today. There is need to correct the misplaced urban oriented priority in favour of rural electrification rural domestic fuel needs than industrial power needs (K.S. Narayana, 2003).

Infrastructure and Rural Development

Rural development is a complex exercise. The more important goal of rural development is to ascertaining about an aesthetically and ecologically sound environment. It over output, employment, infrastructure (health, education, transport, commerce, power supply, water control), political and social systems in a rural society. A strategy for rural development should therefore be based on a comprehensive survey of appropriateness to the local environment, mass mobilisation through a process of education and equitable sharing of available resource. This strategy can work satisfactorily if proper precautions are taken at the conceptual level.

The welfare of rural masses depends on the consumption, distribution and production pattern prevailing in a regional economy. This was again dependent on the level of development in agriculture and other economic activities in the rural economy, which greatly depend on the quantum of rural infrastructure available.

Rural development is handicapped by the back lay of rural poverty, unemployment, underemployment and tip backwardness. The primary focus of the varied programmes and strategies adopted in the basic necessities to the rural poor who are ignorant and superstitious and do not participate in the development programmes initiated by the government. In the present context, the government conceives rural development with the assistance of urban intelligentsia, who has no knowledge of rural India and Rural poverty. Rural development is necessary not only because an overwhelming majority of the population lives in villages but because the development of rural activities is essential to accelerate the hour is rural development of the county. The need of the hours is rural development aiming at: removal of unemployment rise in the standard of living, adequate food, clothing and shelter, clean environment, access to education and sound health etc.

An examination of the Rural Development Programmes in India reveals that most of these programmes have aimed to create rural economic-social and institutional infrastructure. The first two plans had concentrated their effort on creating an institutional set up (Formation of Community Development Blocks, Panchayati Raj Institutions, etc.). The third and fourth plan targeted to develop agriculture, which is one of the important physical infrastructures in the rural area. Specific effort on certain of all types of rural infrastructure stated in the fifth plan through the minimum need programme. Concurrently several employment oriented programmes where also lunched with the objective of creation of socio-economic overheads in rural areas are have been in practice till now. Emphasis was given in the recent years on the participation of financial institutions in establishing the foundation of the rural economy. Three decades of experimentation with rural infrastructure development programmes with certain of employment opportunities as a by-product has thrown many challenges and lessons. Investment of huge public money in these programmes also demands careful assessment of their impact on the productive capacity of the rural economy.

To sum up, infrastructural development is key to economic transformation and India has to go a long way in this context, so as to find its place in the competitive atmosphere in the era of globalisation.

REFERENCES

1. Dasgupta, K.R., *Rural Development: Programs in India—Concept and Strategies,* Kurukshetra, August 1997.
2. Dwarakanath, Dr. H.D., *Policies and Programmes for Rural Development,* July-1997.
3. Ghosh, B. & Chattapadhyay, K., *Regional Imbalance in Infrastructure and Income in India,* IEA 1st Amrit Jubilee (80th) Conference, Hyderabad, 1997.
4. Government of India, Economic Survey (various issues 1996-97, 1997-98, 2003-04, Ministry of Finance, Economic Division.
5. Guha, Biswajit, *Economic of Infrastructure in India—A Case Study of the State of West Bengal,* IEA, 1st Amrit Jubilee (80th) Conference, Hyderabad, 1997.
6. Kaur, Kuldip, *Infrastructure and Growth-Evidence from Major State of India,* IEA, 1st Amrit Jubilee (80th) Conference, Hyderabad, 1997.
7. Narayan, K.S., Unending Debate on Rural Development Issues: A Relook at Diagnostics; Kurukshetra, Jan. 2003.
8. Raju, K.N., *Rural Road Networks: Some Issues,* Kurukshetra, Sept. 2000.
9. Shridharan, L. "Providing Infrastructure Needed Paradigm Shift in Thinking", *Yojana,* Feb. 2002.
10. World Bank, World Development Report, Infrastructure Development, Oxford University Press, 1994.

8

Rural Development Through Rural Roads

*Deepak Bishoyi**

Adequate quantity, quality and reliability of infrastructure are important preconditions to determine a country's success or failure in diversifying production, expanding trade, coping with population growth and reducing poverty. Availability of adequate infrastructure raises productivity and lowers cost of production (Kaur, 1997). Infrastructure being a sine qua none of economic development, its development is not a luxury but necessity. Like every other development activity, infrastructure development has several players and it cannot be taken as a responsibility of a single institution/agency, infrastructure is a multifaceted phenomenon of provisioning socio-economic inputs. It is not the "engine" but the wheels of economic activity (Ghosh and Chottapadhyay, 1997). Development of infrastructure based of an economy accomplishes the following tasks:

(i) Product diversification and trade expansion by raising the volume of exports;

(ii) Increase employment opportunities and raises standard of living with enhanced income;

(iii) Reduction in cost due to economics of scale;

*Ph.D. Scholar, Institute for Social and Economic Change, Bangalore.

(iv) Optimal resource allocation;

(v) Improving environmental conditions.

This paper makes an attempt to evaluate the role of road transport as a factor, leading to ail round development of rural areas. Besides, road transport development during 1995 to 2001 has been portrayed to emphasize its significance in the rural economy. Both secondary and primary source of data have been used for the present study.

Importance of Road Transport

Transport has always been the core factor to the evolution of mankind. Transport and communication networks are the arteries of an economy without which the development of industry sector and agriculture sector is possible. It is one of the most important infrastructure services needed for the rapid growth of an economy. Transport brings people of different areas into place and migration of people from one place to another in made possible, goods and services are made for sale at different localities (Sivaprakash, 1997). Transport can be divided into many categories like roads, railways, harbour, airways etc. (Basu, 1997).

Among the various modes of transportation road transport occupies a dominant place and play a vital role in integrating production, marketing and consumption function of the economy (Raman and Kumar, 1998). This sector is highly labour intensive and employment oriented. There are different types of roads: National Highways, State Highways, P.W.D. roads, system etc. Widening and strengthening the existing highways, reconstructing, widening of weak and narrow bridges, converting crossings to high level bridges and construction of expressways to provide unhindered high speed and safe movement of vehicles are necessary to meet the transport demand.

Rural Roads and Economic Development

Inadequate rural connectivity and lack of mobility pose constraints to rural development in India. Infrastructure facilities and improvements in delivery of services can reduce the costs and time of the various economic and social activities taken up by the rural people. Rural road connectivity to market center will provide remunerative price to the farmers for their agricultural process. Road transport has promoted agricultural growth, contributing directly to lower transport costs and facilitating the expansion of services sector activities in rural areas. In addition, an adequate road network can help to reduce regional variations in food prices by facilitating the movement of food and agricultural commodities in the areas of surplus to areas of deficit especially in the case of foodgrains, vegetables, fruit, fish, poultry, dairy products etc. which cannot be stored for a long period.

Moreover, the cost and availability of public transportation/connectivity become key factors for expansion of employment opportunities as well as efficient delivery of services in rural areas. There is a great need for development of rural transport network as basic infrastructure support to strengthen the rural economy to promote equitable distribution of benefits of development between producers and consumers in rural areas (Bishoyi, 2004).

Present Status of Road Connectivity

In the last 30 years, roads have grown in prominence as a mechanism for moving goods and people in the country. India has an extensive road network of more than 3.3 million kms making it one of the largest in the world. The road network comprises of national highways, state highways, district roads and special purpose roads (for military, ports etc.) out of total roads network of all types in India, Panchayat roads constitute 42.6 per cent, while P.W.D. roads account for 38.0 per cent, urban roads from 9.4 per cent and projected roads account for 10.0 per cent. The surfaced roads account for only 56.5 per cent of all types of roads in India. The majority of Panchayat roads remain unsurfaced which constitute about 63 per cent of total Panchayati road length. The National Highways, State Highways, and other P.W.D. roads had almost surfaced (83%) in India (Raju, 2000).

Table 8.1: Operation of Road Transport

Sl.No.	*Types of road*	*1995-96*	*1997-98*	*1998-99*	*1999-2000*	*2000-01*
1.	Length of roads ('000 kms)					
	Total	2302.5	2457.7	2526.0	N.A.	N.A.
	Surface	1263.4	1401.7	1448.6	N.A.	N.A.
2.	Length in NH ('000 kms)	34.3	38.4	49.4	—	58.112*
3.	Length in SH ('000 kms)	132.9	134.3	135.7	N.A.	N.A.

NH—National Highways; SH—State Highways; NA—Not available

* National Highways are surfaced and the total length is 58.112 km (as on March 31, 2002)

Source: Economic survey 2002-03, Government of India.

It is informed from the Table 8.1 that there have been a remarkable progress in the construction of roads in terms of kms as a crucial infrastructure from 1995-96 to 1998-99. The increase has been impressive so for as National Highways road construction is concerned during 1995-96 to 2000-01.

The total length of the road increases 2302.5 thousand kilometres to 2526.0 thousand kilometres in the year 1995-96 to 1998-99. Out of these the surfaced road has increase 1263.4 thousand kilometres to 2448.6 thousand kilometres during the same period. Similarly the length of the National Highways in the year 1995-96 was 34.3 thousand kilometres and on March 31, 2002 it is 58.112 kilometres.

The share of roads in the total public sector outlay/ expenditure has declined over the plan periods. There was a decline of 2.5 percentage points, from 5.5 per cent during the fourth plan period to 3 per cent Eight Plan period. Out of the total expenditure of Rs. 15,611.92 crore incurred under IRY from 1989-90 to 1995-96 an amount of Rs. 3260.91 crore was spent rural roads, which constitute about

21 per cent (Table 8.2) About 6.7 lakh kms of rural road was laid under JRY during 1989-90 to 1995-96.

Table 8.2: Expenditure on Construction of Rural Roads under Jawahar Rojgar Yojana Programme

Sl. No.	*Year*	*Total Expenditure under JRY*	*Expenditure on rural roads*	*Percentage of expenditure on rural roads to total expenditure*
1.	1989-90	1939.51	576.24	29.70
2.	1993-94	2938.91	610.29	20.80
3.	1994-95	2488.96	382.14	15.40
4.	1995-96	1523.98	126.21	8.28
	Total	15611.92	3260.91	20.90

Source: Annual Report 1995-96, Ministry of Rural Areas and Employment

At the existing level of availability of funds it may take several decades to establish road connectivity in the all the villages in the country. Once the roads are built, they must be maintained at least to a minimum level of reasonable standard. The funds available for maintenance are only about 20 to 30 per cent of the actual requirements. During the Ninth Plan the estimated requirements of funds for maintenance was about Rs. 5000 crore per annum for the rural road development with the present level of funding, serious constraints on the availability of funs could be discerned

Road Lead to Economic Prosperity

In this backdrop a study has been conducted in Digapahandi Block of Ganjam District (Orissa). Two village named Narsinghapur and Birbadia have been purposively selected to the present study. Village Narasinghapur is well connected with road transport and Biribadia is regretted from other parts due to lack or road link. Villages Narasinghapur is located in Gokarnapur Gram Panchayat at about 11 kms from the block headquarters, while village Biribadia is located in the same Gram Panchayat at about 1 3 kms from the block headquarter.

A Tentative questionnaire has been prepared to assess. The level of literacy extent, from agricultural output, use of scientific equipment, health status of the people magnitude of employment, level income, migration, social awareness etc. For the purpose of comparison we have selected 40 rural households on random sampling technique constituting approximately 20 per cent of total household of each village. We can bright analyse them and derive the inforrences from the study.

It is clear form the Table 8.3 the village which is linked with the nearest town/block headquarter with fair weathers road is more developed as compared to unconnected village. This is evident from the all socio-economic indicates link level of literacy, extent of agriculture out put use of scientific equipments, health status of all people, magnitude of employments level of income, migration social awareness etc.

So far as agricultural production and marketing is concerned the village is linked with road transport is found using scientific and technological methods of cultivation i.e. use of tractors and powetillers HVV seed fertilizer pesticides and insecticide etc. This in enhances and enables to sale their products i.e. vegetables fruits milk and milk products etc. in the nearest town at better price.

The level of literacy shows that the village linked with road has higher literacy level as compared to the delinked villages. In both the villages the through the primary educations is available but for the higher education they depends on the nearest town. Thus the people the delinked villages face more problems specially the girls for their higher education. So the level of literacy is low.

Poor health condition are intimately linked with almost every aspect of life. The availability of almost every other items of consumption like foodstuffs, house, cloths, sanitation and educational facilities is relevant to maintain good health conditions. So the health status of road connectivity village is comparatively better then the unconnected village. There

Table 8.3: Socio-economic Indicators of Village Connected/Unconnected with Road Links

		Villages	
	Socio-economic indicators	*Narasinghpur connected N=40*	*Beribadia unconnected N=40*
1.	Level of literacy	55%	23%
2.	Agricultural production	16.5 Quintal paddy per Ac.	11.6 Quintal paddy per Ac.
3.	Agricultural marketing, vegetables, fruit milk etc.	Can get better price for their products	Don't get remuneration price of their agricultural produce
4.	Per capita income of household	36 thousand per year	17 thousand per year
5.	Employment through outside village	156 days	63 days
6.	Health	Can avail health care facilities by contacting health personnels at Digapahandi	It becomes extremely difficult to contact doctor or health care facilities
7.	Bus	4	-
8.	Mini bus	2	-
9.	Auto rickshaw	5	
10	Tractor	2	-
11.	Taxi	1	-
12.	Two wheeler	15	-
13.	Cycle rickshaw	6	-
14.	Tubewells	2	-
15.	Wells	3	2
16.	Use of latrine	42	2
17.	TV	10%	1%

Source: Field study.

is low infant mortality rate and high life expectancy because of linked village people are depends on the nearest health care centre in time.

The study also reveled that the mobility of the road linked village population improved appreciably with the development of road and transport infrastructure. Many landless households started supplementing their income through labour in construction works by commuting to the work sites in private buses and trucks. Labour contractors too started connecting the village with tracks to transport workers to the construction sites. This apart same members of the households the road connected village found employment as bus conductors, trucks drivers and their assistants. Self-employment through investments in cycle rickshaws, autorickshaws, taxis and mini buses for hire become possible because of road connections. Moreover, to maintain the growing transports sectors a network of service establishments come up, adding to the employments avenues for the people.

Due to the education and contact with the outside of people and urban areas of the villages connected with road transport are found socially well aware then the delinked village. The used of tubewell water TV sets, latrine etc. and drainage system could possible in the road linked village. But the road unconnected villages people are lack of social awareness.

Thus, it goes without saving that road transport is highly indisposable for socio-economic and cultural development of a community.

Problem Encounter in the Development of Road Transport

(i) Inadequacy of Finance

The country is facing a formidable challenge to expand, modernize, upgrade, maintain and manage its vast rural road net work due to serious constraints of funds. The cost of building roads and maintaining them is increasing with every passing year. While more budgetary resources will certainly case the situation but this is inadequate of their actual requirement Rural Road Organisation, have to do more with scare resource by optional utilization of the available funds by increasing their efficiency level.

(ii) Bureaucratic Corruption

It is observed that because of the bureaucratic corruption the funds are not invested in properly. Approximately 30 per cent of the allotted funds are invested for the purpose of road construction and remains are misappropriated.

(iii) Problems of Proper Management

Inadequacies in infrastructure limit the access of poor people to essential basic services which often stems from weakand contradictory incentives built in the current institutional and organizational arrangements. In many countries outputs and inputs are not closely measured monitored, or managed and the rewards of supplies have little relation to the satisfaction of users.

(iv) Training and Technologies

Technical skills of the functionaries, especially of those implementing rural roads programmes should be upgraded through training and also disseminate appropriate road technologies which were developed by central Road Research Institute or other research stations.

The Panchayat bodies and Public Works Departments (PWD) have to play important role build, operate and transfer (BOT) of rural roads since the private sectors may not come forwards to take up rural road network project on the Basic of BOT as the paying capacity of the rural people towards usages of roads is low. Further, the volume of traffic, both men and material passing through may also vary according to seasonality of agriculture in rural areas.

Policy Paradigms

From the agro-processing point of view it is as necessary to modernize and improve the rural transport sector as to tray to avoid transportation to the extent, possible, especially of the raw farm products. The objective is to reduce costs as also to prevent damage to the produce during hawage. In fact value addition, when done by keeping the supply logistic in view becomes an instrument curing needless transportation of the superfluous parts of the produce. It is for instance much difficult and costlier to transport voluminous products like say melons but much simple to move their juice or pulp. For this, the processing units need to be set up as close to the production centers as possible. Nobody would obviously want to set up processing unit in an area not even connected with a reliable road.

In its present form, the Indian rural transport sector consists in general, largely of old-age, traditional modes, The bulk of the produce is still handled manually, carried as headloads or in human or animals driven carts in the absence of good roads. It is the availability of motorable road that encourage the use of tractor-trolleys as means of transport in rural areas. Indeed, according to estimates nearly 50 per cent of the tractor usage time goes in the for either haulage of the farm produce or as family transport vehicle (Sul, 2002).

It is apparent form the analysis that road transport is the basic and key factor of the development of a backwards economy. India being a country of village there should be high priority on road transport development, as it is labour intensive with high employment and augments the growth process in multi-dimensional ways.

REFERENCES

1. Basu, K. (1997), "Infrastructure Development of Major States of India", *IEA Conference*, Hyderabad.

2. Bishoyi, D. (2004), "Development of Infrastructure in the era of Globalisation", *National Seminar Preconference*, Warangal.

3. Ghosh, B. & Chattapadhyay, K. (1997), "Regional Imbalance in Infrastructure and Income in India", *ITA Conference*, Hyderabad.

4. Government of India, *Economic Survey* (Various Issues 1996-97, 1997-98, 2002-03).

5. Kaur, K. (1997), "Infrastructure and Growth-Evidence from Major State of India", *IEA Conference, Volume,* Hyderabad.

6. Ministry of Rural Areas and Employment, *Annual Report* 1995-96.

7. Raju, K.N. (2000), Rural Road Networks: Some Issues", *Kurukshetra,* September.

8. Raman, P. and Kumar, P. (1998), "Productivity in Infrastructure", *Yojana,* January.

9. Shridharan, L. (2002), Providing Infrastructure Needed Paradigm Shift in Thinking", *Yojana,* February.

10. Sud. S. (2002), "Rural Connectivity: Current Issues and Future Plans", *Kurukshetra,* September.

9

Interstate Imbalance in Agriculture Production and Marketing in India

*Deepak Bishoyi**

In India agriculture is the largest sector of economic activity. With around 27 per cent contribution to the Gross Domestic Product (GDP) at current price and 40 per cent to the National Income, employment nearly two-thirds of the work force, agriculture occupies the central stage of Indian economy. If the Indian agricultural is thoroughly analyzed imbalance in this sector.

The agriculture production is not the same in all the states in India. Some states produce more while others less. The production, which is expected, is not received in production to the expenditure incurred on inputs. In different states we get different level of production for different crops. The following table gives a clear picture regarding the production of different states (Table 9.1).

Table 9.2 shows that Uttar Pradesh produces more agricultural items then other states. Sikkim is the backward state from the point of view of agricultural production. Sikkim's contribution is quieting negligible to total production.

In overall the production of Northern states i.e. Uttar Pradesh, Haryana, Punjab and Uttarakhand are dominating

* Ph.D. Scholar, Institute for Social and Economic Change, Bangalore.

Table 9.1: Foodgrains Production Fluctuation in 1999-2002

State	Production of foodgrain (Million tones)			Share of state in all India foodgrains production		
	2001-02	*2000-01*	*1999-00*	*2001-02*	*2000-01*	*1999-2000*
1	*2*	*3*	*4*	*5*	*5*	*6*
Andhra Pradesh	14835.8	16029.2	1369.2	7.0	8.0	6.5
Arunachal Pradesh	217.5	215.3	210.2	0.1	0.1	0.1
Assam	4024.0	4166.5	4042.0	1.9	2.1	1.9
Bihar	11849.7	147777.8	14387.6	5.6	7.4	6.9
Chhattishgarh	5811.1	2901.3	0	2.7	1.5	0
Goa	136.0	153.0	219.8	0.1	0.1	0.1
Gujarat	4898.7	2539.0	4051.8	2.3	1.3	1.3
Haryana	13301.1	13294.4	13063.2	6.3	6.7	6.2
Himachal Pradesh	1571.6	1112.2	1443.3	0.7	0.6	0.7
Jammu & Kashmir	1325.8	1114.5	1328.5	0.6	0.6	0.6
Jharkhand	2008.5	2011.0	0	0.9	1.0	0
Karnataka	8771.0	10986.0	9859.3	4.1	5.5	4.7
Kerala	729.3	765.3	793.3	0.3	0.4	0.4

(Contd...)

Table 9.1: (Contd...)

1	*2*	*3*	*4*	*5*	*5*	*6*
Madhya Pradesh	13057.5	10185.4	21272.1	6.2	5.1	6.1
Maharashtra	1187.5	10134.9	12700.9	5.3	5.1	6.1
Manipur	460.5	395.8	375.7	0.2	0.2	0.2
Meghalaya	217.8	216.0	208.7	0.1	0.1	0.1
Mizoram	126.3	124.0	105.6	0.1	0.1	0.1
Nagaland	255.4	322.7	210.5	0.2	0.2	0.1
Orissa	7556.4	4984.2	5622.5	3.6	2.5	2.7
Punjab	24886.9	25324.5	25201.4	11.7	12.7	12.0
Rajasthan	13984.9	10040.6	10684.1	6.6	5.0	5.1
Sikkim	98.7	103.2	103.1	0	0.1	0
Tamil Nadu	8472.3	8616.9	8968.8	4.0	4.3	4.3
Tripura	634.4	523.1	513.5	0.3	0.3	0.2
Uttar Pradesh	43119.8	42714.9	45649.6	20.4	21.4	21.8
Uttarakhand	1707.5	1726.4	0	0.8	0.9	0.0
West Bengal	16501.3	13815.0	14915.6	7.8	6.9	7.1
Union Territories	166.7	242.5	173.2	0.1	0.1	0.1
All India	212033.8	199535.6	209800.5	100.0	100.0	100.0

Source: The Economic Times, 27 October 2003, p. 10.

in this connection. There are several reasons for such imbalances in agricultural production.

Table 9.2: Rainfall Deficiency—Per cent Deviation from Normal

A&N Islands	–24
Arunachal Pradesh	–22
East UP	–24
West UP	–21
Haryana & Delhi	–26
Punjab	–36
Himachal Pradesh	–20
West Rajastan	–71
East Rajastan	–60
Gujarat Region	–22
Saurashtra, Kutch & Diu	–25
Coastal Andhra Pradesh	–26
Telangana	–23
Rayalseema	–33
Tamil Nadu & Pandicherry	–45
Coastal Karnataka	–30
North Interior Karnataka	–31
South Interior Karnataka	–44
Kerala	–35
Lakshadweep	–45

Source: Economic Survey, 2002-03.

- Irrigation
- Agricultural subsidy
- Fertilizer
- Seeds
- Agricultural credit

- Agricultural mechanization
- Training and research, and
- Public distribution system (PDS)

- **Irrigation:** The economic conditions of North-eastern states are not sound. These states mostly cover hilly areas and lack irrigation facility. If we focus our attention on methods of cultivation and the facilities given to these states are inadequate. Mainly the monsoon plays a major role in determining the quantity of agricultural production. All states in India do not get equal rainfall. Some states get excess and some states suffer from drought condition. In 2001-02 the western part of Rajasthan could not get the blessings of the monsoon. This region expressing 71 per cent of less than the normal rainfall. Whereas Himachal Pradesh received 20 per cent less than the normal rainfall. So lack of water caused a serious problem for agricultural productivity. Had there been adequate irrigation facilities more production would have been expected. The percentages of net irrigated area in different states are not same, in some states more lands gets irrigation facilities. Whereas in some other states such facility is inadequate. The following table shows the percentage of net area irrigated in 1998-99.

Table 9.3 reveals that Punjab gets, maximum irrigation facility i.e. 94.5 per cent of land area and Mizoram is very backward in this respect only 8.3 per cent of its land area get irrigation facility. As a result of which the agricultural production suffers in those states where the prospect of irrigation is bleak causing it, a serious imbalance in agricultural production.

- **Agricultural Subsidy:** Agricultural subsidy given to the farmers during different natural calamities is not enough to compensate their loss. Natural calamities and insurgencies greatly effect the production in agricultural sector. Due to this there exists imbalance in supply of agricultural products and their demand.

Table 9.3: Percentage of net Area Irrigated to Net Area Sone—1998-99

State/U.T.	*1998-99*
Andhra Pradesh	41.4
Arunachal Pradesh	19.5
Assam	21.2
Bihar	49.6
Chhattishgarh	NA
Goa	15.5
Gujarat	31.6
Haryana	78.3
Himachal Pradesh	18.8
Jammu & Kashmir	42.2
Jharkhand	NA
Karnataka	23.8
Kerala	16.6
Manipur	46.4
Meghalaya	24.7
Mizoram	8.3
Nagaland	24.1
Orissa	34.6
Punjab	94.5
Rajasthan	34.2
Sikkim	16.8
Tamil Nadu	53.6
Tripura	12.6
Uttar Pradesh	72.2
Uttarakhand	NA
West Bengal	35.1

- **Fertilizer:** In most of the state the crops are rot harvested in more quantity for the want of fertilizer, insecticides and high yielding varieties of seeds. As most of the farmers are poor they are unable to buy fertilizer, insecticides and HYV seeds. So if these are not supplied at subsidized price the agricultural productivity will decrease. Now farmers in same poor states of India experience it. Hence consumption of fertilizer, seeds etc. are important to enhance the productivity. The consumption of fertilizers. Nitrogen (N), phosphates (P) and potash (k) have been steadily increasing over the years. In nutrient terms, the fertilizes consumption rose by more than three times from 5.5 million tones in 1980-81 18.07 million tones in 1999-00. A great deal of variability is observed in fertilizer consumption between the states.

Amongst states in the plains per hector consumption was highest in Punjab, Haryana, Andhra Pradesh and Tamil Nadu. It was lowest in Madhya Pradesh, Rajasthan and all northeast starts. All India average was 90 kgs per hectare. (Table 9.4).

- **Seeds:** The National seeds Policy 2001 provides the framework for growth of the Seed sector. It seeks to provide the farmers with a wide range of superior the farmers with a wide range of superior quality seed varieties and planting materials.

The adoption of high yielding varieties (HYV) of wheat and rice, which were seen to possess vast potential for raising grain production. This policy her been helpful in several ways. From a situation of massive storages, India has emerged as a grain surplus country and food security has been attained at the national level. A strong base has beer, created for grain production and for meeting grain demand in the medium term. The food policy has been highly favourable to rice and wheat production and has resulted in a shift of good quality in a shift of good quality land and other resources to these crops. This has created serious imbalances in demand and

Table 9.4: Per Hectare Consumption of Fertilizer for Cropped Area During—2001-02

States/U.T	*2001-02*
Andhra pradesh	143.46
Karnataka	101.48
Kerala	60.72
Tamil Nadu	141.55
Gujarat	85.52
Madhya Pradesh	39.96
Maharashtra	78.24
Rajasthan	38.98
Haryana	155.69
Himachal Pradesh	41.40
Jammu & Kashmir	64.55
Punjab	173.38
Uttar Pradesh	130.44
Bihar	87.39
Orissa	40.91
West Bengal	126.82
Arunachal Pradesh	2.88
Assam	38.81
Tripura	30.45
Manipur	104.94
Meghalaya	17.16
Nagaland	2.13
Mizoram	13.72
Sikkim	9.72
All India	90.72

Source: Economic Survey, 2002-03.

supply of several agricultural commodities in the country. On one hand the country is holding more than one-fourth of the annual production of rice and wheat in public stock, and on the other every fifth Indian is underfed even by the standard of minimum calorie requirement for a healthy and active life. Similarly, the country has been facing large shortages of pulses and edible oils and has now to meet about one-tenth of demand for pulses and close to half of the demand for edible out from imports. These imports are in turn having an adverse impact on produces in the unfavourable dry land areas. Where the surplus of wheat and rice is being disposed of as export at a huge cost to the state exchequer.

- **Agricultural Credit:** Agricultural credit is also a vital to raise productivity during the reaping, ploughing and harvesting. If loans are given to the poor farmers they can be able to rise more production. The total credit flew to agriculture and allied sector during the Ninth plan (1997-02) is expected to have reached Rs. 233,700 crore as against the projection of Rs. 2,29,000 crore. For the Tenth Plan period (2002-07) the credit flow into agriculture and allied activities from all banking agencies is projected at Rs. 7,36,570 crore, which is more than three times the credit flow during the Ninth than three times the credit flow during the Ninth plan. The target for credit flow for the agriculture and allied sector for the current year is Rs. 82,073 crore (Table 9.5). So agriculture credit is very important for production.

- **Agricultural Mechanization:** Agricultural Mechanization plays a vital role to raise productivity. Tractors and power tillers have become the main source of motive power for tillage, threshing and transport, contributing about 44 per cent of the total farm power requirement compared to that 7.75 per cent in 1971-72. During this period the total power availability has increased farm 0.29 kW/ha to 1.231 kW/ha in 2001-02, which is likely to increase further with more use of tractors and power

Table 9.5. Flow of Institutional Credit to Agriculture

Institutions	*2000-01*	*2001-02*	*2002-03 targets*
Co-operative Bank	20,784	27,080	35,111
Per cent share	39	42	43
Regional Rural Bank	4,219	4,956	5,745
Per cent share	8	8	7
Commercial	27,711	31,369	41,217
Per cent share	53	50	50
Total	52,714	60,000	82,073
Per cent share	14	21	28

Source: Economic Survey, 2002-03.

tillers. Uttar Pradesh, Madhya Pradesh and Punjab are using more tractors and West Bengal, Tamil Nadu and Assam use of power tillers is more. (Table 9.6).

- **Training and Research:** Adequate training facilities to the farmer and role of research institutions in providing this is vital for more production. So research institution should be setup and proper training should be given to the farmer which is turn will enable them to increase the productivity and maintain the balance.

- **Public Distribution System (PDS):** Another causes of the imbalance in agricultural production are lake of implementation of Public Distribution System (PDS). The main goals of PDS are to:

    - make goods available to consumers, especially the disadvantaged/vulnerable sections of society at fair prices;
    - rectify the existing imbalances between the supply and demand for consumer goods;
    - check and prevent hoarding and block marketing is essential commodities;

- ensure social justice in distribution of basic necessities of life;
- even out fluctuations in price and availability of mass consumption goods;
- support poverty-alleviation programmers particularly rural employment programmers, (SGRY/SGSY/ IRDP/Midday meals, ICDS, DWCRA, SHGS and food for work and educational feeding programmers).

Table 9.6: Number of Tractors and Power Tillers Sold

Tractors		*Power tillers*	
State	*2001-02*	*State*	*2001-02*
Uttar Pradesh	9	West Bengal	4866
Madhya Pradesh	32.496	Tamil Nadu	1865
Punjab	23039	Assam	1103
Rajasthan	17666	Orissa	990
Haryana	25904	Karnataka	979
Bihar	14949	Maharashtra	765
Gujarat	14616	Kerala	584
Andhra Pradesh	12703	Tripura	455
Tamil Nadu	10205	Andhra Pradesh	429
Maharashtra	9870	Gujarat	277
Karnataka	9669	Bihar	244
Orissa	2822		
Other states/ Uts and Exports	9576	Other states/ Uts and Exports etc.	1006
All India	2,25,280	All India	13,563

Source: Economic Survey, 2002-03.

Even though food production in the country has improved and there is no space in FCI godown to store the foodgrains. Large numbers of Foodgrains are rotten and damaged. But on the other hand there is large regional inequality, because pressure on budgetary resources and political pressure from surplus states for higher prices and subsides have emerged as major problem.

To overcome the problem of imbalance in agricultural production there was a need of project agricultural marketing. For ensuring growth of the agriculture sector along with other sectors, a remunerative price to the farmers for their produce is necessary and so the role of marketing becomes important. Agricultural price to the farmers for their produce is necessary and so the role of marketing becomes important. Agricultural products, because of perishable nature of the products, seasonality of production, bulk quantities; variation is quality, irregular supply, small size holdings and seated production. Marketing problem for agricultural production is no less important. It generates life and blood in the farmers to undertake the next vantage in the coming years. If the product are not marketed well and are not sold in reasonable prices the farmers willingness to work (cultivate), save will be hampered. So their commodity should be marketed at reasonable prices in time.

Agriculture Marketing Reforms in India

Government of India in the ministry of Agriculture appointed an expert committee on 19th December 2000 to review the present system of agricultural marketing in the country and to recommend measures to make the system more efficient and competive. The committee in its report dated 29th June 2001 has suggested various legislative reforms as well as the reorientation of the policies and programmes for development and strengthening of agricultural marketing in the country.

With a view to examine the findings and recommendations of the expert committee and to suggest measures to implement them. The ministry of agriculture constituted a task force on 4th July 2001, under the chairmanship of the additional secretary in the department of agriculture and cooperation.

The Task force thereupon identified nine priority areas to work out a road map for strengthening the agricultural marketing system in the country. The areas identified are:

- Legal reforms
- Direct marketing
- Market infrastructure
- Pledge financing
- Warehousing receipt system
- Forward and future markets
- Price supports policy
- IT in agricultural marketing and
- Marketing extension, training and research.

Legal Reforms: Legal reforms can play an important role in marking the present marketing system more effective and efficient by removing unnecessary restrictions and by establishing a sound framework to reduce the uncertainty of the markets.

To encourage private sector to make massive investments required for development of alternative marketing infrastructure and supporting services, provisions of the Agricultural Produce Marketing Regulations Act (APMC) would need modification to create a lawful rote for the private sector in market development. Governments role should be that of a facilitator rather them that of having control over the management of markets.

To attract the promoting agencies to take up these market infrastructures projects, the central/state governments additionally need to extend support in following areas:

(a) Deregulation of areas where new markets will be set up, along with forward and backward linkages from the purview of the agricultural produce marketing act.

(*b*) Allocation of suitable and sufficient land with necessary approvals to set up agricultural produces markets.

(*c*) Provision of village land for farmers associations and collection centers.

(*d*) Long terms credit for initial capital investment.

Direct Marketing: Innovative Marketing Channels Direct marketing by farmers is being encouraged as an innovative channel. Some examples of these channels are Apni Mandi, Hadaspar Mandi, Rythu Bazars and Uzhavar Sandies.

(*a*) *Apni Mandi:* In Apni mandi there is a direct contact between the farmers and ultimate consumes;

(*b*) *Hadaspar vegetable Market:* This is one of the ideal market in the county for marketing of vegetables. In this market, there are no commission agents/ middlemen. The market has modern weighing machines for weighing produce directly to the farmer in cash;

(*c*) *Rythu Bazars:* With prime objective to provide direct link between farmers and consumers in marketing of fruits, vegetables and essential food items. Both produces and consumers are benefited from rythu bazars as produce's share in consumer's rupee is more by 15 to 40 per cent and consumers get fresh vegetables fruits and food items and 2.30 per cent less prices than the prevailing prices in nearly markets;

(*d*) *Uzhavar Santhaigal:* In these markets farmers enjoy better marketing infrastructure free of cost and receive considerable high prices for the products than what then receive from middlemen at villages of primary markets at touns. Farmers also get good quality seeds and others inputs in the market itself.

Marketing Infrastructure

- *Regulated Markets:* The benefits available to the farmers from regulated markets depend on the facilities amenities available rather than the number of regulated markets in the area. The basis facilities viz. Internal roads, boundary walls, electric light, loading and unloading facilities and weighting equipments are available in more than eighty per cents of the markets. Farmer's rest houses exist in more than half of the regulated markets.

- *Grading Facilities at Producer's and Market Level:* Grading of products as per their quality standards before sale fetches higher price to the farmers. To bring uniformity in grading overtime and space, the Agricultural Produce (Grading and Marketing) Act, 1937 was enacted. Under this Act, grade standards for number of agricultural commodities have been prescribed for sale in domestic market, for export and for farm level grading.

- *Transportation:* Although there has been a considerable increase in the railway route length, total road length, the length of national highways and state highways in the country, however, the states of rural connectivity, which affects the farmers mast, continues to be poor, so for only 48.4 per cent of the villages are connected with roads.

- *Storage:* The scheme of warehousing was initiated at the center and state level after the enactment of the Agricultural Produce (Development and Warehousing) Corporations Act, 1956. The total covered storage capacity available with CWC, SWC and FCI including hired capacity is estimated at 40.7 million tones at the and of 2000. Cooperative sector has also built storage capacity of 13.55 million tones.

- *Cole Storage:* Cold storage units are an important infrastructure for storage of perishable and semi-perishable agricultural commodities viz. fruits, vegetables, dairy, poultry and marine products. The cold storage capacity increased from 300 thousand tones in 1960 to 4.0 million tones in 1980, 8.7 million tones in 1996 and further to 15.32 million tones by the end of March 2001. Presently a total of 4199 cold stores with the capacity of 15.38 million tones exist in the country in different sectors. The direct involvement of government in cold storage units is negligible. The present storage capacity available with 4199 cold stores is sufficient only for 10 per cent of the production of fruits and vegetables.

- *Processing and Value Addition:* Processing industry provides a ready market for agricultural raw materials like cotton, jute, sugarcane, oilseeds, pulses and several other commodities, reduces losses in the marketing chain and expands markets in addition to creation of employment opportunities. The occurrence of technological changes for processing and availability of new processing and preservation, higher consumers awareness about processed products, increasing urbanization and increased income of the consumers, lead to the growth of processing industry at commercial level.

Pledge Financing

Credit flow to agricultural sector may be substantially stepped up to meet increasing demand for capital expenditure for developing marketing infrastructure and for pledge finance. Pledge financing enables farmers to take advantage of favourable prices and improve their net margin.

According to the RBI guidelines advances up to Rs. 1.00 lakh can be given against pledge/hypothecation of agricultural produce (including warehouse receipts) for a period not exceeding six months subject to the condition that farmers have been given loan for raising the produce and provided the borrower draw credit from some bank. Such advances are included as direct finance to farmers. Besides all the conditions that have been decided upon, there are a few points that need to be improved upon:

(i) That the banks while advancing such loans emphasize on the collateral surety from the member, which is either the cooperative society as, marketed. In case of default by the members, the cooperative societ/mark fed is passed on the liability by virtue of their being second/collateral guarantor, which should not happen.

(ii) The pledge loan advance is on stock security.

(iii) The period of months for repayment of pledge loans is extended to up to 12 months.

(iv) The quantum of pledge loans to farmers for agricultural commodities especially for high value crops be enhanced from Rs. 1.00 lakh to Rs. 5.00 lakh.

(v) The produce adopted for pledge financing needs to be simplified.

Negotiable Warehousing Receipt System

The states of warehouse receipts has to be enhanced through legal changes for creating an effective system of regulatory oversight and be instituting a secured central electronic—register allowing for the reeking of all change in ownership and liens on warehouse receipts. Following short term and long term measures in this regard area

Short-term Measures

(i) The central warehousing corporations and the state warehousing corporations should evolve commercially acceptable quality standards in respect of various commodities in order to ensure quality maintenance of the stored goods over a sufficiently longer period of time.

(ii) The warehousing corporations should enforce standards both for quality and quantity at the warehouses, for which required of grades and standard need also be put in place, so as to reduce

disputes on account of quality and quantity standards and to improve the credibility of the warehouse receipt.

(iii) The warehousing corporations are also required to year up appropriate market intelligence on the prices of various commodities linked with the grades/standards.

(iv) The government of India is already considering value added tax all over the country. The other barriers particularly, the level of public intervention in the market need to be completely stopped or greatly liberalized in order to allow free flow of trade in agricultural commodity all over the country.

Long Term Measures

(i) A central legislation on the pattern of the Multimodal Transportation of Good Act, 1993, needs to be enacted for the warehouse receipts to be made fully negotiable instrument. Law should be farmed in such a way that it gives full enforceability and transparency of the warehouse receipts.

(ii) The CWC being the premier warehousing agency at the national level, it should be the ideal institution to be classified as the accreditation agency. In the long run some new institution has to be established for the purpose of regulation, as the players cannot be the monitors.

(iii) The legislation should also take care of care of securing a system of central electronic register like in the stock exchanges, for allowing the tracking of all changes in the ownership and liens in respect of the warehouse receipts. As the fluctuations of the prices in the market varying farm place to place play a great role, necessary safeguards have to be provided to present any political interventions.

Forward and Future Markets

Introduction of a negotiable werehouse receipt system to facilitate increased liquidity in rural areas, lower cost of financing, shorter and more efficient supply chains, enhance reward for other productivity, enhancing agricultural services and better price risk management.

Amendments to some of the provisions of the forward contact (Regulation) Act, 1952 are currently with the parliamentary standing committee. These amendments include defining futures trading, removal of ban on options trading, provision of registration of brokers, strengthening of FMC by including professionals at part time members, enhancing the penalty provisions etc.

Price Support Policy

Government intervention in purchase of agricultural commodities under minimum price support programme, procurement of foodgrains, market intervention scheme (MIS), monopoly, purchase, open market purchases of commodities by NAFED, CCI, JCT and state oilseed federations etc. have attained importance in recent years. The entry of these public and cooperative agencies has altered the existing channels and also their importance in terms of quality marketed through them. The basic objective of entry of these agencies in purchase of different commodities is to safeguard the interest of producer farmers alongside the protection of consumers form excessive prices in same years.

IT in Agricultural Marketing

Strengthening of ongoing central sector scheme of establishing market information Network and making it as a vehicle of market led extension, provides facility of electronic trading or e commerce on the Market Information Network portal to enable producers to directly transact business with the buyers. Use of information technology in agricultural marketing is becoming increasingly indispensable. Encouragement needs to be provided to generate and host useful portals, websites, databases, information packages and other software, generic as well as customized, on agricultural marketing. Info kiosks should be encouraged to be set up in the markets and with farmer's organizations, associations of traders and other functionaries for on line demand of different products. The information that is important and useful regard to quality, pack size and packaging material, quantity and time frame of supply, transport cost involved and the marketing charges likely to be incurred in the market where the goods are to be delivered, facilities available to the farmers in the buying market, rules and regulations of the distinction markets if they are located outside the state at a distant place, other specific information as may be conducive for the seller to transact the business with the purchases and the legal provisions related to storage, transportation and photo-sanitary requirements.

Marketing Extension, Training and Research

Agricultural marketing research undertaken so for is both descriptive and analytical. The institutions presently engaged in conducting agricultural marketing research are:

- Directorate of Marketing and Inspection, Government of India
- State Agricultural Marketing Boards (SAMBS)
- Indian Council of Agricultural Research (ICAR)
- National Institute of Agricultural Marketing (NIAM)

On the job/in service training of different durations are arranged by Directorate of Marketing and Inspection (DMI), National Institute of Agricultural Marketing Boards (SAMBS) and state Agricultural Universities. These training are meant both for fresh recruits as well as for those in service to refresh them. Important areas of research are:

- structure conduct and performance analysis of agricultural markets;
- role and effectiveness of marketing institutions;

- study of cost and margins of important agricultural horticultural crops;
- export effectiveness of agricultural and horticultural crops;
- information needs of stakeholders in agricultural marketing;
- marketing of organically produced commodities;
- price discovery mechanism of different agricultural commodities;
- implication of WTO on agricultural marketing;
- risk management in agriculture, etc.

Co-operative Marketing

The marketing of agricultural production through cooperative societies considered as an alternative pattern to the traditional marketing system, since it is expected that it will remove all the defects of traditional marketing and ensure faire price to the producer and consumer both. With this view in end co-operative marketing is a system in which a group of farmers join together to carry on some or all the process involved in marketing. It may purchase the produce of their member at current price and sell it in the market like a trader. Co-operative marketing of agricultural product is necessary not only for stabilizing marketing condition by means of orderly and regulated supply of commodity but also improve bargaining power of cultivators. During 1993-94, co-operatives have marketed agricultural produce worth over Rs. 7400 crore against the achievement of Rs. 6800 crore during the previous year registering an increase of 8.82 per cent.

Aim and Objective

- To sell the members product directly in the best market and in a state which attract best price.
- To help the members to produce the best products and those are most in demand.
- To give fair weight.

- To grade the produce in such a way that best price is obtained for all qualities.
- To provide fair trading practices and to use its influence against rings and manipulation of prices.
- To help the members to finance himself while he is waiting for his crop to ripen.
- By give a farmer a better understanding of all stages in marketing process.

Functions of Co-operative Marketing

The co-operative marketing societies have been perform three important function i.e. sale of agricultural product, sale of agricultural requisites and sale of consume goods.

Apart from these it perform some other functions, which are as follows:

- Marketing of products;
- Distribution of fertilizer, seeds and agricultural machinery;
- Grading, processing and pooling of produce;
- Provision of storage facilities;
- Provision of financial assistance;
- Export of commodities;
- Co-operative cold stores.

Future Strategy

- Developing co-operatives as economically efficient organizations capable of meeting the challenges of new economic environment.
- Accent on creation of additional marketing and infrastructure facilities in potential areas and sectors.
- Encouraging and facilitating co-operatives in forging collaborative alliances partnership with other co-

operatives, private/public sector in areas of strategic importance including marketing tie-ups.

Investment for Market Reforms

Market Infrastructure

The investments for development of market infrastructure have been projected. During the next five years a total investment of Rs. 40306 million has been envisaged for development of marketing related activities such as market infrastructure, Grading, Standardization, Quality, Facilities, Marketing Information Network, Market Research Surveys etc.

Storage Infrastructure

The Government of India has also formulated a National Storage policy aimed at harnessing the resource of the public and private sector for augmentation of infrastructure to handle food grains including construction of bulk storage facilities as also conventional godowns under "Gramin Bhandaran Yojna" Total additional storage capacity of 130 lakh tones is likely to be created in the country with total investment of Rs. 34800 million including back-ended subsidy of Rs. 5700 million from Government of India.

Cold Storage and Cool Chain Infrastructure

In view of the expected market surplus of fruits and vegetables by 2007 and the available cold storage capacity, it has been envisaged to create an additional capacity of 56.50 lakh tones during the Tenth plan period. The total outlay on construction/creation of cold storage capacity and cool chain would be Rs. 47200 million, which includes back-ended subsidy of Rs. 11750 million from Government of India.

Conclusion

After the "Green Revolution" which ensures abundant production and food security in India, we are gearing ourselves to have Marketing Revolution with all its rainbow colors so as to size the opportunities provided by the liberalized international market. This would not only maintain the balance of agricultural production but also ensure availability of qualitative products to the consumer at reasonable prices.

REFERENCES

1. Chand Ramesh (2003), "Minimum Support Price in Agriculture: Changing Requirements", *Economic and Political Weekly*, July 1925.

2. "Co-operative Marketing-Status", (1996), *NCDC*, June-August.

3. Dr. Bhattacharyya and Dr. Bihari Krishana (2003), "Scope of Organic Farming in India", *Jojana*, November.

4. Desai Gunrant, M. (1985), "Farm Price Structure", *Indian Journal of Agricultural Economics*. Vol. 40, No. 4.

5. *Economic Survey*, 2002-03, Government of India.

6. *Economic Survey*, 2002-03, Government of Orissa.

7. Jena, A.C. (2002), "Public Distribution System: Impact, Status and Future Programmes", *Kurukshetra*, October.

8. Mahanti Tushar, K. (2003), "India's GDP to grow at 7.4% in 2003-04, Courtesty Higher Agri Growth", *The Economic Times*, October 27.

9. Mishra, P.K. (2002), "Agricultural Marketing Co-operatives in India", *NCDC*, December.

10. Rudrappan, D. (2003), "Economic Reforms and Agriculture" *Yojana*, November.

11. Sidhu, D.S. (1986), "Policies Pertaining to Agricultural Marketing and Input Supply", *Indian Journal of Agricultural Economics*, Vol. 41, No. l.

12. Sidhu, D.S. (1987) *Marketing Indian Journal of Agricultural Economics*, Vol. 42, No. 1.

13. Singh, P.K. (2003), "Reforms in the Agriculture Sector", *Yojana*, November.

14. "Statistical Outline of Orissa" (2002-03), Government of Orissa.

15. Subbarao, K. (1985), "Incentive Policies and India's Agricultural Development: Some Aspects of Regional and Social Equity", *Indian Journal of Agricultural Economics.* Vol. 40, No. 4.

16. Urs, D. Shrijay Devaraj (2002), "Agricultural Marketing: Status, Future Policies and Strategies", *Kurukshetra,* October.

10

Entrepreneurship and Infrastructure in Tribal Kandhamal

*Govinda Chandra Panda**

Introduction

The economic status of Kandhamal District in the State of Orissa is in low profile. In spite of our serious economic interventions, still 70 per cent of the people of this district are living below the poverty line. These people mostly belong to ST and SC communities. This happens mainly because the district suffers from certain economic deficiencies and contradictions. The deficiencies are low saving, low capital stock, low investment and low capital formation on the one hand and low education, low health, low quality of life and to human resource formation on the other hand. This altogether results in low entrepreneurial and technological advancement in the utilisation of existing resources. In addition to this, the district is also legging behind in terms of provision of better infrastructure and institutional arrangements. Another important reason for the economic backwardness of the tribes is their mental unpreparedness to participate in the process of natural resource management. Such a situation also leaves a wide space for the nontribes to impose the economic supremacy over the tribes while utilizing

* Mr. Panda is Head, Department of Economics, AMCS College Tikabali, Kandhamal, Orissa.

the rich resource potentialities of the district. It is also worth to mention that the tribes mainly supply raw materials and sell their labour power even at non-remunerative price to the manufacturing units usually run by the non-tribal people. This actually creates a big gap between the tribes and non-tribes in the tribal regions in general and tribes in particular. So it is quite pertinent to sort out the deficiencies in the management of resources so as to make the approach holistic and integrative with a view to bring back the tribes into the mainstream of the development.

The approach to natural resource management is not self-determining and isolative in nature. Rather, the approach is integrative and multi-factorial. It is integrative as it aims at............

1. Economically optimum utilization of resources i.e. optimality in production.
2. And, other economic and non-economic viabilities to sustain development for a longer period, i.e. sustainability of production.

It is multifactorial as it calls for a perfect combination between inward and outward factors. Inward factors are capital Investment, decisive capacity, technology adoption and innovative applications, Outward factors include availability of resources, supply of labour force, and other such institutions facilitating finance, market, transport, power supply and training etc. Inward factors imply entrepreneurship and ensure optimality in production. Out ward factors do mean social overheads i.e. infrastructure and lead to sustainability of production, Since economic development is a multilateral and multidirectional movement, abundant resources both physical and financial, are bound to be grossly misutilised in the absence of development of human capital i.e., entrepreneurship and social overhead, i.e. infrastructure, Thus, the right mix of these two factors can make Least-Cost Combination possible in the process of production.

Moreover, the industrial promotion and economic development of an economy just happen only by the way of entrepreneurisation of the society where the infrastructure plays a supportive or secondary role Entrepreneurs is the life blood of an economy, more so in the developing economy. As such, entrepreneurs are crucial to development than other economic and non-economic factors; inter-alia they play a vital role in the process of resource utilization and economic development. When development linked human minds are absent development will hardly take place in the economy. Hence, development of entrepreneurship is pre-condition for stimulation and sustenance of economic progress. To conclude, entrepreneurs are the real risk-takers, decision-makers and prime-players in resource utilization and production.

In this backdrop attempts have been made in this research write-up to explore the following objectives.

Objectives of the Study

The study has the following objectives.

(i) To highlight the socio-economic conditions of the tribes of the district under study.

(ii) To present a picture on the resource potentiality of the study economy.

(iii) To focus on entrepreneurship vis-a-vis industrialization in Kandhamal district.

(iv) Shortcomings, concluding remarks and suggestion for further policy options.

Methodology

Keeping in view the above objectives, the district of Kandhamal has purposively been selected for its tribal concentration, Tribes, mostly the Kandhas, are the principal inhabitants of the district and constitute nearly 52.02 (2001 Census) per cent to the total population of the district. Socio-culturally the tribes are rigid in nature and economically they lead a simple life.

The study has been made mainly depending on secondary sources of data. Papers, journals, magazines official records and other information have extensively been utilized to complete the study. The researcher has also adopted investigation and observation method to infer conclusions, Some previous literatures have also been taken resort to.

Resource Potentiality of Kandhamal

The economy of Kandhamal is Agro forest in nature, Forest and agricultural determine the economic life of the people and provide the sources for earning livelihood and generating income and employment of the district. Similarly, the industrial development of the district also, by and large, depends upon its resource potentiality. So let us have a bird's eye view on the resource potentially of the district under study. The district possesses vast scopes for development of resource based industries in the following broad based area.

Agriculture

Agriculture is the primary sector of the district and the followings are the major crops of the district depicted with production data for the year 1999-2000.

(i)	Paddy	:	10325.43	MT
(ii)	Maize	:	20365.41	MT
(iii)	Turmeric	:	50776.95	MT
(iv)	Niger	:	4909.29	MT
(v)	Mustard	:	2194.27	MT
(vi)	Ginger	:	24591.80	MT
(vii)	Potato.	:	7844.44	MT
(viii)	Sweet Potato (Local Variety)	:	10301	MT
(ix)	Pulses			
	(a) Arhar dal	:	5175.96	MT
	(b) Moong dal	:	444.83	MT

(*c*) Biri dal : 1739.83 MT

(*d*) Kulthi dal : 1878.18 MT

Turmeric is the main spice of the district. Local turmeric, containing 2.36 per cent of curcumin, 12.15 per cent oleoresin and 5.33 per cent of volatile oil is cultivated in an area of about 14000 hectare Improved turmeric with 5-7 per cent of curcumin, 10-15 per cent of oleoresin and 2-4 per cent of volatile is grown in a area of about 700 hect. The area and production of improved turmeric is increasing day by day.

Ginger is another important spice item available in this district. Local Ginger with 7-10 per cent of crude fibre, 4.28 per cent oleoresin and 1.83 per cent volatile oil is cultivated in an area of 1700 hectare. The improved ginger with 4-5 per cent of crude fibre, 4-8 per cent of oleoresin and 0.9-1.3 per cent volatile oil is cultivated in 100 hectare. This is also increasing from year to year. All these spices in Kandhamal district are organic in nature. The tribal farmers are traditional organic growers without application of fertilizer and pesticides. SKAL Certifying Agency of Holland have issued certification for turmeric of Kandhamal district as "organic". Therefore, spices of the district has the potentiality of entering into the global market and as a matter of fact the spices of the district have been exported to many Foreign Countries during last year.

Plantation: This district has ideal climate for growing fruits and vegetable crops. There are 3 nos. of Horticulture division at Phulbane, Balliguda and G. Udayagiri and ongoing programmes are implemented for increasing the fruit and vegetable production through cultivation of banana, apple, orange, mango, grape, cocoanut papaya, pine apple etc.

(*i*) Mango 12666 MT

(*ii*) Sapata 73 MT

(*iii*) Ber 44 MT

(iv)	Lemon	8119	MT
(v)	Litchi	92	MT
(vi)	Pine apple	1062	MT
(vii)	Guava	2379	MT
(viii)	Banana	6091	MT
(ix)	Papaya	27954	MT
(x)	Jack fruit	6000	MT
(xi)	Misc. fruits	34663	MT

Coffee Plantation: Coffee is also grown in G. Udayagiri, Daringabadi and Raikia blocks. From 1999, one acre coffee plantation scheme has been introduced in the District for BPL family with total project cost of Rs. 28,000/- per acre to be financed over a period of 4 years. If this programme will come out success then every family will have permanent income for coming 50 years.

Animal Husbandry: Animal and Husbandry is an important sub-sector of agriculture economy. On going projects are on the full swing in the dairy development and animal husbandry sectors relating to the following activities.

(i) Fodder development.

(ii) Mobile veterinary laboratory.

(iii) Mini mixing unit for cattle and poultry feed.

(iv) Chilling plant.

(v) Goat rearing.

(vi) Fisheries.

Forest Resources: 67 per cent of geographical area are covered by forest with trees of Sal, Asan, Devadaru, Kendu, Karada, Kusuma, Beja, Siali, Bamboo, Mango, Jack fruit and Cane trees. There are also abundant availability of Nim, Mahua, Karanja, Bahada etc. Licences could be obtained from the TDCC/GPs for promotion of SSI units. Processing and packing of Arrowroot can also be done by utilising the available raw material from the forest resources.

Tamarind is naturally grown in the forests and backyard of the farmers. Annually about 940 MT of Tamarind is produced in the district of Kandhamal. Basing on the availability of the Tamarind units like Tamarind concentrate, pulp and powder, starch from Tamarind seeds can be set up by inviting suitable entrepreneurs.

Mineral Resources: Occurrence of Bauxite has been reported from Madagura, Kotagarh, Belghar, Gurlinise area. Graphite is available at Tumudibandha and Belghar reserve forest area. Lime store is located at Khajuripada. Deposits of managanese has been reported to be at Karlangi near Belghar and at Sirikajodi near Gochhapada in Phiringia block. Coal are also found at Katringia and Gochhapada area. It is also reported some precious and semi-precious stones like cat's eye and aquamarine stones are also available in the District. The exact quantity and quality of deposit of Gem stones, Bauxite, Manganese and coal are yet to be ascertained by the Mining Department. The estimated deposit of graphite in the district is around 1.68 lakhs MT basing on which a graphite purificiation plant may be set up in this district by deserving entrepreneurs.

Sericulture: At present 400 Ac. of land is utilised for mulberry cultivation. There is scope for expansion of the programme to 2500 Ac of land with in next five years. About eight thousand kgs of cocoon is produced at present during 1998-99. There is a plan to take up production of 15000 kgs of cocoon. At present these cocoon is being sent to Mahendragiri in Ganjam district where spinning of silk yarn are done. At least 15000 kg of cocoon are required for running the mulberry cultivation centre and such quantum is not available in the district, and as such the cocoon are being sent to the aforesaid.

Place in Ganjam for production of silk yarn. There is also a scope for utilising the silk yarn in nearby districts of Boudh, Bolangir and Sonepur. In the long run such production can also be taken up in the district of Kandhamal by developing entrepreneurship.

Existing Infrastructural Facilities

1. (a) Communication	Railway Link - Nil State Highway - 340 km. Major District Road - 182 km. Other District Road 63 km.
(b) Road ways	Forest Roads - 323 km. G.P. Road 15651 km Classified Village Road - 279 kms, P.S Roads - 532 km. Village Roads, 682 kms as on 2000.
3. Water	The district receives high rainfalls. Water conservation capacity the district is abysmally low. Major Irrigation Project - 11 Nil, Medium Irrigation Project - 4 Nos.
3. Electricity	Hydroelectric Project - Nil, Thermal Power Plants - Nil. The district gets power supply from Machkund and Hirakud through radial 33 KV feeders from Aska and Balangir power station respectively. Ironically, Kandhamal district is the lowest consumer of power in the state.
4. Growth centers.	There is one industrial Growth center identified and land have been earmarked for development of S.S.I. sector at Majuribida - Near Phulbani with a patch of 748.5 Ac.
5. Industrial Estate.	There is one industrial Estate at Phulbani town with total land area of 10 Ac. And having 12 sheds. At present 4 nos of SSI units are operational in this industrial Estate. However, industrial activities are yet to be visible in this industrial Estate on full scale.

6. Training facilities. The Industrial Training Institute. Phulbani is having good scope for training in various trades. The names of the different trades and its intake capacity are as follow.

i.	Welder	24
ii.	Fitter	32
iii.	Motor Mechanic	16
iv.	Wireman	32
v.	Draughtsman civil	16
vi.	Draughtsman Mech.	16
vii.	Electrician	32
viii.	Electronics	32
ix.	Stenography	16

Besides this, the ITI is regularly training the youths from different block areas under the sponsorship of DRDA, ITDA and other promotional agencies.

Existing Industries as on 1999-2000

a.	Large/Medium scale industries	:	Nil
b.	Small scale industries.	:	496
c.	Handicrafts and Cottage industries	:	711

Industrial Scenario of Kandhamal District Problems and Prospects

1. *Achivements Up-to-date*

District Industries Center, Phulbani was created in the year 1978 with a view to provide greater momentum to the industrialization of the district. But in spite of the presence of vast natural resources and abundant manpower the district could not make desirable progress in the field of industrialization.

A. Small Scale Industries

The industrial scenario of the district up-to 1999-2000 is as follows.

Table 10.1: Industrial Scenario of Kandhamal District (1999-200)

Sl.No.	*Categories of industries*	*No. of units*	*Investment (Rs. in lakh)*	*Employment*
1.	Food & Allied	203	127.28	496
2.	Glass/Ceramic	19	21.05	116
3.	Chemicals	7	44.28	206
4.	Elect. & Electronics	12	3.35	24
5.	Engg. & Metal	25	24.59	113
6.	Repairing & Servicing	113	78.01	267
7.	Forest & Wood based	14	6.24	
8.	Textile Based	63	19.99	208
9.	Livestock/Leather	5	0.93	10
10.	OSI	6	46.67	60
11.	Mis. Ind.	24	30.39	51
12.	Rubber/Plastic	2	4.39	05
13.	Paper & Paper Products	3	4.01	15
	Total	496	411.18	1768

(During the year 1999-2000, 57 no of SSI units have been promoted in Kandhamal district with investment of Rs. 79.04 Lakh generating employment to 207 persons.)

B. Prime Minister's Rozagar Yojana

For eradication of unemployment in the district and for upliftment of the socio-economic condition of the unemployed educated youth the DIC has implemented the PMRY scheme since 1993-94. The target and achievement under PMRY sector is tabulated below.

Table 10.2: The Target and Achievement under PMRY Sector from 1993 to 2000

Year	*Target*	*No. of cases*	*Percentage*
1993-1994	8	4	50%
1994-1995	60	31	52%
1995-1996	100	88	88%
1996-1997	100	88	88%
1997-1998	130	107	82%
1998-1999	140	104	74%
1999-2000	140	28	
Total	678	450	

C. *Handicrafts*

Artisans in the district of Kandhamal are practicing different crafts under Handicraft Sectors. Accordingly, to support the artisans in a particular craft, societies have been organized. List of crafts under the Handicraft Sector, promoted by DIC, Phulbani with the of H&CI and Development Commissioner (Handicrafts) have assistance of directorate been illustrated below.

1.	Applique works.	Phulbani
2.	Stone Garbing.	Pusangia, Iballiguda
3.	Artistic mat.	Darnerika, K. Nugaon
4.	Wood Carving.	Phiringia
5.	Sisal Works.	K. Nuagaon
6.	Dhokra Casting.	Barakhama, Balliguda, Kurtamgarh, Tumudibandha
7.	Cane & Bamboo.	Tumudibandha.
8.	Bamboo works.	Sukumpa, Khajuripada, Nandini (Chakapad)
9.	Clay Terra. Cotta.	Tellapali, Keradi (Phulbani)
10.	Tribal Jewelery.	Pusangia (Phiringia)

The societies which are in existence manifested below.

Table 10.3

Name of the District	*Name & address of the CS*	*No. of member working*	*Name of the craft*	*Present status*
Kandhamal	1. Kasturibai Women's Handicrafts Coop. Society Ltd., Phulbani	136	Readymade Garments, Embroidery and Applique works.	Working
	2 Lahabadi Mat Weaving Coop.	52	Mat weaving	Defunct
	3. G. Udayagiri Appliuique Works Indl. Coop. Society G. Udayagiri	57	Applique	Defunct

D. *Cottage Industries*

The Cottage and Village Industries Programme are implemented in this district with the assistance of Orissa Khadi and Village Industries Board. The no. of Cottage and Village industries promoted in the district till date are illustrated below.

Table 10.4

Sl.No.	*Category of village industry*	*No. of units*
1.	Pottery	112
2.	PCPI	95
3.	RE Industries	125
4.	Fibre Industries	65
5.	Bee Keeping	10
6.	Cane & Bamboo	102
7.	Service	24
8.	Leather	59
9.	Textile	65
10.	Lime	5
11.	Village Oil	2

12	Fruit and Vegetable processing	14
13.	Cottage Match and Agarbati	6
14.	Collection of forest plant	2
15.	NEO soap	1
16.	Marketing	2
17.	GK Industries	7
18.	Bell metal	5
19.	Hand made paper	1
20.	Poly vastra	8
21.	Adivasi Jewellery	1
	Total	711

K&VI Societies functioning in the District of Kandhamal are as follows.

Table 10.5

Sl. No.	*Name & Address of CS*	*No. of members*	*Activities*
1.	DGMCS Ltgd, Phulbani	71	Central CS for marketing
2.	Phulbani BLAIMCS Ltd.	387	Multipurpose industrial activities and training
3.	Tikabali BLAIMCS Ltd.	126	-do
4.	G. Udayagiri BLAIMCS Ltd.	353	-do
5.	Raikia BLAIMCS Ltd.	333	-do
6.	Daringbadi BLAIMCS Ltd.	106	-do
7.	Rameswar AIMCS Ltd.	202	-do-
8.	K. Nuagaon Sisal Fibre Indl.	53	-do
9.	Pattakhanda AIMCS Ltd.	597	-do-
10.	Bhairabi AIMCS Ltd.	173	-do-
11.	Kotagarh BLAIMCS Ltd.	136	-do-
12.	Phiringia BLAIMCS Ltd.	222	-do-
13.	Khajuripada BLAIMCS Ltd.	846	-do-
14.	Chakapad BLAIMCS Ltd.	206	-do-

Shortcoming, Suggestions and Concluding Remarks

The erstwhile Phulbani District (named before the re-organization of District in Orissa 1994) had no place in the industrial map of Orissa. Industrially the district is legging behind in comparison to other District of Orissa. Development of entrepreneurship in the study district is a big challenge. To conclude development of entrepreneurship and resource utilization of district are abysmally low owing to the following disadvantages.

1. Major areas of the district are inaccessible because of hills, slopes, plateaus, mountain and forest. The transport system clearly reveals the absence of national highways and railways in the district. The development of road transport is still under progress leaving many parts of district untouched. Even today, the G.P. headquarters are yet to be connected to Panchayat Samiti with fair-weather roads. Thus, due to lack of communication and transport facilities essential raw materials are not procured properly and finished products cannot be delivered in time also.

2. Supply of Power and Electricity is another major problem in the district. Power generating capacity of the district is zero, because of non-existence hydroelectric power projects and thermal power plants. Even though electricity is available, there are load shedding, frequent power cuts and blockouts for hours together.

3. Water is also not found adequately in the district. Ironically, the district lies under heavy rainfall zone but due to lack of water conservation capacity water becomes absolutely insufficient even to meet the drinking purposes of the people in non-rainy days.

4. Another important huddle of the district is psychological in nature. The aborigines of the district are normally shy in nature. They live within their group boundaries. They don't have exposure to the outer world. Their expectations are minimal and limited, which keeps them in backward to shoulder the risk of entrepreneurship.

5. Today, crores of rupees are being spent in tribal regions to alleviate poverty. Excess implementation of poverty eradication programmes also provide some economic relief to the tribes leaving them in a lower complexity of non-shouldering any risk in the life.

6. Usually, the people of this district are economically poor. Originally, the people were nomadic in nature, moving from place to place and hence don't own much legitimate landed property. Most of the land belongs to Forest Department and they inhabit in the area without legal entities. As the financial condition is alarming they never show interest to set-up micro enterprises.

A perusal of the study clearly manifests that the tribes are leading a subhuman life in their own world of isolation and despair. It is because of low human capital formation in tribal reason. This is the single largest reason causing low development of entrepreneurship. Secondly, inadequacy of infrastructure also debars the district to advance rapidly in the path of industrialization. As a result, in today's "Globalized Village" the district has been pushed back into the corner leaving the people amidst poverty.

So to break up the industrial backwardness of this district the following measures should immediately be taken.

1. The district needs railhead and improvement of existing connecting roads within the district and to other neighbouring districts.

2. Sensitization programmes and awareness camps in relation to entrepreneurship developments have to be conducted using audio-visual shows/Stage shows to make the tribes understand the trend of changes and match with the pace of development.

3. More training institutions should be opened to meet the training needs so that awareness and motivation among the tribes can be generated for the entrepreneurization of the society.

4. Entrepreneurship Development Training Programmes with Special Margin Money Assistance are to be provided in under to enable them to switch over to entrepreneurial activities in the Industries/Service/Business and other vital sectors.

5. Adequate provisions should be made for power supply to the district for industrial use.

6. Industrial Growth Centers and Industrial Estates should be opened to create a congenial atmosphere for growth of SSI Units, Ancillary unit's and tiny sectors.

7. Course modules and training modules especially for the beneficiaries under PMRY and SGSY, as a part of Entrepreneurship Development Programme and Entrepreneurship Awareness Programme should be prepared. For this purpose funds are to be mobilized from Directorate of Industries, SIDBI, NABARD, NSIC and other promotional and supporting agencies.

To conclude emphasis should be given to inject motivational and behavioural inputs for creating an entrepreneurial culture in the district of Kandhamal.

REFERENCES

1. Panda, G.C., "Empowering Tribal Women through Self Help Groups—A Study in Kandhamal" in Tripathy S.N., Sahu R.K. Edited Book *Empowerment of Women.* Anmol Publication, New Delhi. 2006

2. Panda, G.C. & Tripathy S. "Impact of Road Transport on Population—A Study in Kandhamal" in Panigrahi R.L. Edited Book *Problems of Population in India,* Discovery Publishing House, New Delhi, 2005.

3. Panda, G.C., "Panchayat Raj Institution and Tribal Development—A Study in Kandhamal", Paper presented in a National Seminar, S.R.T.M. University, Nanded, Maharastra.

4. S.S., Khanka, *Entreprenerial Development,* S. Chand & Company Ltd., New Delhi, 2001.

5. Vasanta Desai, *Dynamics Entrepreneurial Development and Management*, Himalya Publishing House, Bombay, First Edition 1992.

6. Dr. D. Himachalam, "Entrepreneurship Development in Small Scale Sector", *Yojana;* Feb. 16-28, 1990, Vol. 34, No. 3.

7. Economic Survey of Orissa, 2005.

8. *Statistical Handbook of Kandhamal*, 2001.

9. District Industrial Report, 2000.

10. Office of the D.R.D.A., Phulbani.

11

Strategies for Marine Fisheries Development in India

*Dr. Tanuj Kumar Bisoyi**

Fishery sector provides the fifth largest agricultural resource accounting for 7.5 per cent global food production and is the chief source of food protein for common people besides providing economic livelihood for many. Since independence, India has gradually emerged as a major fish-producing nation in the world being second in total aquaculture production and third in the overall fish production. India with a coastline of over 8143 kms and Exclusive Economic Zone (EEZ) of around 2.02 million sq km. Central Marine Fisheries Research Institute's potential yield estimate is 3.9 million tones from total EEZ of this 1.7 million tones is available from outer continental shelf while the inshore water are being exploited to their full capacity. India is also having vast and varied inland water resource. Both capture and culture fisheries, the potential yield for inland fisheries has been estimated to be 4.5 million tones.

Since fisheries is a broad term, the methods and strategies for its development can be discussed under headings such as:

* Dr. Bisoyi is a lecturer in Economics, Kabisuriya Baladev Mahavidayalaya (Ganjam), Orissa.

(*a*) Resource for marine fishery

(*b*) Existing aquaculture

(*c*) Environmental issues

(*d*) Harvest and post-harvest technology

(*e*) Human Resource Development and socio-economic issues.

Resources for Marine Fishery

The marine fisheries in India have transformed its nature from subsistence level activity to the fishing for commerce towards the turn of 19th century. The commercial orientation was further strengthened during the 20th century. The most rapid development in the marine fisheries sector came during second half of the current century. These developments were mainly directed towards increasing fish production and foreign exchange earnings.

Our marine living resources are spread in the Indian Ocean, Arabian Sea and Bay of Bengal covering an area under EEZ. The Indian Ocean has total area of 51 million sq kms. after declaration of EEZ in 1997, the available for fishing is estimated as 2.02 million sq kms. Comprising 0.86 million sq kms. On the west coast, 0.56 million sq kms. On east coast and 0.60 million sq kms. Around Andaman and Nicobar islands. The present scenario of marine fisheries in the Indian EEZ is that of mixed status with coastal fisheries nearing optimum level of development and deep-sea and oceanic fisheries receiving scant attention. The euphoria of acquiring the vast area on the seas around the peninsula and envisaged development through the exploitation of rich fish stocks within the Indian EEZ could bring in certain deep-sea fishing schemes but they had limited positive impact. Our future effort should be in the line of optimizing the use of potential resources by application of eco-friendly technologies, maximizing use of fish that is caught by these technologies for human consumption and minimizing post-harvest losses.

Preservation of ecological balance through sustainable exploitation of resources and management measures aimed at continuance of stock potential to meet the nutritional demands of ever growing human population.

In the inland sector of India, problems of resource management are not the same as in all other developing countries. A good many problems of India are peculiar and many others are similar to other developing countries. Some of the common problems of developing countries are, dearth of natural resources and suitable technologies, population explosion, poverty, ignorance as indigenous fish fauna. We face problems of diversity of natural resources, topographical and agro-climatical differences, varying types of indigenous fish fauna, vagaries of nature etc. Management policies are needed to be formulated keeping in view their regional nature.

Table 11.1: Water Resource Potential in India

Items	*Units*	*Quantity*
Length of the coastline	Km	8118
Exclusive Economic zone	Million km^2	2.02
Continental Shelf Area	000 km	506
Length of rivers, Canals K.M.		191,024
Brackishwater Area	Million ha	1.23
Reservoirs Area	Million ha	3.15
Tanks and Ponds	Million ha	2.25
Beels, oxbow and Derlict waters	Million ha	0.82
Marine fish potential	Million tones	3.93
Indian fish potential	Million tones	
Marine		2.83
Inland		2.82
Total		5.65

Table 11.2 Resource Potential of Exclusive Economic Zone ('000 tones)

Coast	*Demersal*	*Pelagic*	*Total*
North-west	756	461	1217
South-west	473	834	1307
North-east	142	178	320
South-east	313	241	554
Total			502
Lakshadweep oceans deep sea total			3900

Source: Journal of Indian Farming.

Existing Aquaculture

World aquaculture dates back to China from the 5th Century, its development has been confined to a few regions and at present there are about 190 sp known to be cultivated of which more than 10 acre being cultured in southeast Asia. The Asian region has been and still is the centre of aquaculture production and diversity. Aquaculture in India has witnessed remarkable progress particularly during the post independence period. Apart from substantial contribution to the national economy it has emerged as a lucrative venture of growing industry. Over the years the country has made great strides not in increasing the total aquaculture production but also enhancing the unit productivity from a subsistence level to mean national productivity of about 2 t/ha/yr through adoption of scientific culture technologies. The production has shown a quantum leap from 0.51 million tones in 1984 to 1.63 million tones in 1994 registering 215 per cent increase during the period. However, bulk of production is contributed by a few species of carps. Though aquaculture in India is carp based and carps contribute, as much as 89 per cent of the total aquaculture production at present, the country possess vast potential in terms of other species resources for diversification.

The catches from the rivers have dwindled considerably and several stretches, once the favourite haunts of the fish and fishermen alike are now depleted of those rich stocks, which they once harbored. While increased fishing pressure is the root cause of this decline, it has largely been compounded by dam construction, water abstraction, domestic and industrial as well as pesticide and herbicide pollution.

The estuaries are a function of the rivers and the impact of the changes upstream is reflected in the ecological disturbances in the estuaries. As such, the major estuaries and lagoon also have not been spared by pollution, siltation and vegetation. The Hoogly estuary, Chilika lake and Cochin backwaters have their own tales of woe and have fallen in disgrace with nature.

Unfortunately, reservoir fisheries development has not been given any serious attention despite the recommendations of the All India Coordinated Research Project on the Ecology and Fisheries of Freshwater Reservoirs to treat them as specific entities. A rule of thumb is applied to all reservoirs with no attention to such details as stocking density/ha, size of fingerlings to be stocked, species-mix, time/period of stocking etc. besides place of stocking or any preparation prior to stocking.

Table 11.3: Status and Trend of Fish Production of India (Million Metric Tonnes)

Year	*Total Production*	*Marine Production*	*Inland Production*
1950-51	0.75	0.53	0.22
1961-62	1.16	0.88	0.28
1970-71	1.75	1.08	0.67
1980-81	2.44	1.55	0.89
1990-91	3.84	2.30	1.54
1999-2000	5.65	2.83	2.82

Never before had the world seen such a fast rate of growth as in brackish water aquaculture. More than finish, it was the crustaceans, which despite there low production and comparatively poor knowledge about their biology and techniques of culture. Shrimp farming which was mainly a traditional activity grew into a commercial enterprise practiced not only by small and marginal farmers but also by the corporate sector.

Table 11.4: Fish Production in India

Year	*Marine*	*Inland*	*Total*
1980-81	15.55	8.87	24.42
1986-87	17.13	12.29	29.42
1990-91	23.00	15.36	38.36
1991-92	24.47	17.10	41.57
1992-93	25.76	17.89	43.65
1993-94	26.49	19.95	46.44
1994-95	26.92	20.97	47.89
1995-96	27.07	22.42	49.49
1996-97	29.67	23.81	53.48
1997-98	29.50	24.38	5.3.88
1998-99	26.96	25.66	52.62
1990-2000	31.22	27.19	58.41

Table 11.5: Fish Production—Projection for Xth Five-Year Plan

Base year	*Marine @2.5% growth rate/year*	*Inland @8% growth rate year*	*Total @5.44 growth rate/Year*
2001-02	2.97	3.29	6.26
2002-03	3.04	3.555	6.59
2003-04	3.12	3.83	6.95
2004-05	3.20	4.14	7.34
2005-06	3.28	4.47	7.75
2006-07	3.36	4.83	8.19

Fish Production in India from 1950-51 to 1999-2000

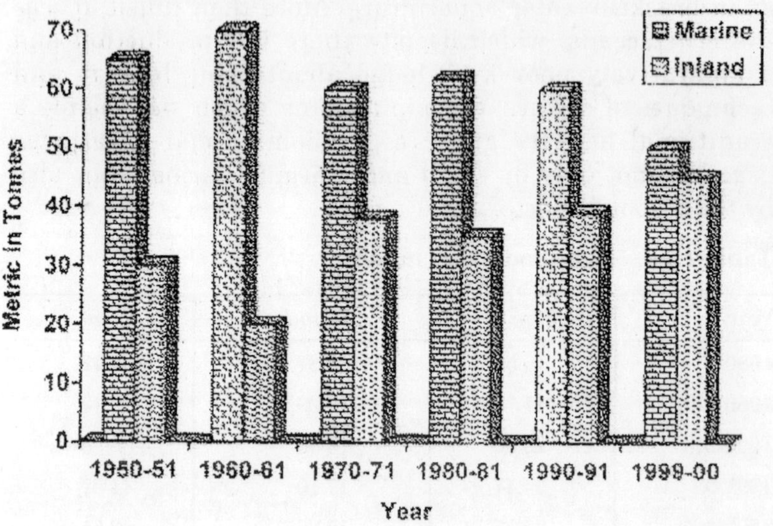

Nutrition Issue

Fish is a good source of animal proteins. Man has realized its importance from the very inception of the evolution of the human race. It has been the sole diet for many island nations before the evolution of farming techniques. Even to day the fish supplies 35-60 per cent animals protein requirement of many Asian countries. It also plays a lead role in foreign trade. Around 180 countries trade marine products on a global basis. India's exports of marine products crossed Rs. 50000 million in 2001 and continue to grow at a rate of 10 per cent annually. From nutritional point of view, aqua-food are unique as they provide not only superior quality proteins but also vitamins calcium and phosphorus essential for health and well being of people, In the view of low energy yielding substance and the presence of essential amino acids, polunsaturated fatty acids retional, and be complex vitamins these food are plane vital role in the food and nutritional security system of the country for attaining the two objective of food and nutritional security for the present and future generation, we can examination in date the current and the future production scenarios and emerging challenges resulting form the unsustainable activities which have far reaching implication on aqua food production in the years to come. Under the changing scenario. We can opines that a pragmatic plan of action meets to be designed with definitive objective and activates by including protection and prevention components in the future aqua food production programme.

Nutritional Status of Aqua Food

From nutritional point of view the aqua foods are valuable as they provide wide range of nutrients besides mineral in high proportion retinal, B group vitamins, calciums, and phosphorus for both poor and reach population of the country. The aqua food is a health food for the rural and urban masses of the country and therefore playing a crucial role to wards preventing, controlling and reusing the multiple nutritional deficiency diseases in the country.

Role of Fish Farming and Development Agencies in the Food Security

Fisheries sectors occupy a very important place on the socio-economic development of the country. It has been recognized as a powerful income and employment generator as it stimulates growth of a number of subsidiary industries, and is a source of cheap nutritious food, besides being a foreign exchange earner. Most importantly, it is the livelihood of a large section of economically backward rural population of the country.

Naturitonal Value

(a) Determination of nutritional requirements of various stages of presently cultivated finfishes and shell-fishes and of candidate species for culture other than those already studied.

(b) Development of suitable diets on the basis of findings of the study on nutritional requirements as suggested above.

(c) Determination of dietary vitamin and mineral requirements for improving gonadal maturation.

Table 11.6: Nutrient Content of Common Food Fishes

Name of fish/Group	*Moisture*	*Protein*	*Fat*	*Carbohydrate*	*Calcium*	*Phosphorus*	*Iron*
Carps	78.0	20.0	1.4	3.1	462	300	0.9
Live Fish	80.0	19.0	1.0	5.2	430	443	1.5
Catfish	70.0	19.2	6.4	2.3	270	170	2.0
Hilsa	54.0	22.0	19.4	2.9	180	280	2.1
Mahseer	78.0	18.0	1.9	2.0	110	80	3.8
Bhetki	80.0	15.0	0.8	3.0	480	350	3.1
Pormphret	75.0	17.0	1.0	0.8	324	278	5.3
Mackeral	77.0	20.0	1.6	0.5	430	300	2.0
Mullet	70.0	19.0	7.8	1.5	357	175	4.4
Oil sardine	76.0	19.6	2.0	0.1	357	350	6.1
Shrimp	77.0	20.0	0.5		32	270	53

(d) Development of least-cost diets through fishmeal substitution by unconventional feed sources.

(e) Petermination of merits of various non-hormonal growth promoters

(f) Development of technology and promotion of commercial scale production of single cell protein (e.g. Spirulina).

(g) Incorporation of 'probiotics' in fish feeds for deriving better-feed conversion and growth.

Environmental Issues

Its true that man is an integral part of nature, the dividing line between man and nature is due to the all-pervasive ego. Unless the ego is dissolved and reconciled with the fundamentals of nature, the conflict between man and nature will continue. The ego manipulates itself in the form of technology, innovations, desire to accumulates desire to exploit selfishness and greed. Only if the ego is dissolved can man function to enable the evolution of a technology, which is humane and will work towards catering of needs and not the fulfillment of greed.

Harvest and Post-Harvest Technology

World catch of fish has increased in the 1970's and 1980's but seems to have stabilized since 1988 to just around 100 million tones. As the human population is ever increasing, the tendency for demand to exceed supply is also increasing, resulting in widening supply/demand gap. This has the inevitable consequences of reduced availability, rising price and a search for alternative resources to close the gap. Limited availability will be particularly severely felt by people in developing countries to whom fish is often the most important source of animal proteins as well as a culturally acceptable food. Action will be required on a variety of fronts and better integration of all the scientific, technical and economic disciplines will be necessary. The post-harvest 6 technologist will have to play a more prominent role in this team.

Human Resource Development

After independence, India has achieved significant progress in preparing trained R&D personnel through the infrastructure built in the form of universities under the UGC and the Central Institutes, fisheries colleges in various states and under the ICAR and CSIR. Three personnel possessing post-graduate degree in general and doctorate and post doctorate research degrees in particular have shown themselves as a potentially useful band to researchers bringing the fisheries research on par with world class R&D elsewhere. The institutions having overlapping objectives and limited financial support are not able to optimally utilize the human resource potential, this is where we need very serious thought as to how to put these personnel in the right places with the institutions having well defined non-overlapping objectives.

It can be stated that, a certain level of manpower available with the various fisheries institutions in the for of scientists, technologists, researchers, administrative personnel and other supporting staff are working on the similar aspects or programmes but in different organizations. If these institutions are recognized with well defined specific objectives, the human resources spread over in many institutions would be really redeployed to achieve more and high degree of excellence with the same resource and simultaneously the duplication in the work as well as the manpower problem will be reduced to a great extent.

On the other hand, the recent setback caused in coastal aquaculture due to disease outbreak has proven beyond doubt the poor entrepreneurial acumen of the workforce involved in fisheries activities of our country. Likewise, inspite of having demonstrated the possibilities of taking production to the tune of over 17,000 kg/ha/yr. The low average yield of 2,180 kg/ha/yr. presently obtained from FFDA ponds speaks of serious lapses on the part of managerial skill of the involved manpower in aquacultural pursuits of the country. Scenarios relating to the management of other fisheries resources are also not much different. All these suggest that our country now needs more of well-trained resource managers rather than resource explorers or exploiters.

Table 11.7: Human Population in the Country

Year	*Total population*	*Average Annual Growth (%)*	*Person/km²*
1951	361.0	1.26	117
1961	439.1	1.98	142
1971	548.2	2.20	178
1981	685.0	2.30	216
1991	846.3	2.50	267
2000	1400		
2025	1400		

Conclusion

India is the sixth largest produce fish in the world and the second largest producer of inland fish the production the production of the country had increased from 2.959 million to 8.388 million from the year 1981 to 2001 at the annual average growth rate of 6.2 per cent, 2.95 yielding and 2.438 million tones about 80 per cent of inland production reported from aquaculture it estimated that the production potential of marine sector is 3.9 million and 2.9 million of inland sector Therefore fish farmers development agency has the main objective of optimizing fish production productivity augmenting export of fish generating employment and improving welfare of the fishermen and their socio economic status.

Strategy for Development in Fishery Sector

The main strategies and thrust area of future development of fishery sector are:

1. Expansion of aquaculture through up gradation of technology.

2. Conservation and optimum exploitation of the reverie fisheries.
3. Production of quality fish seed and feed for aquaculture.
4. Development of coldwater fisheries.
5. Shrimp and prawn culture for meeting export requirements.

It is time to recall that India was one of the pioneers amongst developing countries to list its biota, especially aquatic fauna back in the last century and develop its cadastral maps by survey of India. Indian advancements in the field of fisheries were foremost in Southeast Asia till the fifties. When Indians were experimenting carp and shrimp culture and demonstrating results, only China was at the same level, while Indonesia, Thailand, Philippines, Taiwan were busy denuding their mangroves for milk fish culture. Today these countries have raced much ahead, albeit with sad experiences of catastrophes of pollutional collapses of shrimp culture due to lack of monitoring of pond environment and knowledge to deal with diseases. Ironically, Singapore advanced fast and fish in international water all over South-East Asia, while we are unable to tap our own EEZ beyond 50 m depth. The lost ground has to be regained and India has to regain her glory. For this several challenges are to be taken by the horn, for which politician, bureaucrats, economists, planners and fisheries experts have to come together.

The globalization of technologies and free trade is a reality and would only get strengthened as we walk into 2st century. So would be the need to protect environment and ensure sustainability of the productive resource base. The conflict would lead to more restricted availability of quality land and water for aquaculture and cut throat competition from abroad for market share facing sea fisheries. These challenges will have to be met by not multiplying institutions but by strengthening and consolidating the available resources and the vast pool of scientific expertise across the country.

Development authorities and decision-makers at the National Planning level would need to give a hard look at the requirements of change at the legal and regulatory frame and assess investment needs and bring equity amongst alternative food production system, preferably by increasingly integrating aqua foods with land based foods and removing bottlenecks facing the enterprising Indian capability in fisheries and aquaculture.

REFERENCES

1. Handbook of Fisheries Statistics, (2000), Ministry of Agriculture, Government of India.
2. Pearce, D.W. (1976), *Environmental Economics,* Longman Group Ltd., London.
3. Pillay, T.V.R. (1994), *Aquaculture Development Progress and Prospects,* Fishing News Books, Great Britain.
4. Price Gittinger, J. (1982), *Economic Analysis of Agricultural Projects,* 2nd Ed., The John Hopkins University Press, London.
5. Rowena M. Lawson (1984), *Economics of Fisheries Development,* Francis Pinter (Publishers), London.
6. Shang, Y.C. (1981), *Aquaculture Economics Basic Concepts and Method of Analysis,* Croom Helm Ltd., Great Britain.
7. Skabo, H. (1983), *Financing Fisheries Project,* Infofish, 5.
8. S. Saroja (1987), USAID Sponsored Training Programme on Planning, Implementation and Evaluation of Agricultural Projects IIPA, New Delhi.
9. Squire, L. and van der Tak, H.G. (1975), *Economic Analysis of Projects,* The Johns Hopkins University Press, Maryland.
10. Subba Rao, N. (1986), *Economics of Fisheries—A Case Study,* A.P. Daya Publishing House, New Delhi.
11. Velayudhan, T.D. (1991), *Journal of Fisheries Economics and Development,* 1(1), p. 27.

12

Peasant Movement for Empowerment

A Mechanism of Rural Development

*Dr. Shrawan Kr. Singh**

A social movement has been broadly perceived as an organised or collective effort to brim, about changes in the thought, beliefs, value, relationship and major institutions of Society and establish new Social order (Blumer, 1951; Toch, 1965; Hebarle, 1951; Gusfield, 1972; Wilson, 1973). For Rao (1987), Collective mobilization; ideology and orientation towards change are basic elements of a social movement where as Rajendra Singh (2001) opines that leadership, ideology, objective and mobilization are the basic components of the Social movement.

Recent trend of Marxist Sociologist (R. Rajendra Singh) has the view that the new social movements have dominated the Indian scenario in the past three decades in the form of' gender movements, peasant movements, dalit movements, ethnic movements, tribal movement, human rights movements and environmental movements, however Singh has view that India is facing a blending of both old and new types. Unlike Rajendra Singh, K. Gough gives six categories of peasant movements: (a) Peasant rebellions to drive out British rulers and restore the Social relations; (b) religious

* Research Officer, A.N. Sinha Institute of Social, Patna-1.

movement, (c) Social banditry; (d) terrorist; (e) mass insurrections; (f) modern peasant movements (Jharkhand, Naxalite).

Peasant movement is defined as a relatively organised and continuous collective action involving violence, or the threat of violence for securing more share in the control or and ownership of land and is produce and to establish injustices which have orison these of and which involves kisan and landless or small landholders (Khetidar Mazdoor).

The central thrust of the process of empowerment, on the other hand is the dynamics of power. Power has widely been defined as one's capacity to influence or control others; if capacity is legitimized it becomes authority. According to Weber there are three main bases for the legitimization of power: traditional, national-legal and charismatic. One group can have effective power to control others by having control over resources and ideology. Those who have power are those who control material and knowledge resources and the ideology which governs path public and private life, and are thus in a position to make decisions which benefit themselves. Hence, the process of gaining control over the self, ideology and the resources which determine power may be termed empowerment (Batliwala, 1993). Empowerment as a social process challenges the fundamental imbalances of power distribution and relations. It is as process of redistribution of power within and between families/societies; and a process aiming at social equality which can be achieved through disempowering some structures, systems and situations (Sharma, 1992). Empowerment, therefore, is a process aimed at changing the nature; and direction of systematic forces which marginalize labourers and other disadvantage sections in a given context. It is also visualized as an enabling process for disadvantaged section Thus labours empowerment can be seen as mean of creating a social environment in which labour can take decisions and make chances of their own either individually or collectively, for social betterment. Since labourers occupy a disadvantage position in society, the process of l labour empowerment will also help men of lower socio-economic strata to liberate themselves from the clutches of traditional bondage, hierarchy and exploitation.

Social movements and empowerment are both social process. Orientation towards change and identified ideology and strategies are the basic components of these processes and both undergo process of progression from self-assertion to collective mobilization. However, collective mobilization, leadership and identified organization are the immediate requirements of a social movement. A social movement may cover various issues (social, economic, political) and may take diversified forms of collective mobilization and resort to diverse ideologies. Empowerment also resorts to collective mobilization, and gradually identified leadership and organization emerge with distinctive ideological orientations of rural equality grass roots organizations for labourers empowerment may be cited as example. Thus a given context empowerment is also a variant of self-conscious social movement.

Through the process of empowerment can achieve the status of social movements in the process of its progression over a period of time the scope of empowerment of labours also is available in latent form in various social movements, especially in peasant and dalit movements.

Labourers and Social Movements

The social and economic roles of labourers in a peasant society are essentially structured by age old traditions, beliefs, values, customs and by the processes of education and socialization. In a system in which resources and power have been concentrated through historical processes in the hands of a few, and the majority are landless or semilandless, labour of lower strata are doubly oppressed. First by being (subjugated in the social hierarchy), then by being members of the oppressed class (subjugated in the class hierarchy). Such concentration of resources and power has a enormous patriarchal bias in which labourers have no control over productive resources. Thus also have no control over knowledge information and ideas and even over their bodies and selves, since their reproductive activities are determined by patriarchal expectations. In the power hierarchy they are relegated to marginality since they have no say in decision-making process, even decision about themselves. The social and economic bases of marginalisation and oppression of labourers are legitimized by traditional norms, values, institutions and scriptures which provide the broad ideological foundation of patriarchy and casteism. The resourcelessness and powerlessness of labourers are widely recognised within the normative framework of society in India, including traditional literature and religious scriptures. (Singh, 2001).

Scholars (Rao 1976; Dhanagare, 1976) have viewed peasant movements as a distinct variant of social movements and have endeavoured to analyse these in terms of their linkages with changes In the organization of production and class conflict. Peasant movement a specific connotation in the Indian context since farmers movement have emerged as a different variety in recent years. At an operational level, a peasant movement may be defined as an organised and collective effort of the peasantry (subsistence and small producers, tenants, sharecroppers and agriculture labourers) to bring about change in the pattern of ownership, control and use of land, share of agricultural produce, wage structure, credit and institutional support system and in other aspects of socio-economic life that have subjugated them in agrarian society. The form and extent of the reposes of the disadvantages sections and labourers towards a peasant movement largely depend on the nature of ideological orientation and the form of mass mobilization which play crucial roles in the dynamics of peasant movements. Peasant movements can broadly be categorised as 'radical' or 'reformative' depending on their particular combination with ideology, form of mass mobilisation and orientation towards change. Radical movements are those that use non-institutional mass mobilisation, guided by an ideology of rapid change in social structure (Singh, 1994).

Though these movements are usually shortlived, they may spread over a large geographical area. A reformative peasant movement, in contrast uses institutionalised mass mobilisation is guided by an ideology of gradual social change, and tends to exhibit a longer life span. Peasant movements, however, are not discretely radical or reformative; rather one way be an extension of another over a period of time.

It is observed that radical peasant movements promise greater scope for empowerment of labourers by denying the norms, values and institutionalized bandage that legitimize the subordination and powerlessness of labourers in the society. The reformative peasant movements in the form of grass roots mobilization, on the other hand, provide limited potential for labourers empowerment since they accept the pre-existing institutional arrangements, norms and values of' class segregation and subordination in one form or of the order (Singha Roy, 1992). Dhanagare almost agreeing with Gough, points out that the nativistic movement (Gough's category 'a') and religious movement are transformative, while social banditry, terrorists, mass insurrections and modern peasant movements or liberal reformist agitations are reformative. Several peasant uprisings and tribal revolts of nativist type occurred in India throughout the latter half of the eighteenth and nineteenth centuries. Worsley suggested that millenarian movements are relatively rare in India. Gandhian agrarian movements, whether in Champaran Kheda, Bardolei or those in UP in 1921 and 1930-32. belonged to the liberal relorinist type Gandhi's notion of Swaraj, Ramrajya or Gramrajya did imply an utopia in which he sought to combine traditional values with the new political culture and aspirations of the masses. Dhanagare labels that as a millenarian appeal (Singh, 1994).

But the fact in concrete reality none of the peasant movements in India seem to coliform excursively to a single 'ideal type' suggests that complex forces operate and peculiar historical conditions shape the form and substance of peasant resistance. And none of the peasant movements culminated in a full-fledged revolution. Moore attributed this lack of revolutionary experience in the Indian peasants and also the peculiarities of the village structure that has not only remained relatively unchanged but also has a built in mechanism to enforce hierarchical submission and to weaken the rebellions impulse of the peasantry. Although agrarian discontent and grievance pervaded in different degrees almost all parts of the country, resistance and revolt never assumed an all-India character (Singh, 1998).

Empowerment of Rural Labourers

The current phase of peasant movements in the state has important implications for the rural labour markets and the socio-economic and political structure of the state. One obvious impact of this massive movement has been the increased consciousness among the poor peasants and agricultural labourers about their socio-economic and political conditions. This growing consciousness has also made an impact on the state. Although the state is far from becoming sympathetic to then in the face of the growing unrest among them, it had to initiate some measures with regard to their welfare. The drive in the acquisition of surplus land over the ceiling limits in mid-1970s was essentially a response of the state to the violent outbreak and unrest among poor peasants and labourers in some of the districts of central Bihar. The occasional pronouncements of the government, more so in recent years, about its promise take effective steps to safeguard interest of the tenants was largely because of peasant movement and their increasing political importance as a pressure group (Sharma, 1998).

An important gain to the credit of the movements is that they have been able to raise agricultural wages in the areas of their influence Wage struggle has been the most important agenda of these organizations for mobilising the labourer. Bihar experienced a significant rise in real wage of agricultural labourers since early 1970s. Most particularly during the 1980s both for males and females. Between 1970-71 and 1988-89, 56.1 per cent increase took place in the case of male labourers and 70.8 per cent in the case of female labourers (Jose, 1988). Although heavy migration of rural labour from Bihar to out of state and some other factors are also responsible. In large parts of the state radical movement of agricultural labourers has been a very important factor behind the rise in this respect because collusion between the labour administration and rich farmers. Of course, the pressure generated the movements of the peasant organizations puts some check even on the government machinery. In about 900 villages in the districts of Bhojpur, Patna, Nalanda, Rohtas, Jehanabad, Aurangabad, Gaya, Siwan and East and West Champaran most successful struggles were launched by the Bihar Pradesh Kisan Sabha (one of the most powerful organisations of poor peasants and agricultural labourers) leading the substantial rise in wages. Sometimes they have been mature to take account the element of land productivity while agitating for increased wages.

Land reform has been another issue on which the poor peasants and agricultural labourers have been mobilised. If a substantial portion of the surplus land was acquired m Bihar in the mid-1970s, it was largely due to the pressure generated by the movement launched by poor peasant organizations. Though the movement to capture gairmazarua and surplus land above the ceiling led to occasional violence in the countryside, it also aroused the government from slumber many cases not only these organisations labour captured gairmazarua land hitherto occupied by rural rich and distributed it among the poor. They have also made provision for irrigation and co-operative farming and in some villages they have produced good result. It is well documented that the sharecroppers organised movement in Madhubhani and Champaran, particularly in the former, has done much to give them security of tenure and raise the tillers' share of produce (Sharma, 1995).

The most important gain of the movements has been the weakening of the feudal system in the rural areas (Singh, 1994). The feudal forces are on the defensive. In several areas upper caste people have started ploughing their lands themselves which was unheard of some years ago. To touch plough was a taboo for most of the families among upper castes. This is to some extent because of the economic compulsion oh small/marginal farmers - they are unable to afford payment of the prevailing wages. It is also because of the fact that now they cannot intimate poor labourers to accept low wages so that the process of substitutability of hired labour by family labour can be observed in many parts of the state (Singh, 2004).

Achievement of Rights and Rural Development

In India more dean 70 per cent of the population dwell in villages. There are about 6 lacks villages constituting more than 600 million people. The problems of rural masses are terrible and innumerable. Even after 58 years of independence, people in villages are found to be economically backward, socially oppressed, culturally suppressed politically exploited, traditionally nullified and in general deprived of facilities like health, education, transportation, communication and even denied basic amenities like protected drinking water, food, clothing shelter etc. As a result they are prone to poverty, illiteracy, ignorance ill health and multitudes of exploitations.

The Rural Development sector policy paper of the world Bank observed that 'Rural Development is a strategy designed to improve the economic and social life of a specific group of people the rural poor'. It involves extending the benefits of development to the poorest among those who seek a livelihood in the rural areas. The group includes small-scale farmers, tenants and the landless. Again a world bank publication defines rural development as "improving the living standards of the masses of the low income population residing in rural areas and making and process of rural development self-sustaining" (Bhose, 2003).

Experiences shows that to achieve rural development in true sense, the participatory approach of the people is indispensable. Participatory approach is the way of bringing the rural people together and involving them in the process of their socio-economic development. Here, the rural people are enabled to decide their needs and requirements and to find out ways to meet them Gandhi gave the first exposition of the participatory approach when he stated that people are the roots, the state is the fruit; that the classes at the top which crushing the masses at the bottom must get-off their backs and that the democracy can't be worked out by twenty men sitting at the top; and that it has to be worked from below by the people of every villages.

As the preceding section illustrates, the struggle issues actively taken up by the peasant movement reflect the practical needs and expectations of its mass base. Those relate primarily to what may be seen as basic economic, social and political rights that have been taken up by the movement are *(i)* land rights; *(ii)* minimum wages; *(iii)* common property resources; *(iv)* housing; *(v)* schemes; and *(vi)* political rights.

Land Rights

It is commonly held in India that "Zamin, Zar, Zanani" i.e. land, wealth and women have all way been the causes of all feuds and violence (Nimbran, 1992). In the birth of peasant movement also, land was the principal factor. But landlessness alone was not the sufficient cause. It was only when poverty and landlessness were accompanied with social oppression that the situation became explosive and resulted in violent out bursts. The movement has contested for 'surplus land' (above the legal ceiling), or misappropriated gairmajurwa (common) land. In some cases, the land belongs to absentee landlord. The movement has also attempted to change tenancy relations for example by demanding the implementation of tenancy regulations and better share cropping terms. In some areas movement has attempted to enforce *batai* (equal shares for landlord and tenant), though this struggle has not been without problems. In particular, when the terms of share cropping improve, landlords sometimes react by reducing the amount of land they lease out. Positive impact of the movement on this issue is that mostly lands which remained barren are being utilized by the rural people.

Minimum Wages

In many villages, prior to a wage struggle, the labourers were given approximately half *paseri kachhi* (1 kg and 750 gms) of coarse rice with some lunch and sometimes also breakfast. There was no knowledge of an officially stipulated minimum wage. Today, they tend to be in range of 3 to 4 kg of grain per day. Though, the wages are not in uniform. However, it has increased minimum double in major parts of the state. Virtually it has raised the income resource of the rural people. That is why very before hardly village seemed to be prospered in housing construction, but today in mostly villages one can find pucca/brick built houses. All are not of rich people, some belong to dalits also. There has also been an increase in the wages paid to the labourers at harvest time. Prior to the wage strike, the harvesters used to receive one *bojha* (headload) for every 21 bojhas of harvested crop; this has risen to 1 bojha for every 10 bojhas. The increased rate benefits not only the casual labourers, but also the *halwaha* or *bandhuas* (attached labourers who are employed for one agricultural year). In addition, some other changes have been achieved including an equal wage for women (even though gender differences persist in some areas), a set number of work hours, and an improvement in the quality of grain paid.

Common Property

The movement has also fought for the rights of the poor to common property resources. In doing so, the movement has asserted the identity of the poor as equal members of a village. These struggles are over gair majurwa land as well as full access to the village pond. Used for washing clothes, bathing buffaloes, etc., these ponds are also an important sources of fish the question of who has rights over the fish has never been settled to an satisfaction of all the villagers. The general government policy has been to auction the fish to the highest bidders. Often the local landlord gets the fish for a low price since his bid goes unchallenged. This system is considered unfair by the poorer sections of the village, for whom fish is a much needed food supplement. The movement has challenged the landlords monopoly, established control over ponds on behalf of the poor and devised a fairer system of distribution.

Housing

Another issue often taken by the movement relates to housing. Owning a residential plot is very important for the poor, since it means some security. Living on home stead land belonging to the landlords (the standard arrangement in earlier days) increases the dependence of labourers on their employers. Now labourers are sometimes able to resettle on reclaimed gairmajurwa an land (Bhatia, 2005).

Schemes

The peasant movement has also helped, albeit marginally, in better execution of government programmes in rural areas in the state. In several cases the issues of wrong selection of beneficiaries under. Integrated Rural Development Programme (IRDP), digging handpump, wells, construction of drainage and houses in dalit localities, non-availability of ration cards to the poor, bribe taking by block and bank officials for disbursement of assets, etc. were taken up actively by them and in several cases the wrongs have been corrected. The movement has greatly contributed to the elimination of several aspects of exploitation in the rural labour markets (Singh, 2001).

Political Rights

Peasant movement has not only achieved its social and economic success but political also which can be said landmark for rural development. The poor and oppressed of rural Bihar who used lo be invisible as far as upper classes and the state were concerned, are now a visible - even - powerful - political force. Agricultural labourers are able to think of themselves as citizens with the same political rights as the landlords, and to a large extent even to assert this equality in practice. Also their perception of poverty as a matter of 'fate' (nasseb) has changed; now they often see it as a matter of injustice. In other respects, too, the poor of Bihar strike the observe for their political consciousness. In both rural and urban areas, people take strong interest in political matters, and are well informed about political issues.

Another important political right which has been denied to many ill south Bihar is the result to vote. People were often kept away from the polling booths by henchmen of the uppercastes and classes who would caste the votes on their behalf in favour of their own candidate. Now they dare to cast their vote for their desired candidate and no one intervens on this issue. Indirect impact of this result is that through their collective votes they influence the leaders to take developmental benefits which was not possible before the movement (Singh, 1996).

Conclusion

The Bihar which was the hub of anti-feudal peasant movement in pre-independent days has experienced a landlord path of capitalist development. This path in the absence of commensurate infrastructural facilities like perennial irrigation and landowners aversion to labour on land in herited from the social culture of permanent settlement, did not make for fast transition from semi-feudal agriculture to capitalist agriculture and manifested in agricultural stagnation. The consequent exacerbation of labour and poor peasantry in the context of high tend democratic consciousness of poor peasants and agricultural caused the gap between rhetoric and reality to manifest in militant articulation of the aspiration of the exploited.

Infact, the peasant movement in south Bihar has fought against exploitative relations in social as well as economic terms. *Izzat* (dignity or honour) is one of the crucial social freedom it has attempted to restore even though the dalits of the region continue to face many deprivations, there is now a greater sense of confidence and autonomy. Most importantly, the peasant movement has been effective in its assertion of dalits as human beings and individuals entitled to equal rights. Now arbitrary beatings are no longer tolerated. Labourers are free to sell their labour to whomever they please. Dalit children are able to go to school. Labourers are able to bear clean cloths, sit in front of their homes on *khatias* (string cot) welcome their guests without interference from the landlords, amongst other gains. All this has come about because the landed are no longer in a position to exercise illegitimate power with impunity. Peasant movement wants not only economic development. It wants development in human capabilities, real freedom, real democracy, life securities, equal opportunities, education and food securities health care without any discriminations for all. Peasant movement urges for abolition of every form of oppression, exploitation and secrecy in the whole society and social institutions.

Virtually movement is a tool to the rural people without knowing the use and way to operate the tool due to their innocence and ignorance people were being exploited. Through these movements all the power centres are to be nearer and easily accessible to them.

REFERENCES

1. Blumer, H. (1951), *Social Movement,* New Outline of Principles of Society, Barnes and Noble, New York.
2. Toch, H. (1965), Social Psychology of Social Movements. Bobbs Merrille, Indianapolis.
3. Heberle, R. (1951), Social Movements, Appleton Century Crafts, New Delhi.
4. Gusfield, J.R. (1992), (ed), *Protest, Reform and Revolt: A Reader in Social Movements,* John Wiley and Sons, New York.
5. Wilson, R.F. (1973), *Introduction to Social Movements,* Basic Books, New York.

6. Sharma Kumud (1992), "Grassroots Organisations and Women's Empowerment: Some Issues in the Contemporary Debate", *Samya Shakti*, Vol. 6. pp. 28-43.

7. Batliwal, S. (1973), Empowerment of Women in South Asia: Concepts and Practices. ASSBAF and FAO, Freedom for Hunger Campaign, Action and Development, New Delhi.

8. Rao, M.S.A. (1987), *Social Movements and Social Transformation*, Manohar, New Delhi.

9. Dhanagare, D.N. (1976), "Peasant Protest and Politics, The Tebhaga Movement in Bengal (India), 1946-47", *Journal of Peasant Studies*, Vol. 3 (33), pp. 613-41.

10. Singa, Roy (1992), *Women in Peasant Movements: Tebhaga, Naxalite and After*, Manohar, New Delhi.

11. Gough, K. (1974), "Indian Peasant Uprising", *Economic and Political Weekly*, Vol. 9 (32-34), August, pp. 1391-412.

12. Singh, Shrawan Kumar (1994a), Peasant Movements: A Conceptual Overview, *Mainstream*, May 7, p. 25.

13. Sharma, A.N. (1998), *Empowering Rural Labour in India*, Institute of Human Development, pp. 408-11.

14. Sharma, A.N. (1995), "Political Economy of Poverty in Bihar", *Economic and Political Weekly*, Vol. 30 (41-42), October, pp. 14-21.

15. Singh, Shrawan Kr. (1998), "Social Movements: A Conceptual Overview", *Third Concept*, August, 33-34.

16. Singh, Shrawan Kr. (2004), *Role of Social Movements in Social Transformation*, October-Dec., Third World Impact, pp. 21-22.

17. Singh, Shrawan Kr. (2001), "Peasant Movements and Empowerment of Rural Labourers", *Third Concept*, July, pp. 34-38.

18. Singh, Shrawan Kr. (1996), Social Movements for Social Justice: A Mechanism of Social Development, Published seminar paper, GIS, Rajghat, Varanasi March 26-27.

19. Bhose, Joel S.G.R. (2003), *NGOs and Rural Development*, Concept Publishing House, New Delhi, p. 2.

20. Bhatia, Bella (2005), "Naxalite Movement in Central Bihar", *Economic and Political Weekly*, April 9, pp. 1542-44.

21. Jose, George (1988), Peasant and Agricultural labour movement in Kerala: Their Contribution to the Genuine Development Efforts in Social Movements for Rural Development (ed.) A.L. Srivastava & S.K. Srivastava, Publications, Allahabad, 1988, p. 243.

22. Singh, Rajendra (2001), *Social Movements, Old and New; A Post-Modernist Critique*, Sage Publication, New Delhi.

23. Nimbaran, Amrik Singh (1992), *Poverty, Land and Violence*, Layman's Publications, Patna, p. 126.

13

Joint Forest Management (JFM) in Orissa Some Issues

*Dr. C.R. Das**

The concept Joint Forest Management (JFM) means different things to different people. According to Jeffery Campbell "Foresters may view JFM primarily as means to ensure forest regeneration; community members may see it as a solution to a growing shortage of biomass, a means to ensure daily requirements of food, fodder and NTFPs, and/ or a way to increase incomes; NGO workers/activists may view the programme as a vehicle for grassroots empowerment, academic researchers may see in JFM an experiment in collection action; while politicians may view JFM as a means to decentralise control over resources. It is a dynamic initiative still very much in its evolutionary stage, full of variation, uncertainty and conflict" (Campbell, 1996). In India the concept of JFM introduced in 1990 when the JIM circular issued in 1990 by the Secretary, Environment and Forests was to set a new policy on involvement of village communities and village assemblies in the regeneration of degraded forest land. The circular took the National Forest Policy, 1988 as its basis for envisaging, peoples involvement in the development and protection of forests. The circular

* Research Supervisor, NKC Centre for Development Studies, Bhubaneswar.

was more in the nature of a direction setting documents outlining the need as the objectives of working out modalities for giving to the village communities, living close to the forest lands usufructory benefits to ensure their participation in the afforestation programmes of the government.

To facilitate participatory forestry management between the forest department, the user community and non-government organisations most of the orders on JIM have annexed a model Memorandum of Understanding (MOU) or some form of agreement between the Stakeholders which lay down the terms and conditions including duties and responsibilities of all parties.

In order to make JFM effective institution to achieve ecology and biomass conservation through development of forests which not only help local habitats to improve their standard of living and provide livelihood support, it must also instill the confidence that the rights to those benefits are secure and cannot be taken away arbitrarily. In past, this sense of security requires the rights and responsibilities of both the communities and the government must be clearly defined. Both patties need to clearly know not only what they stand to gain but also what they are expected to demand what the consequences will be if they fail to live upto agreement. A lack of clarity simply creates fertile ground for disagreement. Similarly, both parties need to know that they have a mechanism of recourse at hand in the event their rights are abridged during the course of the agreement (Lindsay, 1994).

In most of the states the JFM termed differently as Van Samirakshana Samitees, Van Suraksha Samiti, Forest Protection Committee, Viliage Forest Protection Committee were registered by the DFO by recording the committee in his/her register. After detecting that the DFO certainly is not a legal authority having powers under the Indian Registration Act or any other registration acts such as those societies or trust acts, the Central Government issued guidelines in February 2000, vide Resolution No. 22-8/2000-JFM (FPD dated February 21, 2000) suggesting that the

JFMs should be registered under the societies Registration Act, 1860. But the spirit and the objective of the societies act which is to promote charitable activities where as JFM is an incentive based management offering usufruct benefits varies with each other will lead to confusion and chaos.

Environment and Forest

The environment can be defined as the physical surrounding of man of which he is a past and on which he is dependent for his activities like physiological functioning, production and consumption. His physical environment stretches from air, winter and land to natural resources like energy carriers, soils, plants, animals and eco-systems. Stability of eco-system depend more on sustainability of forests. Forests not only sustain environment but also provides economic pursuits to society in general and to forest dwellers communities in particular. Stability of bio-diversity of a region/country also depend on stability and sustainability of its forest and eco-system. It is therefore, important to put bio diversity of India in following Table 13.1.

Table 13.1: India's Bio-Diversity

Sl. No.	*Groups*	*Number of Species India (SI)*	*Number of Species in World (SW)*	*SI/SW %*
1.	Mammals	350	4629	7.6
2.	Birds	1228	9702	12.6
3.	Reptiles	428	6550	6.2
4.	Amphibions	197	4522	4.4
5.	Fishes	2546	21730	11.7
6.	Flowers & Plants	15000	250000	6.8

Source: http://www.terrn.org/biodiv/status.htm

India possess only 7.6 per cent of mammals, 12.6 of birds, 6.2 per cent of reptiles, 4.4 per cent of amphibions, 11.7 per cent of fishes and 6.0 per cent of flowering plants prevail in world.

Therefore, it is important to examine various factors which affects sustainability and stability of our eco-system in general and forests in particular.

Sustainability of forest, too governed by various natural, political, socio-economic, administrative factors. Administration also carried out by a domestic manner such as legislation, execution of such measures and enforced by government machinery as well as judicial interpretation instructions and orders in case of conflict arise due to various questions arise in the process of execution. In this chapter, it is proposed to analyse various important factors in brief such as institutional, legal framework and conceptual issues arise in present scenario of emergence of co-management of forest by people and government known as Joint Forest Management (JFM).

Forest Policy During British Rule

The British Government asserted control over extensive forest lands resulting in the decline in traditional conservation and management systems around the forests (Gadgil and Guha, 1992). The tradition of tribal society had been dwelling in and around the forests and its economy was a community resources meant to be used according to human needs as well as preserved posterity, thus respecting ecological ethos. The communal character was all pervasive including their land, forests and other natural resource management and also their social and political structures (Roy Burman, 1985). The symbiotic relationship suffered a set back during British rule, when the forest was looked upon only as a source of maximization of profit and not a vital link between human habitat and the larger environment (Sachidananda, 1998). Heavy destruction of forests occurred in the latter part of the eighteenth century and early part of the nineteenth century. Teak forests along with the cost of malabar were over exploited to meet requirements of the British Navy. He sandalwood trees of south India were exploited and marketed in Europe. The first conservator of forests was appointed in 1806 to organize timber supplies from the west coast. The early years a railway expansion saw an unprecedented assault on the more accessible forests (Rao, 1995). The world wars accentuated destruction of forests to meet the requirements of fuel and timber during the first world war and char coal need of army during second world war.

After independence, the early post-colonial forest policy differed little from the colonial period. The National Forest Policy, 1952 did not consider the needs of local people, its aim being supplying timber for industrial needs. Commercialization of forests was emphasized, like the colonial regime, at the cost of the local people. The post-colonial government in the Forest Policy of 1952, continued to envisage the commercial exploitation of forests, now for the natural rather than colonial interest. Recognition of the importance of forests the policy level is reflected in the constitution which states: The state shall endeavour to protect and improve the environment and to safeguard the forests and wildlife of the country. Constitutionally it has been enjoined upon every citizen of India as a fundamental duty, to protect and improve the natural environment including forests, lakes, rivers and wildlife, and to have compassion for living creatures (Kashyap, 1990).

Conceptual, Institutional, Legal Framework and Benefit Sharing

The concept of village communities and state forest departments jointly managing forest lands has been rapidly gaining popularity in South Asia and in many Indian states in particular. Over thousand villages in Orissa have formed FPCs in lieu of protection and conservation of village forest resources where the village communities have been granted rights by the FD to the extent of 50 per cent of all regenerated timber and 100 per cent of minor forest products. Needless to say that there are two linked problems which seem to have been reconciled in jointly managing the forests; first, the FD lacks the organisational capacity to control forest degradation, unless required co-operation and participation of the villagers are sought for; second, the villagers have little incentives to participate in the management of forests, unless they directly derive some benefits and have sufficient authority to make effective.

An attempt is made in this chapter to discuss some relevant concepts used in JFM for ensuring effective forest management, and also, several forest protection committees (institutions) to strengthen participatory forest management.

Forest Protection Incentives

Here, villagers are granted a great deal of incentives to take care of the local forest resources not only for enabling them to increase their access, but also to exercise control over the local resources. The basic purpose is to trade increased access so as to ensure increased management responsibility and authority. On the contrary, the FD has also granted a lot of concessions. However, access to these resources is directly linked to village agreements to reduce activities causing forest degradation. The basic idea however is do away with destructive forest uses through watch and ward even by establishing fines for violating forest rules in order to improve forest conditions and also, to create strong incentives for forest protection by linking access to resources with protection responsibilities. In this context, sharing management authority is the key element underlying effective linkages between rights and responsibilities.

Banerjee (1989) indicates that joint management cannot be approached with the "I do, you participate" attitude which seems to underlie so many attempts at peoples' participation. In point of fact, for a variety of historical, economic, social reasons, villagers most often do not trust the Governmental Agencies (including FD) to act in their best interests. Therefore, the user groups should have sufficient management authority to ensure; (a) the products they desire are produced; (b) they will get the product in time and in manner agreed upon; (c) they can enforce joint management decisions. In this connection, the villager may be reluctant (observed in many sample villages located in various districts of Orissa in the context of recent policy decision of the GoO) to allow timber harvesting which may threat many other forest products they are now receiving from regenerated forests, besides increasing threats to precious biodiversity, environment and livelihood of the local forest-dependent population. As a result, there is a direct contradiction between village community and the FD conceptions of appropriate management. However, there are numerous examples of contradictions over the concepts in many parts of the country with respect to sharing of benefits, sharing management authority, access to forest resource, sharing authority etc. because, there is no linkage between benefits and management responsibilities.

Equity

The basic purpose of JFM is to ensure equity in sharing of benefits, in, participation in the community management, and also, equitable distribution of resource access. Therefore, equity issues are linked to the conceptual requirement for community management. The equity aspect has been considered crucial in 'joint management' as a valid goal in itself, since it is considered to be the best possible way to provide benefits/resources to disadvantaged sections of society. Besides, the basic need in the joint management is guarantee of representations from all communities, who need to share the benefits equally. However, the primary goal of joint management is to strengthen the linkage between management efforts and access to forest resources, and also, strengthen strong incentives for ensuring better and effective forest protection as well as conservation. Though, increasing equity in joint management seems to be crucial, the conceptual basis to link equity to management is very weak and therefore, needs further operational development.

Strategy

Though a number of basic factors attribute to local institution development so as to formulate the strategy for ensuring successful 'joint management', often, these are not available at the grassroots level-leading to failure of the scheme. It is indisputable to say that in 'joint management' a very distinct clear, enforceable, demarcation of rights and responsibilities are essential. In such a situation, it is not only difficult to demarcate rights and responsibilities very clearly, but also to enforce those. Therefore, 'joint management' system performs better where villagers are homogeneous in caste, with minor economic class divisions. This homogeneity itself improves the quality of joint management to achieve the objectives of equity, in sharing benefits and efficiency resource management (due to equivalent interest in forest resources) where the elite powerful groups are relatively less effective.

Thus, 'joint management' could resolve many forest resource problems in the following situations; first; where a direct link could be established between improvement in degraded forests and increasing access to forest resource; second, where a single village is the user of a specific forest area; third, where available forest resources are shared by the villagers in lieu of increased forest protection; fourth, where the village is homogeneous in terms of caste and economic class and fifth, where the villagers have higher degree of dependence on forest resources for their livelihood. In point of fact, these are some ideal conditions in which the 'joint management' of forest resource at the village level may perform better. But, the grass root level realities suggest that most sample villages of our study do not necessary suggest non-existence of such ideal conditions.

Despite widespread interest and a great deal of 'joint management' activities in thousands of villages in Orissa, the very core objective of peoples' participation depends upon how the goal is interpreted to achieve sustainable source of livelihood notwithstanding conservation of precious species, rich biodiversity and environmental security.

In course of series of Government orders with respect to Participatory Forest Management (PFM), a number of different forest protection committees have been constituted in Orissa at different points of time.

Eco-Development Club (EDC)

Protection of assigned forest are by the people under Governmental patronage in the form of VSS/FPC is possible in case of forest except sanctuaries as declared by the forest and environment ministry. As in case of sanctuary area it is impossible to assign such area for protection of people due to legal and technical hindrances. Moreover, without people's registered organization developmental expenditure in the area for improvement of environment is difficult. In order to sort out such problems eco-development club (EDC) has been constituted. It is the initiative taken by various group of people who are interested to protect forest living around various sanctuary area. In Orissa, there are 309 number of EDC formed by the end of June 2005.

(a) Van Samrakhyan Samitis (VSSs)

As per the Government Resolution of July 1993, the total number of VSSs formed in different districts and the total number is 9549 till the end of June 2005 (PCCF, Orissa, Bhubaneswar). The highest number VSSs are noticed in the Bhawanipatna Circle; 1526 followed by Koraput circle; 1992 and Berhampur circle; 1235. These VSSs have been formed for undertaking and implementing the resolution/scheme. So far, as much as 843058 hectares of degraded forest land (though some RF areas also have been assigned to the VSSs) are now under the direct supervision of VSSs for protection and conservation of forest (till June 2005). Many existing forest protection committees and unregistered organisations engaged in protection of village forests have been gradually converted in to VSSs resulting in number of VSSs and protected area to cause a spectacular increase.

(b) Forest Protection Committees (FPCs)

On the basis of the recommendation of a State Level Steering Committee Constituted vide the Resolution of July

1993, the existing FPCs constituted prior to the Resolution of 1993 may be allowed to function as such till they are reconstituted as VSSs. There were as much as 5520, FPCs in the state of Orissa by March 2004, who were assigned an area of 65154 hectares for protection in terms of their active participation. FPCs were constituted in each assigned village. Following the government of India's JFM guidelines issued on June 1, 1990 (GoI, 1990), the Orissa government modified the earlier circular to provide representative to women and minorities in the FPCs (GoO, 1990).

Further, the village woodlots and social forestry plantations raised under the SIDA assisted social forestry project 1984-94, have been declared village forests and have been brought under the purview of JFM. Hence, the village Forest

Committees (FCs) created for protecting these forests are also part of JFM. In 1996, the Orissa Government issued another resolution to provide encouragement for protection of forests by adjoining villagers and confer right to the villagers protecting these forest (GoO, 1996).

(c) Unregistered Groups Engaged in Forest Protection

Apart from FPC, and VSSs there are a number of unregistered self-initiated groups like Yuvak Sangh protecting forests. As per available information, there are as much as 640 such unregistered groups protecting a forest area of 89864 ha in the state.

These different peoples' organisations namely the FPCs, VSSs and VFCs have members, who are tribals and non-tribals, but bulk of them depend on forests for their livelihood. Since NTFP collection and sale are crucial to their subsistence economy, it was possible to involve these well organised groups for improving the current management practices of NTFP collection, processing and marketing in order to provide the primary collectors better returns for their labour and time involved in NTFP collection.

NTFP Management

It was visualized that better management of incentive structure could not only improve the performance of JFM programme, but also, promote the goals of livelihoods creation and sustainable management of forest resources. The best way of meeting the twin challenge of maximizing collectors income from NTFPs and of ensuring sustainable harvesting therefore was to involve VFCs/VSSs in NTFP collection and marketing. NTFP collection could also be a powerful strategy for transforming VFCs into robust, autonomous people's organizations by imparting to them a strong economic drive. For this, the interventions required may be:

- Restricting collection within revenue boundaries of the village to avoid conflicts between villages and poaching in one another's territory.
- Rationalization of conflicts between contractors and the VFCs.

One plausible option was with respect to demarcation of the boundaries of the areas to be managed by each VFC, as prescribed in the JFM resolution. However, the experience gained over the years bought home the merits of mainstreaming. It is important that within the current system of NTFP trading and marketing, space should be created for VFCs. Especially in case of nationalised NTFPs, when the government agencies appoint private parties as sub-agents, is also possible for them to appoint the VFCs and their collectors as sub-agents, it for the areas, where VFCs are operational.

Apart from capacity building measures, financial assistance was essential for the VFCs to undertake this assignment. The capital provided to making prompt payments to collectors for the NTFPs sold could either be an investment from the Government or could be recovered from the VFCs from the profits they would make from the trading operations. The VFC collective endeavour had definitely an economic scale of operation to gain a strong bargaining position in the market. With sizable quantum of NTFPs coming from the VFC areas they could influence and force changes in the current system.

Another option was to promote user groups of NTFPs and involve them in forest management along with VFCs wherever they exist. The FD may be required to lend its support to these groups to strengthen them. Especially in the JFM areas the FD would need to change its policy (Saxena et al., 1997):

- It should claim no share in NTFP collection by VFC members
- VFC should charge a marginal fee from sale proceeds for providing local storage and monitoring over exploitation.
- The VFC should be free to sell its collection to agency, which provides them the best deal.

The main goal of involving VFCs in NTFP collection was not to earn revenue for the FD, but to ensure sustainable harvesting and value addition through efficient processing and marketing. In such a scenario the FD was supposed to bring in improvements by prevailing upon the collectors to ensure scientific methods of collection, harvesting, storage etc. in order to sustain and improve the quality of the product.

Role of VFCs/VSSs/FPCs and the FD

Through the Protection Committees, it would be important for the FD to provide assistance to them to undertake the responsibilities of protection and conservation. Committees should take care of all aspects related to collection and marketing of NTFPs, under the guidance of FD, as follows:

- Promote the economy of NTFPs that remain unexploited due to lack of market arrangements
- Make arrangements under which collectors get best reward/price

- Control over-incentive to prevent unsustainable extraction levels of NTFPs

However, free competition might not be the best alternative to the current situation because:

- FDs revenue from NTFPs could decline
- Large number of tiny operators may not be able to build and sustain linkages with upcountry markets, and the entire NTFP economy might shrink.
- High collection prices could strengthen over incentives in unsustainable harvesting.

The second option could be promoting a small number, say 6-8 licensed contactors in a self-contained territory for a license fee. This would increase FDs revenue and may also take care of volume of each operator, but it would still create incentives for over-harvesting. This can be avoided by promoting user groups of NTFPs and then involving them in forest management along with VFCs. This would not only eliminate the risk of illegal removals but also make monitoring easy, in such a situation the FDs machinery can lend its support to such groups by preventing smuggling.

The seriousness of the situation can be well appreciated from the following facts

- Dependence of tribals on forests is increasing and shifting from a constructive to a destructive dependence.
- the collection of NTFPs provide more than half of the total person days of employment (58.0%) per household, with women accounting for a longer percentage.
- Nearly, 40.0 per cent of the total annual income (Rs. 1940) of a tribal household is derived from sale of NTFPs. This increases with the poverty of the households

Apart from changes in the policy guidelines that need to be formulated with respect to processing, marketing and use of NTFPs; there needs to be other changes with respect to the management strategies also. Separate Working Circles should be created in Working Plans for the management of NTFPs, so that operational prescriptions can be incorporated for improved silviculture and utilisation practices. Appropriate harvesting schedules should be developed which will promote biodiversity conservation (Sharma undated).

Financial Assistance to JFM Programme

Financing JFM programme to execute some of the forestry activities at the grassroots level is an issue of concern. As per the proceedings of 20th meeting of the State Level Co-ordination Committee of the World Food Programme (WFP), it was decided to provide financial assistance to various items of JFM programme; such as: Orientation training to the VSS members, construction of Forest Awareness Centre-cum-Meeting Room, Preparation of Micro Plan for rehabilitation of degraded forest in 13 Forest Divisions of the state.

State Plan Scheme

The government of Orissa had granted around Rs. 70 lakh during 1995-96 to execute JFM programmes in the state. It was decided to finance two micro plans in each forest division in order to cover at least 167 ha in case of Tribal Area Forest Divisions and 202 ha in case of non-tribal area forest divisions. However, during 2003-04, the Government of Orissa reported to have spent Rs. 3965.51 lakh on RLTAP, (Revised Long Term Action Plan), Economic Plantation, Jagannath Vana Prakalpa; and Natural Afforestation Programme funded by FDA.

Legal Issues and Statutory Provisions:

According to government orders, following the suggestion of the DFO/Range Officer/Forester, the Gram Panchayat will convene a meeting of all adults living in the selected villages, where the forest officials will explain the scheme of JFM and depending on the response and motivation of the villagers, formation of VSS may be possible by the Gram Panchayat (GP). The members of the VSS include two adults from every household including one female member.

The VSS through its Executive Committee executes an MoU with the concerned DFO for active participation in the task of protection, regeneration and management of the forest area assigned to it, and also, for implementation of programmes as per JFM Plan. As a per the provisions, the members of the VSS are entitled to collect fallen and dry leaves, small timber, bamboo branches, leaves, grass, various fruits free of cost after the execution of MoU. Thus, 100.0 per cent usufruct rights are granted to the members for collection of minor forest produces from the protected area. The former VFPCs constituted at the village level are being motivated by the FD to form VSS, but the VSS does not enjoy any legal powers to try individuals or the State for non-compliance with the guidelines of the 1993 office order. Thus, lack of legal provision is reflected in insecurity on the part of VSS members. Further, the legal ambiguities noticed in the institutional structure put serious hindrances in the normal functioning of JFM in the state of Orissa. In the absence of legal power, the VSS faces difficulties to ensure equitable distribution of usufructs. Besides, occasional threats of the adjacent villagers, forest thefts, forest fire, entries of timber smugglers cannot be restricted/prevented.

In point of fact, some conflicting and changing policies without commensurated changes in statutory forest rules and acts, several legal and institutional ambiguities seem to have prevented the poor. In the Forest Laws, Acts and regulations formulated and implemented in Orissa till date, the primary intention has been obviously to improve the socio-economic conditions and level of living of the forest dwellers. Customary rights have been bestowed in the local tribes in some areas for their bonafioed consumption (not for sale).

However, participatory forest management in Orissa was initiated well before the passage of the June 1990, GoI guidelines through the Orissa Village Forest Rules, 1985 and were framed under powers conferred under Sections 31, 32 and 82 (d) of the Orissa Forest Act, 1972. These rules are statutory in nature, in nature and therefore, cannot be amended except by issuing similar statutory notifications (Mishra, 1998). Since then several government resolutions have been effected in 1988, 1990, 1993 and finally 1996 dealing with village forest management. However, none of these changes have been incorporated within the existing statutory rules of 1985, a necessity to avoid confusion and to give the current resolutions validity since as it currently stands no resolutions can supersede these statutory rules. This laxity has led to much uncertainty and confusion and a lack of legal standing for various forest committees. Thus, because of all these different resolutions, a number of Village Forest Committees (formed under the 1985 rules). Forest protection committees (under the 1988 resolution) VSS (formed under the 1993 and 1996 resolutions) and unregistered committees are functioning simultaneously in many of Orissa. This has, "led to utter confusion in the field as to legal status, powers and functions of these committees" (Mishra, 1988).

A number of other legal issues have further compounded the confusion. While it is widely believed that the 1988 resolution formally launched participatory forest management in Orissa, in fact the formalization of participatory forest management predates even this resolution and owes its origin to the 1985 rules. Therefore, the scheme for participation of local communities in the protection, development and management of village woodlots and social forestry block plantations raised under the SIDA assisted Social Forest Project between 1984 and 1994, came under the purview of participatory forest management through the 1985 rules. This was almost a decade before the GR of 1994 (7/12/94) which is erroneously believed to be the resolution that integrated the Social Forestry Project with JFM, (Mishra, 1988) and according to which "All the village woodlots, and Social Forestry block plantation raised under the SIDA assisted

Social Forestry Project between 1984 to 1994, after being notified as village forests, will also come under the purview of this scheme."

This has further led to confusion as to whether the committees can be formed in reserve or protected forests. Under Section 30 of the Orissa Forest Act, 1972, no reserve forest or any part there of can be constituted/converted as a village forests without the prior approval of the Central Government as laid down in Section 2 of the Forest (Conservation) Act, 1980. Only protected forests can be constituted as village forests by the procedures laid down in Chapter III of the Orissa Forest Act, 1972 (Mishra, 1998). The 1990 resolution however, ignored this stipulation by clubbing protected and reserve forests together and ignoring the legalities involved—that is the legal distinction of Reserve forests, while protected forests were equated with reserve forest without the obligatory requirements of constituting them as Village Forests in accordance with Chapter III of the Orissa Forest Act, 1972.

The solution to this problem is easy once, recognition of legal identification of these two distinct forest classifications are made. This will not prohibit JFM from being carried out in both these forest types but it will provide legal sanctity to the entire area. According to Mishra, 1998, while there is no difficulty in introducing JFM in Reserve Forest areas since it is the absolute property of the State with no rights of private individuals or the community, a protected forest is burdened with rights and privileges of local communities. The only way then is to constitute Village Forests in pursuance of the provision of Chapter 3 of the Orissa Forest Act, 1972. Chapter 3 empowers the State Government to constitute village forests on "any land at their disposal." However it is the revenue department which owns the land outside of Reserve Forests. Therefore, Village Forests on Protected forest cannot be created without the concurrence of the revenue department. Therefore, the Forest department in order to create village forests on protected forest land needs to demarcate the village forest boundaries, and publish notifications to that effect with the assistance of the Revenue Department (Mishra, 1998). The social forestry organization in Orissa has paved the way for this action by declaring nearly 4800 blocks of forests as VF under Section 30 of the Orissa Forest Act, 1972.

There also exists some degree of uncertainty regarding the connection between Panchayati Raj institutions and JFM in the State. While the 1993 and 1996 resolutions provide ample scope for linkages between the two institutions, the framing of the resolutions has been done without carrying out due consultations with the concerned departments. There also exist several ambiguities between the formation of village communities vis-a-vis the panchayat involvement as specified in the GRs and what the 1985 rules allow. Therefore, discussions with concerned departments will have to be carried out to resolve these legal implications.

The notification of village forests for PF area is also a step which will help resolve a diverse range of issues relating to NTFP collection, transportation and marketing, the rights of tribals and other special categories, or the transference of ownership of NTFPs to Gram Panchayats in Scheduled areas of the State under Orissa Gram Panchayats (Amendment) Act, 1997 as per the 73rd Amendment of the Constitution of India (See section on Panchayats and JFM). This is because the rights and concessions of local communities have to be determined under Section 32 of the Forest Act before various provisions can be allowed for village forests constituted in PF areas.

As mentioned earlier legal ambiguities have given rise to a bewildering variety of committees. In a meeting of the State level steering committee constituted under the 1993 Resolution, it was decided that existing Forest protection committees may be allowed to function till they are reconstituted as VSS. Village Forest Committees were also constituted under the Social Forestry Project and are functioning in accordance with Rule 3 of the Orissa Village Forest Rules, 1985. All these can be clubbed together as VSS or VFC so that the benefits of the 1996 GR are theirs. This can be done by conferring statutory status on them as per Rule 3 of the Orissa Village Forest Rules, 1985. While reconstitution of the FPCs as VSS was envisaged, this process is moving very slowly. In Dhenkanal district for instance out of a total of 159 VFPC's only 40 have registered as VSS.

Another issue relates to the 1996 GR decision not to allow residents of areas/villages other than those close to the forest to share the forest usufructs in lieu of protection. This has far-reaching implications, since traditionally, people within these area have been enjoying concessions in accordance with the Schedule of Rates for Forest Produce in Orissa Rules, 1977. According to these rules, tenants of a particular area paying forest cess are entitled to obtain forest produce from neighbouring forests (PF only) on payment of royalty at concessional rates. This *nistar cess* is collected by the Revenue Department. Therefore, this decision will not be implantable unless the cess and rights of local tenants in PF is abolished, since otherwise the people cannot be deprived of their rights to the usufructs of a Village Forest.

Following a seminar, many Legal issues were emerged at Bhubaneswar on October 10, 1998, the recommendation are as follows.

- For taking up JFM in Reserve Forests, no change in their legal status is required. JFM can be undertaken in reserved forests and a Memorandum of Understanding (MOU) will be enough for allowing the benefits to Village Level Organisation (VLO) members.
- JFM resolution/rules concerning JFM areas in reserved forest should be constituted as protected forests in accordance with procedure prescribed for the purpose in the Orissa Forest Act (1972). The protected forests to be brought under JFM should be constituted as Village Forests under the Orissa Forest Act.

- JFM rules for protected forests brought under JFM and declared as village forest should be in accordance with Village Forest Rules (1985) which should be revised and updated to bring them in line with the policy of the government on JFM.
- The cess should be abolished and consequent settlement of rights should be done through proper inquiry as laid down in Orissa Forest Act for the constitution or Protected Forest or Village Forest as the case may be.
- The position with regard to the ownership of minor forest produce in favour of Panchayat/Gram Shashan/Pali Sabha/VSS needs to be resolved. Necessary discussions should be held for the purpose between relevant departments of Orissa government. It needs to be attended on priority before any rules are framed for the purpose under the relevant act.
- The acts, rules and regulations concerning collection, processing and marketing of NTFPs by VLO members need to be reviewed to empower VLO members to undertake such activities.
- VLO need to be given legal status. Such a status will be available when JFM resolution/rule would have been framed under relevant act as recommended under (ii) and (iv) above.

Benefit Sharing

One of the major challenges in sustaining forest conditions, uses and values is to understand the dynamic relationships among people, forest resources and environmental services provided by forest and overall standards and quality of human life (Aplet et al. 1997). In the absence of use-effectiveness, some vested interests and forest staff seem to have been involved in damaging wood-cutting practises. The poor understanding of people's behaviour has not only remained incomplete, but also, has been simplistic for sustainable forest management. Therefore, the top-down approach in decision-making has successfully defeated deforestation activities. In such a situation, the poor and the disadvantaged group of population have compelled to adopt strategies that are environmental damaging. Their herds overgraze, there shortening fallows on steep slopes and fragile soils induce erosion, their need for off-season income drives them to cut and sell firewood and to make and sell charcoal (Myrdal, 1968). It was NFP 1988 that took a radical step in formulating a policy strategy for meeting the basic needs of the people, essentially fuel wood, fodder, small timber for rural people in general and tribal population in particular.

The benefit sharing arrangement in JFM is a two-way process in which the people benefit from the usufructs they re entitled to in lieu of protection and conservation of local forest resource and the government/state benefits as well as from both protection and management activities carried out by the community leading to improved forest conditions as well as productivity. Accordingly, benefits flow from of fuelwood, fodder, grass, NTFPs through a mechanism worked out by the people. Benefit sharing is crucial in the context of JFM in order to ensure improved forest productivity and as per the government orders 1993, 1994, 1996 where 50.0 per cent of the final harvest of timber will be shared with the communities. Besides, the dead wood and small timber collected form forests will be given to the community free of cost and so also, timber for house construction. In particular, according to 1993 resolution, usufructs like leaves, grasses, fodder, thatch grasses, broom grasses, thorny fencing materials, brush wood and fallen lops and taps and twigs used as fuel wood would be available to the members of the community in terms of collection free of charge. In addition to this, according to 1996 resolution, each resident family, who is member of VSS is eligible to gather wood, small timber, bamboo from the protected forest, free of any cost.

Similarly, though kendu leaves collected by members will have to be delivered to the Departmental Agency against payment of prescribed wages, in 1996, with little amendment it states that the people have full rights to collection from the protected forest area, to possession as well as storage and processing of the products for preparation of other communities with specific provision of disposal to the authorized lessees/agents or officials. However, all the intermediate yield (if any) in the form of small wood, firewood, small wood etc. would be equally distributed among the members by the Executive Committee. As regards timber and poles obtained form the major harvest, it will be either equally shared by the Forest Department and VSS or the net sale proceeds available for distribution in cash may be distributed. Further, an amendment to 1993 resolution was specific to state that the village woodlots and other social forest plantation raised under SIST sponsored Forestry Project would be brought under JFM and the village community will be entitled for 100.0 per cent usufructs including final harvest of the plantation.

Villagers in Orissa have been enjoying varieties of forest access rights, concessions and privileges and these rights indeed are according to the types of forests and their tenurial status. In Orissa, while 48.0 per cent of forest land falls under the jurisdiction of Forest Department (FD) the rest 52.0 per cent comprise under control of protected forests and forest land under the direct control of Revenue Department. Similarly, while the Reserve Forests (RF) rests with the FD, the other areas including the gramya Jungle (Village forests on revenue lands) and other forests that lie within revenue village boundaries are administered by the local Panchayats under the Orissa Gram Panchayat Act, 1968, who is responsible for their management (Sarin M. and Rai A., 1998), and within communities under JFM, CFM in Capacity Building for Participatory Management of Degraded Forests in Orissa, India (Scandia consult Natura AB/Asia Forest Network).

A close look at the forest rights granted by the FD to the people for collection of fuelwood, fodder and other forest products to meet subsistence and commercial needs suggest that people had similar access to such forest produce even during the pre-JFM period. Access to forest was however regulated by certain restrictions, but were specific to meet bonafide needs. Sarin and Rai (1998) report that in this context, only 'B' category forests and PF's were demarcated for peoples' use. In most cases, however, people were entitled to pay some amount of cess. However, with the introduction of JFM, fuelwood collection is opened to forest-users free of any changes payable to the FD. Similarly, the members of VSS are allowed to collect fodder grasses though lack of grazing land and lack of alternate supply of grasses cause a lot of pressure on forests.

Apart from the benefits of usufruct rights over the NTFPs and major share from timber following final harvest, wage employment in forestry activities under taken by the FD is also another benefit to the village people, especially during agricultural lease seasons, when they have in fact very limited opportunities for subsistence. In many of the JFM areas, we visited during field survey, it was reported that due to the introduction of JFM it has indeed granted some rights over the forest produce and the scope for opportunities to earn some income from forests has been immensely increased.

According to Sarin and Rai (1998) empowering NTFP collectors to increase their incomes from NTFPs through unambiguous rules, processing and sale rights would not only increase their livelihood security but also, contribute to forest conservation objective by reducing their dependence on damaging and unsustainable activities like firewood head loading or working for timber smugglers to earn wages for survival. In point of fact, NTFPs in Orissa are not freely available to forest communities. Though, as per 1993 government order, usufructs like fodder grasses, leaves, broom grasses, brushwood and fallen lops and tops, twigs and firewood etc. are available as major incentive to the villagers in lieu of protection and conservation of precious forest resource, nationalised products like kendu leaves, sal seed and bamboo are delivered to the Departmental Agencies against prescribed wages for collection and delivery. Attempts by the government of Orissa to minimize involvement of middlemen and exploitation by setting up of Orissa Forest Develop Corporation (OFDC), Tribal Development Cooperative Corporation (TDCC) have yielded very limited success. Unlike many states, Orissa has nationalised many precious forest produces and that seems to have limited/restricted livelihood opportunities of tribal committees in a big way, besides increasing bureaucratisation and delaying process of payments.

Table 13.2: District Wise Number of VSS, Forest Area Brought Under JFM through VSS in Orissa as on End of June 2005

Sl. No.	*Name of the Divisions*	*Total No. VSS Formed*	*Total Forest area brought under JFM through VSS*	*VSS Registered under society Registration Act/Regd under FDA*
1.	Angul	160	25485	45
2.	Athamallik	147	10563	0
3.	Dhenkanal	270	33390	0
4.	Athagarh	117	10815	20
5.	Cuttack	68	6112	10
6.	Satkosia (WL)	17	383	17
7.	Khurda	76	11854	23
8.	Nayagarh	218	21947	218
9.	Chandaka (WL)	19	1241	0
10.	Chilika (WL)	19	1068	0
11.	Puri (WL)	17	4170	15
12.	Rajnagar (WL)	22	1170	0
13.	Mahanadi (WL)	0	0	0
14.	City Forest	9	218	0
15.	Ghumsur (N)	154	22571	84
16.	Ghumsur (S)	126	16027	88
17.	Phulbani	482	30718	0
18.	Boudh	130	11612	0

(Contd...)

19.	Baliguda	283	20610	26
20.	Parlakhemundi	518	27510	156
21.	Berhampur	57	6245	57
22.	Kalahandi (N)	447	34976	0
23.	Kalahandi (S)	364	24472	0
24.	Khariar	403	31459	0
25.	Sunabeda (WL)	0	0	0
26.	Bolangir (E)	245	18437	185
27.	Bolangir (W)	253	27746	253
28.	Rayagada	759	48822	0
29.	Koraput	515	27212	426
30.	Jeypore	404	25381	0
31.	Malkangiri	202	11695	2
32.	Nawranngpur	182	23098	182
33.	Sambalpur (N)	16	3002	16
34.	Sambalpur (S)	276	24567	63
35.	Rairakhol	142	13082	83
36.	Baragarh	244	32345	73
37.	Bamra (WL)	183	22042	176
38.	Hirakuda (WL)	0	0	0
39.	Sundararh	311	33881	0
40.	Bonai	105	6519	5
41.	Deogarh	222	34472	62
42.	Rourkela	228	21213	0
43.	Keonjhar	207	21096	0
44.	Keonjhar (WL)	51	6781	32
45.	Baripada VSS	298	29734	0
	Vipc	82	8980	0
46.	Karanpa	67	5353	0
	Vipc	186	17201	186
47.	Rairangpur	114	14656	114
48.	Balasore (WL)	100	8667	0
49.	Bhadrak (WL)	34	2387	34
	Total	9549	843085	2651

Source: Office of the PCCF, Orissa, Bhubaneswar.

JFM in Orissa: Retrospect and Prospect

In the light of the NFP 1988, JFM has been considered to be the right intervention for ensuring livelihood improvement of the forest-dependent poor in Orissa, who are unorganised and under-privileged due to their poverty, ignorance, and impoverishment - thus, the poor people are found increasingly vulnerable. These people indeed are principally focussed in JFM concept, bringing into play the principle of equity and empowerment. This is how JFM distinctly distinguishes itself from other participatory management practices.

Further, it was realised that the FD, who is the custodian of much Orissa's forests, is ill-equipped to withstand the onslaught of human and livestock populations, and therefore, faces overwhelming odds to deny or even regulate access to rural communities. Similarly, it is equally very difficult on the part of a few thousands of forest officers to restrict the activities of 3.13 crore rural population, who are dependent on the forests along with an immense population of livestock. Therefore, the realisation that mere policing by the FD is not the answer to Orissa's deforestation problem and therefore, has given rise to the emergence of a new approach to forest management, such as; JFM. It is based on participatory processes and recognition of peoples' developmental needs. Besides, it establishes forest management within the wider context of natural resource management. It encourages communities to take a decisive role in forest management, not only based on the concern for the environment, but also for food security and employment.

Though, there are evidences of peoples' participation in forest protection and management in Orissa in the recent past, the Government of Orissa (GoO) recognised these attempts in 1988 vide GoO Resolution, 1988. Accordingly, the villagers were assigned some specific roles in the protection of Reserve Forests (RF) adjoining their villages, and in turn, were granted certain concessions in the matter of meeting bonafide requirements of firewood and small timber. Forest Protection Committees (FPCs) were constituted in each assigned village. Following the Government of India's (GoI's) JFM guidelines issued on June 1, 1990 (GoI 1990), the Goo modified the earlier circular to provide representation to women and minorities in the FPCs (GOO 1990). However, the JFM programme has now become the central point of future forest development programme in the forestry sector of the state of Orissa.

In point of fact, participatory management system in Orissa was in the past and now continues to be of crucial significance due to substantial dependence on wood fuel as an energy source. A wood balance study conducted in 1989 suggests that RFs and PFs together continue to account for the lion's share of domestic fuel, of which 76.0 per cent is fuelwood and 49.0 per cent consists of brushwood and twigs (Saxena, 1996). But, as forest resources dwindle, forest dwelling communities are forced to resort to poor quality fuels, such as; cowdung cakes, palm frouds, stalks of pulses, dry leaves, non-wood residues of rice and maize etc. The extreme shortage of forest produce and fuelwood make local communities aware of the need for forest regeneration and also, forest protection activities.

Evidently, Orissa is one of the pioneering states for Participatory Forest Management (PFM) systems, many of which seem to have in existence prior to JFM initiatives. Such PFMs and a number of such Community Management Forest (CMF) systems have spontaneously emerged across the State of Orissa. The factors which attribute to such emerging forest management systems are aesthetic and religious feelings of the forest-dependent communities, besides the positive response to increasing forest degradation and a consequent upheaval in the livelihood strategies of forest-dependent economics. However, such management systems are essentially different from JFM, since these are self-initiated and carried out without the assistance of the FD. Further, many of these community management initiatives devise their own rules to regulate extraction of forest resource and to carry out protective as well as conservative measures. A study (Ravindranath et al., 1998) reports that the spread of CFM in Orissa is extremely significant and there are as many as 1181.

In point of fact, JFM seems to have emerged in Orissa much before the formulation of Guidelines in June 1990. Similarly, Community Forest Management (CFM) seems to have begun as early as in 1940s, though community efforts for protecting forests were fully recognised in 1985 by way of its incorporation in Village Forest Rules, 1985, which were framed on the basis of powers conferred under Sections 31, 32 (d) of the Orissa Forest Act, 1972. The rules may be weak, but they provide statutory status to forests demarcated exclusively for use of villagers (Sarin and Rai, 1998). Following this, several resolutions have been effected in 1988, 1990, 1993 and finally in 1996 dealing with Village Forest Management. However, as per the Resolution of the Forest, Fisheries and Animal Husbandry Department in the Government of Orissa on 1st August 1988, the villages adjacent to RF were assigned some specific roles in the protection of RF adjoining their villages in lieu of some concessions in the matter of meeting their bonafide requirement of firewood and small timber duly incorporated in Section 24 of the Orissa Forest Act, 1972 (Singh, 1997).

Accordingly, the concerned DFO is to assign peripheral reserved forest to adjoining villages and constitute a Forest Protection Committee (FPC) in each assigned village. The above Resolution was further amended on 13.10.1988, giving effect from 'Gandhi Jayanti' of 1988 by the Departments of Forest, Fisheries and Animal Husbandry, GoO. As a result, "the committee should be constituted in consultation with the local villagers, and the non-official members of the forest protection committee should be selected by convening a meeting of the concerned villagers". These Resolutions were further amended vide No. 10F (Prm) 4/90/29525/FFAH dated 11.12.1990, and accordingly, the protected forests were also included for assignment to adjoining villages, and the forest protection committees should include women and persons belonging to SC, ST and landless categories.

In order to make effective involvement of the local villagers in forest protection, the GoO's Resolution No. 16700-10F(Pron)20/93F&E dated 3.7.1993 was more transparent. Therefore, the involvement of the local community in protection of adjoining forests, formation of Vana Samrakshna Samittees (VSSs), their Executive Committees, execution of duties and responsibilities of the VSSs and Executive Committees etc. are detailed in the order. But, how far these duties and responsibilities of different stakeholders are practically executed at the grassroots level is a moot point. Following this, another Resolution was passed in 1996 and the salient features are the followings:

- Village is considered as the unit of management
- Exclusive legal rights over Reserve Forests and other forest patches are defined through notification as village forest
- Grant of community primary usage and management rights in terms of a scheme of management developed by the community and approved by the concerned DFO
- Freedom to enjoy community rights to collection of fuelwood, small timber, bamboo etc. free of charge as authorised by the VSS
- Grant of full rights over collection, possession, storage and processing of NTFPs and subject to disposal only to authorised agents, lessee, and also authorised officials.

Despite grant of usufruct rights to the community over the forest products in the protected forest areas so as to provide a great deal of incentives to the adjoining villagers, around a quarter (26.0 per cent) of the statutory forest land has been brought under the JFM in Orissa till date.

Observations suggest that though participation of JFMs and area protected actively under their jurisdiction are somewhat less.

Table 13.3: Status of JFM in Orissa as on June 2005

Sl. No.	*Type of Committee*	*Number*	*Forest Area Protected (In Ha)*
1.	Village Forest Committees (VFCs)	9055 (*5683)	121460 (**78646)
2.	Village Forest (Protection Committees (VFPCs)	5520	662012.28
3.	Vana Samarakshyan Samittees (VSSs)	9912 (*5981)	(**596269.19)
4.	Unregistered Groups	640	89864

Source: Office of the PCCF, GoO, Bhubaneswar.

*Active Committees ** Forest Areas Actively Protected

The above peoples' organisations namely: VFCs, VFPCs, VSSs have members both from the tribals and other categories of forest dwellers, who primarily depend upon forests for their food sustenance and livelihood. Indeed, collection of NTFPs, restricted minor processing at the household level and sale of these forest products in the local markets are crucial to their subsistence economy. Therefore, it was visualised the best way of meeting the twin challenges of maximising collectors' income from sale of NTFPs and of ensuring sustainable harvesting by involving VFCs, and VSSs in collection and marketing in a big way. It is evidently noticed that such a participatory management approach through formation of VSSs has been immensely effective in increasing the biomass production in many naturally regenerated forests of Orissa and also, have successfully met the needs of fuelwood, fodder, small timber, bamboo and other minor forest produces of the local communities into a very great extent. By June 2005 the total number of VSSs constituted for purpose of protection is 9549 covering 843085 hectares of forest area. But, how far, the emerging institutional as well as participatory issues in due course of its functioning in many parts of the scheduled and partially scheduled districts have been adequately addressed is a moot point.

It may be concluded that JFM is a different concept based on practical experiences of both local forest users and professionals employed by the state to act as custodians. The combined effort of community and government is the ultimate solution under the prevailing circumstances. In most areas, local user community failed to utilize forests due to over-exploitation of forest resources as a equal of numerous factors. This has resulted in lack of availability of fuel, fodder, medicines, food articles, small timber for domestic and agricultural uses as well as less of soil fertility and water conservation.

It has also been observed that actual forest cover reduced day by day than recorded forest area by Government. It is also matter of great concern for forest department to protect forest cover as regeneration of such common resources leg behind than the resources withdrawn from its area. It has also resulted in disappearance and extinction of various species as well. VSSs in general considered as an entity for overall development of the village resources and its people, not only to develop degraded forests, but also for a new initiative by the people to get ride of rural poverty trap. The forest department which is the main implementing agency need to motivate people by providing strong support to such organizations. It also requires for top-level commitment at both political and official levels, armed with sincerity, transparenty and greater scope for good JFMs, as considered by forest officials, to work with NGO's, and other Civil Society organizations.

In Orissa, involvement of people in forest protection and regeneration backed by forest officials seems to be satisfactory and effective. Its success will strengthen joint effort of people and forest department to achieve sustainable forest development.

REFERENCES

1. Aplet, G.J. Chuson G.N., Olson J.T. and Sample, V.A (1997), Defining Sustainable Forestry (Eds) The Wilderness Society, Island Press, Washington D.C., Covelo, California.

2. Banerjee, U. (1989), *'Participatory Forest Management in West Bengal'* Malhotra and Poffenferger (Eds) Forest Regeneration Through Community Protection: The West Bengal Experience, West Bengal Forest Department.

3. Campbell, Jeffery, Y. (1996), Second Generation Issues in JFM, Introduction to Panel Presentation, May 14.

4. Chambers Rebert, N.C. Saxena and Tushar Shah (1989) *"To the Hands of the Poor"*, Water and Trees Oxford & IBH, New Delhi.

5. Clay, J.W (1996), Generating Income Conserving Resources-20 Lessons from the Field. World Wildlife Fund : Washington, D.C.

6. CPSW (1996), *Livelihood of Forest Dwellers and NTFP Policy in Orissa,* Bhubaneswar.

7. FAO (1995), "Non-Wood Forest Products For Rural Income and Sustainable Forestry", Technical Papers, No. 7, *FAO,* Rome Italy.

8. Fernandes, W., Menon, G. and Vieges, R. (1988), Forests, Environment and Tribal Economy: Deforestation, Improvement and Marginalisation in Orissa, ISI, New Delhi.

9. Fernandes, W. (1996), "Drafting A Peoples Forest Bill: The Forest Dwellers-Social Activist Alternative", ISI, New Delhi.

10. Gadgil, M. and Guha R. (1992), *This Fissured Land--An Ecologial History of India,* Oxford University Press, Delhi.

11. GoO (1981), Orissa Forest Produce (Control of Trade) Act, 1981. Forest Department, Bhubaneswar: Government of Orissa.

12. GoO (1961), The Orissa Kendu Leaves (Control of Trade) Act, 1961. Forest Department, Bhubaneswar: Government of Orissa.

13. GoO (1962), The Orissa Kendu Leaves (Control of Trade) Rules, 1962, Forest Department, Bhubaneswar: Government of Orissa.

14. GoO (1964), The Orissa Gram Panchayat (OGP) Act, 1964. Rural Development Department, Bhubaneswar: Government of Orissa.

15. GoO (1972), Orissa Forest Act, 1972 Forests Department, Bhubaneswar: Government of Orissa.

16. GoO (1976), The Orissa Excise (Mahua Flower) Rules, 1979. Excise Department, Bhubaneswar: Government of Orissa.

17. GoO (1977), The Schedule of Rate (Forest Produce in Orissa) Rules, 1977, Forest Department, Bhubaneswar: Government of Orissa.

18. GoO (1980), Supply of Bamboo to Artisans including Cooperative Societies (Orissa) Rules, 1980, Forest Department, Bhubaneswar: Government of Orissa.

19. GoO (1980), The Orissa Timber and Other Forest Produce Transit Rules, 1980, Forest Department, Bhubaneswar: Government of Orissa.

20. GoO (1983), Orissa Forest Produce (Control of Trade) Rules, 1983, Forest Department, Bhubaneswar: Government of Orissa.

21. GoO (1984), The Sal Seed Nationalisation Act, 1983-84, Forest Department, Bhubaneswar: Government of Orissa.

22. GoO (1997), The Gram Panchayat (Amendment) Act, 1997, Rural Development Department, Bhubaneswar: Government of Orissa.

23. GoO (2000), Policy on Procurement and Trade of Non-Timber Forest Produce. Resolution 5503, 31st March 2000, Forest and Environment Department, Bhubaneswar: Government of Orissa.

24. GoO (2000), Procurement of Sal seeds of 2000 crop. Resolution 5FC8/2000.1831/F&E, 22nd January 2000, Forest and Environment Department, Bhubaneswar: Government of Orissa.

25. Rameshwari, VLV (2002), Gendered Communications and Access to Social Space—Issues on Forest Management, *Economic and Political Weekly*, Vol. XXXVIII.

26. Kashyap, S.C. (1990), *National Policy Studies,* Tata McGraw-Hill Publication Co. Ltd., New Delhi.

27. Kumar, N and N.C. Saxena (2002), India's Forests: Potential for Poverty Alleviation (eds), *Managing a Global Resource: Challenges of Forest Conservation and Development, World Bank* (eds) by U. Lela Series, Vol. 5, Transaction Publishers, New Brunswick.

28. Lind Say, Jamathan (1994), Law and Community in the Management of India's State Forests. Lincoln Institute of Land policy, Cambridge Workins Paper Series.

29. Mahapatra, L.K. (1993), Customary Rights in Land and Forest and the State in Continuity and Change in Miri, M (ed.) Tribal Society, Shimla India Institute of Advanced Study.

30. Mallik, R.M. (2004), Forest Management and Tribal Livelihood' in the Human Development Report prepared by the NCDS, Bhubaneswar for submission to UNDP.

31. Mallik, R.M. (2004), "In Sustaining Food Security and Tribal Livelihood in Orissa: Issues and Practices of NTFP Management," *Forest Usufructs*, Vol. 5, No. 1/2, Dehradun.

32. Mallik, R.M. (2004), *Sustainable Forestry development in Orissa: Some issues and Policy Options in Reviving Orissa Economy*, (Eds) by R.K. Panda, APH Publishing Corporation, New Delhi.

33. Mallik, R.M. and C.R. Das (2004), Access to Forest Resource and Management: A Study of Forest/NTFP Policies and Tribal Livelihood, Poverty Task Force, Government of Orissa.

34. Mehta A.K. and Amita Shah (2003), "Chronic Poverty in India: Incidence, Causes and Policies", *World Development* Vol. 3, No. 3.

35. Ministry of Environment and Forests of India (1998), Report of the Expert Committee on Conferring Ownership Rights of NTFPs on Panchayats, New Delhi (Unpublished).

36. Myrdal, G. (1968), *Asian Drama: An Enquiry in to the Poverty of Nations*, Vol. 3, Penguin Books.

37. National Commission on Agriculture (1976), M/o Agriculture, Government of India.

38. National Forest Policy (1988), M/o Forest and Environment, Government of India.

39. National Institute of Rural Development (2000), India Rural Development Report Regional Disparities in Development and Poverty NIRD, Hyderabad.

40. National Institute of Rural Development (2000), India Rural Development Report.

41. Regional Disparities in Development and Poverty, NIRD, Hyderabad.

42. Rao, P. Narayana (1995), Environment and National Forest Policy, Procedings of BKMU Workshop, Sept. 1-5, New Delhi, BKMU Publications.

43. Roy Burman, B.K. (1982), Report of Committee on Forest and Tribals in India, Tribal Development Division, New, Delhi, Ministry of Home Affairs.

44. Roy Burma, B.K. (1985), Challenges of Development and Tribal Women in India in Singh J.P, Vyas NN Mann, R.S. (ed.) Tribal Women and Development, MLU Tribal Research and Training Institute, Tribal Area Development Department Rajasthan Udaipur.

45. Sarin M. and Rai A. (1998), Rational Distribution of Benefits between Communities and Forest Department.

46. Sachidananda (1998), "Survival Strategies of India Tribes" in Dube S.C. (ed.), *Antiguity to Modernity in Tribal India: Continuity and Change Among Indian Tribes*, Vol. 1, Inter-India Publishers, New Delhi, pp. 47-69.

47. Saxena (1997), *The Sage of Participatory Forest Management in India*, CIFOR, Indonesia.

48. Saxena, N.C. (1995), "Forest, People & Profit: New equations for Sustainability", Centre for Sustainable Development, Lal Bahadur Shastri National Academy of Admn., Mussorie, Natraj Publishers, Dehradun.

49. Saxena, N.C. (1996), "Forest Policy and the Rural Poor in Orissa", *Jagruti Vani*, Vol. II, No. 4 and Vol. 12, No. 1, March.

50. Saxena, N.C. (2000, 2002), Forest in India, World Bank Washington D.C., U.S.A.

51. Singh, R.V. (1997), Evolution of Forest Tenure in India-Implications for Sustainable Forest Management, Unpublished Ph.D Thesis, The UBC, Vancouver, Canada.

52. World Bank (1992), World Development Report: Development and Environment, Washington, D.C, U.S.A.

14

Regional Rural Banks and Agricultural Development

*Bhagaban Padhy**

India's economy has been predominantly rural in character. This is evident from the very high proportion of India's population living in rural areas. Even today majority (around 70 per cent) of the total population live in villages and about 60 per cent its work force is engaged in agriculture and allied activities in rural areas. However, the British didn't give due importance to agricultural development. The Britishers completely ruined the rural economy of India. After independence, the situation was aggravated as Nehruvian concept of industrialization and Gandhiji's vision of rural India was neglected. Keeping in view the industrialization, in the first two five-year plans importance was given to rapid industrialization. This led to lopsided development, which compelled the planners to feel that Indian economy largely depends on agriculture. Without its development Indian economy cannot grow. Credit is highly essential to lead the agrarian/rural economy of India. Besides, globalisation has brought a multi-dimensional changes which needs a strategic discussion. Because supply of credit, plays very important role for the survival and growth of argarian economy of India.

* Bhagaban Padhy is Head, Department of Economics, A.N. College, Dharakote, Ganjam, Orissa. e-mail: bhagaban_padhi@sify.com

In this backdrop, an attempt has been made to explore the following objectives:

(*a*) To examine financial support to agriculture and allied sectors by Regional Rural Banks in India.

(*b*) To focus on the constraints faced by RGBs in financing the agricultural needs of the undivided Ganjam District of Orissa.

(*c*) To suggest some further policy measures.

Methodology

Keeping in view the objectives of the study, field studies are undertaken in 8 villages, selected on the basis of simple random technique from among four branches of 76 RGBs in the undivided Ganjam District of Orissa. The branches are selected on the basis of simple random technique. Interview and observation methods have been adopted to collect data from the field. 15 agriculturists from each villages thus 120 beneficiaries have been selected for the purpose of data collection and interview to collect their views. For the collection of secondary data periodicals, journals, magazines and other published sources including the RGB reports have been taken resort to. Statistical devices like averages and percentages have been used to infer-conclusions.

The study is made in 6 sections as mentioned below.

Section I : Introduction

Section II: Institutional arrangements and brief profile of RRBs in India.

Section III: Supply of credit to rural economy in general and agriculture in particular by RRBs.

Section IV: Study on RGBs in the Ganjam District of Orissa.

Section V: Problems faced by RGBs.

Section VI: Suggestions and concluding remarks.

SECTION I

Credit is an important input in the process of development and an accelerator of development. Ensuring the provision of timely and adequate credit to the large segment of the rural population has been one of the major policy initiatives of the present day planning in India. Credit needs of the rural people arise out of productivity as well as unproductive purposes. Such requirements emerge from the various rural economic activities like agricultural operations both under traditional and modern methods, processing and marketing of agricultural products and undertaking allied activities. And today, rural credit in India is being provided by three agencies viz., Co-operatives, commercial Banks and Regional Rural Banks where RRBs play very significant role.

That is why a number of committees, study groups and study teams were appointed by the Government of India and the Reserve Bank of India to study and recommend suitable measures to meet the rural credit requirements. Among these Gadgil Committee, Talwar Committee, Hazari Committee, Tandon Committee, Kamath Committee, Desai Committee are worth mentioning. Most of them have expressed, time and again, the need of rural institutional credit system for rural development. However, in 1972, Sariya Committee recommended for the creation of new credit agency namely "Rural Banks" to meet exclusively the credit needs of the rural poor. With a view to find the feasibility of such Rural Banking and their functioning the Government of India appointed a committee under the Chairmanship of M. Narasimham. This committee in its report strongly recommended for setting up of such rural Banks which should be rural and owned by the Government. These banks are to work as supplementary credit agencies to the existing ones. As per the recommendation of the committee, the Government of India promulgated the Regional Rural Banks ordinance on September 26, 1975, which later on known as the Regional Rural Banks Act, 1976. It was made effective from the date of the ordinance.

The objectives of the RRBs are to mobilize deposits from its regional rural area and deploy them in the same region. The RRBs have a key role in lending productive credits to the weaker sections of the society comprising small farmers, marginal farmers, land labourers, persons engaged in trade, commerce and other productive activity.

The agricultural credit given by RRB, may be grouped under three categories.

(a) Direct Agricultural Advances

The financial assistance granted to farmers and landless agricultural labourers are treated as direct agricultural advances. Such loans can be given to eligible persons as investment credit for the creation of fixed assets or production credit for meeting seasonal requirements. Thus RRBs are expected to take up the following schemes:

- Scheme for crop production credit.
- Scheme for loans against pledge of cold storage receipt.
- Scheme for loans for irrigation.
- Scheme for land development.
- Scheme for equipments and implements.
- Scheme for cart and draft animals.

(b) Allied Activities

Apart from the agricultural credit, RRBs are expected to provide loans for allied agricultural activities viz. dairying, poultry, piggery, sheep and goat rearing etc.

(c) Indirect Agricultural Advances

The RRBs may also finance the primary agricultural co-operative credit societies (PACS) and Farmers Service Societies (FSS), which have a preponderance of small and marginal farmers, landless agricultural labourers etc.

Need for an Alternative Credit Source in India

(a) Non-availability of timely and sufficient agricultural credit by the institutional agencies.

(b) Enroute of savings from rural to urban centers by the Commercial Bank.

(c) Lack of sufficient funds for agricultural development from by the Commercial Banks.

(d) To save the farmers from the clutches of moneylenders providing conditional loans at exorbitant rate of interest.

(e) Profit motive and high cost structure of the Commercial Banks.

(f) Unjust distribution of funds by the commercial Banks.

Section II

Table 14.1: Institutional Arrangement for Rural Credit

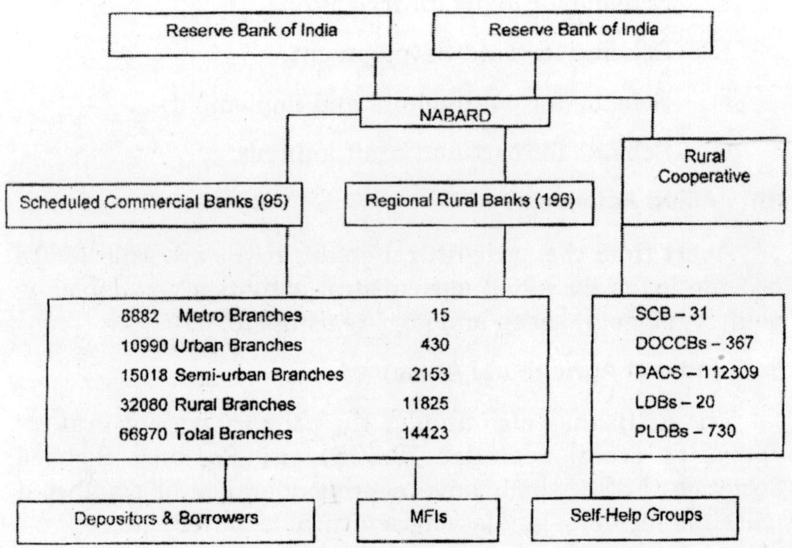

Table 14.2: Profile of RRBs (As on March 2005)

Total No. of RRBs	196
No. of RRBs that made profit	167
Deposits	Rs. 62143 crore
Borrowings	Rs. 5524 crore
Investments	Rs. 23200 crore
Total Assets	Rs. 77866 crore
Outstanding Advances	Rs. 32871 crore
Operating Profit	Rs. 1009 crore
Net profit	Rs. 750 crore

Source: Secondary Source.

SECTION III

RRBs in India

As per the ordinance of 26th September 1975 initially a total of five RRBs have been set up at Moradabad and Gorakhpur in Uttar Pradesh, Bhiwani in Haryana, Jaipur in Rajasthan and and Maida in West Bengal. These Banks were sponsored by the Syndicate Bank, State Bank of India, Punjab National Bank, United Commercial Bank and United of India respectively. In due due course, the number of RRBs has came upto 196 as on March 2005 with more than 14,500 branches. Each RRB is sponsored by a nationalized Bank known as a sponsoring Bank, which provides all sorts of help to these RRBs. The area of operation of these Banks is specified. The jurisdiction of each RRB is confined to specified districts in a State. The number of districts varies between one to five and each branch office covers one to three blocks covering at least five to ten farmers service societies.

Table 14.3 shows the finance provided to agriculture by different financial institutions. The role of RRBs is appreciable in comparison to that of other financial institution.

Table 14.3: Micro-finance by different Institutions in India

Bank	*Cumulative Number of disbursement per SHGs provided Bank loan SHG*	
	Upto March 01-02	*Upto March 04*
Public Sector Banks	118855	516697
Private Sector Banks	5391	21725
Regional Rural Banks	84775	405998
Cooperatives	12773	134671
Total	221794	1079091

Source: NABARD, 2004.

The Table 14.4 shows that the number of RRBs has remained constant since 1990, only the number of branches which has gone up marginally, is not sufficient to support the vast agrarian economy of India. Deposit position is also not very significant.

Table 14.5 shows that co-operative institution which are struggling for survival in India have been playing very important role in providing institutional credit to agriculture in India. So also Commercial Banks but the role of RRBs is not significant which is probably due to lack of funds.

Table 14.6 shows the improvement in the recovery by the RRBs starting from 1993 to 2003. No doubt the recovery position is sound, but not sufficient so far as the position of others financial institutions is concerned.

Table 14.7 shows that the total agricultural advance as on March 2003, Public Sector Banks (PSBs) was only 15.3 per cent and Private Sector Banks 10.8 per cent against the target of 18 per cent. But in the case of RRBs, it was 46.3

Table 14.4: Expansion of RRBs During 1975-2003

Period Ending	*Banks*	*Branches*	*Loans (in Rs. Crore)*	*Deposits*	*Period Ending*	*Banks*	*Branches (in Rs. Crore)*	*Loan (in Rs. Crore)*	*Deposits*
Dec. 1975	6	17	0.10	0.20	Mar. 1988	196	14,508	8,486.62	19,325.65
Dec. 1980	85	3,279	243.38	199.83	Mar. 1999	196	14,508	9,367.21	23,597.61
Dec. 1985	188	12,606	1,407.67	1286.82	Mar. 2000	196	14,311	13,814.89	32,204.34
Mar. 1990	196	14,443	3,554.04	4,150.52	Mar. 2001	196	14,311	15,816.30	38,271.87
Mar. 1995	196	14,509	6,290.97	11,150.01	Mar. 2002	196	14,390	18,629.22	44,539.15
Mar. 1997	196	14,508	7,852.66	15,423.42	Mar. 2003	196	14,433	22,157.85	50,098.34

Source: Annual Report NABARD (2002-03).

Table 14.5: Flow of Institutional Credit to Agriculture

(Rs. in crore)

Institutions	*1997-98*	*2000-01*	*2002-03*
Cooperative Bank Share (%)	14085 (44)	20,801 (39)	24,296 (34)
Regional Rural Bank Share (%)	2040(6)	4,219(8)	5647(8)
Commercial Bank Share (%)	15831 (50)	27,807 (53)	41,047 (58)

Source: NABARD.

Table 14.6: Recovery Performance of RRBs (as on 30th June 2003)

(Rs. in crore)

Year	*Demand*	*Collection*	*Balance*	*Recovery*
1993	2,726.65	1,123.49	1,603.16	41.20
1994	3,159.95	1,460.85	1,699.10	46.20
1995	3,669.07	1,870.36	1,798.71	51.00
1996	4,426.88	2,439.18	1,987.70	55.10
1997	5,503.29	3,143.08	2,360.21	57.10
1998	5,890.29	3,559.28	2,331.01	60.42
1999	7,034.23	4,519.30	2,514.93	64.24
2000	8,026.36	5,473.59	2,552.77	68.20
2001	9,617.93	6,789.53	2,828.40	70.59
2002	11,569.82	8,274.34	3,295.48	71.52
2003	13,246.95	9,738.80	3,508.15	73.53

Source: Annual Report NABARD (2002-03).

per cent. It indicates the RRBs are specially designed financial institutions for financing agriculture.

The Kisan Credit Card Scheme is an innovative mechanism for facility access to ST credit to farmers. The survey indicates that the KCC Scheme has a positive impact on the cost of borrowings with a reduction in interest cost in

Table 14.7: Public Sector Banks Private Sector Banks (RRBs)

End March	*Public Sector Banks*		*Private Sector Banks*		*RRBs*	
	Amount Outstanding	*% of net Bank Credit*	*Amount Outstanding*	*% of net Bank Credit*	*Amount Outstanding*	*% of net Bank Credit*
1999	37632	14.2	3467	9.1	5460	48.1
2000	45296	14.3	4023	8.3	6227	47.5
2001	53571	15.7	5634	9.6	7217	45.7
2002	63082	15.9	8022	8.5	8405	45.2
2003	73507	15.3	11873	10.8	10261	46.3

Sources:(i) Annual Report, RBI, 2003-04, p. 137.

(ii) Consolidated RBI Report on Trend and Progress of Banking in India.

both the formal and informal sector. However, the restrictions imposed while issuing should be made liberal.

Table 14.8: Number of KCC Issued and Sanctioned

Agency	*Cumulative Progress up to September 30, 2004*	
	Card Issued (In lakh)	*Amount Sanctioned (Rs. crore)*
Cooperative Banks	258.6	65,233
RRBs	44.6	11,265
Commercial Banks	132.4	34,961
Total	435.6	1,11,459

Source: NABARD.

Table 14. 9: Purpose-wise Disbursements of Loans and Advances of Regional Rural Banks

(Rs. in Crore)

Sl. No.	*Category*	*1982*	*1985*	*1990*	*2002*
I.	**Agriculture Sector**				
	Short Term crop loans	108.64 (18.83)	264.16 (18.77)	620 (17.42	3812 (36.06)
	Term Loans for Agrl. & Allied Activities	238.20 (41.27)	551.40 (39.17)	1230 (34.55)	782 (7.40)
	Sub-total	346.84 (60.10)	815.56 (57.94)	1850 (51.97)	459 (43.46)
II.	**Non-Agricultural Sector**				
	Rural Artisans, Village and Cottage	30.63 (5.31)	79.90 (5.68)	280 (7.86)	305 (2.89)
	Industries, etc.				
	Retail trade, self employed etc.	124.70 (21.61)	366.00 (26.00)	1100 (30.90)	1279 (12.10)
	Other loans	74.94 (12.98)	146.21 (10.39)	330 (9.27)	4393 (41.56)
	Sub-total	230.27 (39.90)	592.11 (42.06)	1710 (48.03)	5977 (56.54)
	Total	577.11 (100.00)	1407.67 (100.00)	3560(100.00)	10571(100.00)

SECTION IV

Brief Profile of Undivided Ganjam District

The district of Ganjam lies on the eastern part of Orissa. it is the largest district in the state and also ranks third in respect of population. According to 2001 census the population of Ganjam was 3161000 out of which 2604000 live in rural whereas 556000 live in urban areas. Similarly the density of population is 385 per sq. km. SC & ST population are 586798 and 90919 respectively. It is an agricultural district with around 60 per cent agricultural farmers belonging to the category of small farmers residing in rural areas. The major source of irrigation is the River Rushikulya. To supplement it there are a number of river projects like Jayamangala System, Dhanei, Baghua, Ghodahada, Daha, etc.

Table 14.10: Branch Network of RGB as on 31.3.1996

District	*Rural*	*Semi-Urban*	*Urban*	*Total*
Ganjam (undivided)	66	9	1	75

Source: RGB 15th Annual Report, 1995-96.

Area Office was at Aska (Ganjam District).

Table 14.11: Branch Network of RGB as on 31.3.2006

District	*Rural*	*Semi-Urban*	*Urban*	*Total*	*Satellite Office*	*Area Office*
Ganjam (Undivided)	48	12	6	66	4	1
Gajapati	9	1		10	4	
Total	57	13	6	76	8	1

Source: RGB 24th Annual Report 2005-06.

Tables 14.10 and 14.11 show the branch network of RGBs as on 31.3.1996 and 31.3.2005 respectively. From the tables it is clear that number of RGBs in the undivided Ganjam District remain unchanged but number of rural branches has came down to only 57 in 2006 from 65 in 1996. This is not a good sign for the rural agricultural economy of the region concerned.

Table 14.12: No. of Kisan Credit Card Issued by RGBs

	31st March '02	*31st March '03*	*31st March '04*	*31st March '05*	*31st March '06*
No. of Kisan Credit Cards	9,500	14,000	18,000	More than 25,000	30,270
Amount	9.5 Crore	17 Crore	22 Crore	33 Crore	40.85 Crore

Source: RGB Annual Reports.

Table 14.12 shows the credibility of RGBs in issuing largest number Kisan Credit Cards during the sessions 2002-03, 2003-04, 2004-05 and 2005-06 in the district. With this RGB maintains its lead position among all commercial Banks. It has provided more than 30,270 cards as on 31st March 2006. The Bank has issued 5270 new cards during the financial year 2005-06. The scheme has been proved as an innovative mechanism for facilitating access to short term credit to farmers, which helped the rural economy to grow fast. The pace has been quickened with the increase in the number of cards in each successive year since its inception.

Table 14.13: Rashtriya Krishi Bima Yojana by RGBs

(Amount in Lakhs)

		2002-03	*2003-04*	*2004-05*	*2005-06*
1.	Sum insured				
	Kharif	1439.40	1789.94	2657.82	3094.56
	Rabi	20.63	27.78	28.17	16.28
2.	Premium paid				
	Kharif	25.76	36.51	60.50	72.93
	Rabi	0.30	0.41	0.69	0.29
3.	Amount settled	Nil	Nil		

Source: RGB 22nd, 23rd, 24th and 25th Annual Reports.

Table 14.13 shows details about the Rashtriya Krishi Bima Yojana by RGBs during the financial years 2002-03, 2003-04, 2004-05 and 2005-06. Under the scheme all eligible crops have been insured which helped the rural economy in general and the farmers in particular. The increased trend of some insured and premium position reveals the key role played by RGB in rural agricultural development. In this manner the RGB has contributed significantly to the agricultural insurance scheme during the aforesaid years pertaining to Kharif and Rabi crops. However, neglect of rabi crop is unfortunate.

Table 14.14:

(Rs. in Lakhs)

	As on 31.03.02	*As on 31.03.03*	*As on 31.03.04*	*As on 31.03.05*	*As on 31.03.06*
Crop Loan	1466.78	2213.81	2830.96	4111.17	5448.68
ATL and Allied Activities	1182.72	1271.85	1741.66	2276.23	2629.96
Growth Rate	2649.50	3485.66 32%	4572.62 31%	6387.40 29.56%	8078.00 26.53%

Source: RGB 22nd, 23rd, 24th and 25th Annual Reports.

Table 14.14 shows that the increase in the total volume of crop loans and financial help for ATL and Allied Activities during the years 2002 to 2006, which is not satisfactory. This is because the amounts are not sufficient to cater to the needs of the increased rural folk over the years. The growth rate has come down to 26.53 per cent in 2006 as against 32 per cent in the year 2002.

Table 14.15: Financial Assistance to Self-Help Group SHGs

Year	*No. of SHGs given*	*Amount*
1998-99	230	22.40 lakhs
2004-05	1622	469.75 lakhs
2005-06	2417	993.79 lakhs

Source: RGB Annual Report.

Table 14.16: Cumulative Position (1998-99 to 2004-05)

Year	*No. of SHGs covered*	*No. of Women covered*	*Financial outlay (Rs.)*
1998-99	230	207	20.03 lakhs
2004-05	5844	77144	14.23 crores
2005-06	8271	114550	24.17 crores

Source: RGB Annual Report.

Table 14.15 reveals the extent of help provided by RGBs to Self Help Groups (SHGs) during the financial years 1998-99 to 2005-06. The number of SHGs covered was 230 with the amount of Rs. 22.40 lakh in 1998-99, which increased to 2417 and Rs. 993.79 lakh in 2005-06. The Table 14.16 shows the cumulative position of the SHGs. As on 31.3. 2006, the Bank financed 8271 SHGs with a loan amount of Rs. 27.17 crore covering 114550, women. Even Bank has entered into partnership with the reputed international NGO CARE-INDIA for taking forward the Micro-Finance Programme of Gajapati District through its 10 branches. RGB has been selected by NABARD as one among 4 RRBs in India for pilot testing DEWTA (Development of women through Area Programme). After launching of DEWTA Programme of NABARD in January 2004 the Bank has imparted the following skill development training to the women of target villages during the year.

Table 14.17 reveals the non-performing assets (NPA) of the RGB during the last three financial years. The study reveals that the percentage of net NPA to Net advances has gone down which is a good sign for the institution. This helps to increase the efficiency of the institution in the desired path.

Table 14.18 shows the response given by 120 rural farmers regarding their choice for sources of finance. The farmers were taken from different villages at random. The study reveals that even today about 35 per cent of the rural farmers are borrowing from non-institutional sources of finance, which are exploitive in nature.

Table 14.17: NPA Management (Loans and Advances)

(Amount in lakhs)

		2002-03	2003-04	2004-05	2005-06
(a)	NPA at the beginning of the year	1182.84	1153.02	1284.54	1360.60
(b)	Deletion during the year	285.40	285.25	268.05	251.46
(c)	Addition during the year	255.58	416.77	344.11	572.72
(d)	NPA at the end of the year	1153.02	1284.54	1360.60	1681.86
(e)	% of gross NPA to gross advances	8.80	8.06	6.97	7.20
(f)	Provisions maintained	476.52	533.31	606.82	806.61
(g)	Net NPA	676.50	751.23	753.78	875.25
	% of Net NPA to Net advances	5.36	4.87	3.96	3.88

Source: RGB Annual Report.

Table 14.18

No. of respondents	*% of respondents on farmer of institutional finance*	*% of respondents in farmer of non-institutional finance*	*Cannot say*
120	55	35	10

Table 14.19 reflects briefly the response made by the respondent which was collected through participatory rural appraisal technique. The figures of the respondents are rounded off. It reveals that only 20 per cent of the total agricultural credit is given as long term financial assistance, which is insufficient for the rural farmers to procure machinery and make a drastic change in farming methods. Similarly, advance of more loans to kharif crop and discouragement to rabi crops is not good sign for the rural economy. More financial assistance rendered by the RGB to commercial crop is a matter of headache for the rural farmers. Because they can not for go the so-called non-commercial crop. The study also reveals that the lion's share of the

agricultural credit given by the RGB is snatched away by big farmers and small and marginal farmers are neglected.

Table 14.19: Types of Financial Assistance by RGB

		No. of Respondents	*Value in %*
1.	**Nature of Loan:**		
	(a) Long Term Loan	20	16.66
	(b) Medium Term Loan	40	33.33
	(c) Short Term Loan	60	50.00
2.	**Advances for Crops:**		
	(a) Rabi	40	
	(b) Kharif	80	66.66
3.	**On the basis of Marketability:**		
	(a) Commercial	70	58.33
	(b) Non-commercial	50	41.66
4.	**On the basis of size of Landholding:**		
	(a) Big farmers	70	58.33
	(b) Small farmers	30	25.00
	(c) Marginal farmers	20	16.66

Source: Field Survey.

SECTION V

Problems Faced

RRBs face multifarious problems due to their peculiar nature and tasks involved. The main issues are as follows.

1. Poor recovery rate and the resultant, mounting losses.
2. Delay in decision-making on account of different agencies being involved in the management process.
3. Capital inadequacy.
4. Staff incompatibility as they find it difficult to cope with rural surroundings and business opportunities.

5. Restrictions in respect of deposit mobilization and scope for investment.

SECTION VI

Suggestions and Concluding Remarks

In the light of the foregoing analysis and the report of the study group on RRBs, the following suggestions are made, considering the need for strengthening intermittent supply of rural finance and effective operation of the RRBs.

Increase in Branch Network

Increasing of the number of branches in general and rural branches in particular is necessary. This is required to strengthen the rural credit base.

Owners and Control

Instead of these Banks working as extensions of sponsor Banks, they must be made to work independently as a separate entity.

Target and Motive

Advances target should be fulfilled at any cost. Almost all the advances must go to the rural sector. There must be flexibility in the interest rates between different kinds of loans such as crop loans, village housing loans, cottage industries.

Coverage Area and Branch Expansion

India has about 5 lakh villages. As the Scheduled Banks have already diverted their attention to urban and metro cities resulting in closure of many rural branches, the only alternative is RRBs, barring the co-operatives. It is essential that all these villages, panchayats, blocks, taluks must come under these Banks. It is essential to multiply the number of branches to cover the entire rural area of our country.

Staffing and Training

The appointment and training of the staff working in

these rural oriented institutions should be given much attention. Every branch should have on its staff, at least one person from the same locality so that it will be easy for the Bank Manager to learn about the local conditions and people. Generally, members from rural communities only should be appointed in these Banks so that the employees do not appear to be out of place in the rural setting. Also they can serve better in the familiar surroundings.

As Market Leader

The RRBs should have the status of the market leader of rural finance. The number of other players must be restricted.

Group Lending

"Group Lending" (between 5 and 20 people) should be made in order to make repayment more effective. In this context the example of Grameen Bank of Bangladesh should be taken into account.

Government Subsidy

Government should give subsidies instead of spending on other forms of public expenditure. This is because it is cost effective and responsive to local felt needs.

Merger of RRBs

Partial merger of RRBs on experimental basis is not sufficient. In order to make the RRBs viable it is necessary to merge all the RRBs operating in the country and form a monolithic structure i.e. an All India Institution called the Grameen Bank of India for meeting the banking needs of people living in the rural areas.

Conclusion

As institutional finance is inadequate in rural areas, moneylenders dominate in rural area. The rural population is ever in the shackles of debt and bondage. The Commercial Banks are closing down rural branches and concentrating on profitability rather than service to the rural poor.

Organized lending through Government institutions is to be reinforced to help the villages recover from debt and poverty, generate employment and productivity. In this context, the RRBs are specially suited to work solely in the rural areas to channelise funds and monitor regional development.

REFERENCES

1. RGB (Head Office Berhampur) Annual Reports 15th, 17th, 18th, 22nd, 23rd, 24th and 25th.
2. Dhingra I.C., "The Indian Economy", *Resources Planning Development and Problems*, Sultan Chand & Sons, New Delhi.
3. Pany R.K., *Indian Economy*, Kitab Mahal, Cuttack.
4. *Kurukshetra*, Vol. 51, No. 10 August 2003.
5. *General Studies, Indian Economy*, Pratiyogita Darpan.
6. *Kurukshetra*, Jan. 2005.
7. *Kurukshetra*, Sep. 2006.
8. *Kurukshetra*, Dec. 2005.
9. *Yojana*, Aug. 2006.
10. Dr. S.D. Misra, Kisan Credit Cards: Among Weaker Sections, pp. 22-25, IBA Bulletin, Dec. 2005.

15

Development of Tribals in Orissa with Special Reference to Koraput District

*Dr. B. Eswar Rao Patnaik**
*Sri Satyajit Hota***

Human development has been visualized "as a process of enlarging peoples choices (U.N. Development Report, 1990). But, at all levels of time, the essential ones are for all people to lead a long and healthy life, to acquire knowledge and to have resources for decent living standards. The inclusion of income it justified on the ground that it enables the exercise of choice with respect to educational attainment and life expectancy. The census of 2001, by Government of India has considered the following ingredients of development: housing conditions, availability of drainage, latrine and bathroom facilities use of electricity possession of assets, like cycle, radio and scooter, provision of drinking water by tap and provision of separate living room for newly married couples within the premises of the house.

Orissa has been the home of as many as 62 different tribal communities. The accent of plan exercises has been on development and welfare of the scheduled castes and

* Reader in Economics, SBR Government Women's College, Berhampur (Orissa).

** Lecturer in Economics, Ronald Institute of Technology, Berhampur (Orissa).

scheduled tribes, promotion of their educational and economic interests and their protection from social injustice and exploitation. Today, the economy of Orissa is on the threshold of commencing Eleventh Five-Year Plan. The schedule caste and schedule tribe population of the State is 142.27 lakhs (2001 census), which is 38.66 per cent of the total state population. Koraput district has hill area backwardness, backwardness due to natural calamities, tribal backwardness and depletion of natural resources.

So, the present study is taken up to analyze the impact of plan exercises on tribal development in Orissa. Few puzzling questions crop up. Where do the tribals stand today? Are they benefited by public action? Are they uprooted? Have they retained their social and cultural identity?

Methodology

The present study is based on both primary data and secondary data. The multi-stage sampling technique was followed in field investigation. Five per cent of villages in three blocks Narayana Patna, Kotpad and Jeypore block (17 villages) were selected for enquiry. For each sample village a list of all households was prepared and 20 per cent of households from each village were selected through systematic Random sampling technique, giving a total of 389 households. The data related to agricultural year 1989. The figures obtained from field studies were tabulated through arithmetic average and they were compared with the corresponding averages of the district in 2001. Secondary data include plan documents of government of Orissa, Economic Survey 2004-05, Government of Orissa, District statistical handbook Koraput 2001, and edited volumes of Dr. S.N. Tripathy. More precision in findings of the study was obtained by using materials from the work "Economic Development of Tribal India 1987" by P.C. Mohapatra.

Section I

Demographic Profile of the Region

Out of 389 households, 66 families (16.96%) comprised general caste population, 229 (58.87%) households have S.T.

background and 94 families (24.16%) hail from S.C. population. The ratio of S.C. and S.T. population taken together was 38.46 per cent in the poverty-ridden economy of Orissa. It follows that, there is a greater concentration of tribal population in Koraput district, compared to the state of Orissa. The percentage of S.C. population to total population of the state has marginally increased by 0.33 per cent over previous census 1991, while S.T. population has decreased by 0.08 per cent in Orissa.

The economically backward district has a total population of 1029577 and its sex ratio is 998.

Urbanization

Koraput region lags behind Orissa in respect of urbanization and the per cent of rural population to total population of the district is 83.19 per cent, below the state average of 85.01 per cent.

Housing Conditions

The world Development Report, 1990 includes lack of income and poverty of assets, in material deprivation. In study areas, merely 25 per cent of households hailing houses from G.C. population have permanent houses. 75 per cent of tribals like Koyas, Kondhas and Saboras live in thatched houses, with meagre ventilation facilities. In India and Orissa 27.58 per cent and 51.80 per cent of population have permanent houses.

There are no drainage facilities, in respect of 75 per cent of households in the backward district, when it is viewed against the backdrop of the state average of 85.11 per cent. Needless to say that latrine facilities are conspicuous by their absence in majority of households of the regions. It seems fair to state that, insanitary housing conditions go a long way in retarding the health and productivity of workers of an area.

Asset Position of People

Household assets, like, radio, T.V., telephone, cycles, scooters and steel utensils were the privilege of nearly 30 per cent of G.C. population. The S.C. and S.T. population possessed assets like pots, bullock carts, brass made utensils wooden plough, plastic glasses and in rare cases owned cycle and radio's.

Use of Electricity

With regard to use of electricity for lighting purpose, the magnitude comes to 22 per cent and 33.11 per cent in Koraput and Orissa regions respectively. What is common is lighting by kerosene.

Educational Status of Tribals

There is agreement that, education enhances the knowledge and skill of workers, the chances to enhances non-form activities and helps rational use of form resources.

The general literacy level of people of study areas is 29.21 per cent and female literacy rate is awefully low i.e. 12.03 per cent. There is no script for their language of Dravidian origin and in the recent past, attempts are made by the state government to encourage tribal literacy by introduction of tribal dialectics in tribal schools and provision of scholarships and Mid-Day Meals Programmes for tribal children.

Plan exercises at state level of have promised a literacy rate of 63.61 in the state and 36.20 per cent in the district. The dark clouds in the silver lining are the lack lustre performance of literacy rates of S.C. (20.18) and S.T. (8.34%) population in the district. In contrast the literacy rates of S.T. population in Orissa is 22.31 per cent and S.C. population is 36.78 per cent (1991). Thus, there is intellectual deprivation of people as manifested in poverty of education and skills and lack of social opportunities and restricted scope of social mobility.

Institutions

In Orissa, merely 15 per cent of households may be categorised as female headed households. As regards marriage, it is universal among people and polygamy is practised by the backward population though monogamy goal is the declared goal.

Tribals believe in Animism deities, magic and celebrate social ceremonies like Chaitra Parva, Holi and the situation remains unchanged today. Drinking liquor has been observed to be an apple in the eyes of tribals, which acts as a growth depressing force on the economy. Regarding the diet of tribals ragi, mango kernel and occasional use of dal are common. Contact with non-tribals has induced them to use vegetable and milk in their consumption baskets.

In respect of clothes the dress of a hills man is of a dal uniformity a scanty lion cloth head clothe and coarse cloth. The Bondas and Koya women wear no garments but a strip of coloured clothes woven from jungle fibre, eight inches wide and two feet long. They wear ear rings and bangles, of late the use of clothes, oil and hairpins are noted among tribals.

Section II

Income Earning Opportunities

There is substance in the statement that, the level of income at a point of time is the sine-qua non of the level of living of a person. The ratio of workers to total population of the district was 64.34 per cent in 1987, which declined to 48.46 per cent in 2001. Dependence on agriculture, wage employment opportunities and collection of Minor Forest Produce provided livelihood for the tribal population till date. Even more tragic, is the increase in the ratio of agriculture labourers to total workers of the district from 27.70 per cent in 1987-88 to 48.46 per cent in 2001.

Contours change are noted in respect of shifting cultivation the magnitude of which has declined in recent years. The average size of landholding was 5.35 acres in 1987 and 1.65 hectares in 1995. Moderate improvement in the extent of irrigation facilities and increase in the cropping intensity of the economy from 129 per cent in 1987-88 to 134 per cent in 2001 are flowers to the garland of plan exercises in Orissa.

The yield rate of rice in Koraput is 15 quintals in 2001, which has picked up from 6 quintals in 1987. The per acre yield of ragi shot up from 3.3 quintals in 1987 to 3.87 quintals in 2001. Area under hyv paddy has gone up from 23 per cent in 1981 to 41 per cent in 2001. The wage rate per a male agricultural labourer has been fixed at Rs. 8 per day and Rs. 6 per day for a female agricultural labourer. The average rate for agricultural field labourers stood at Rs. 33.43 per day for a female worker and Rs. 25.33 for a female worker in 2000-01.

The average income of a person in Koraput district was Rs. 124 per month and 68 per cent were below this income level. The Orissa Development Report, 2002 states that, a vast segment of population in Koraput did not have per capital income of Rs. 500 and hence it is no eighth wonder of the world that 71.40 per cent of population of the district live below poverty line.

Factors like small size of holding, skewed land ownership, extreme drought conditions, employment of traditional tools and equipment's, illiteracy, seasonal nature of agriculture, lack of entrepreneurship and slender irrigation base of the economy have accentuated the problem of rural poverty in the district.

Agriculture is not a remunerative occupation. The net income accrued for cultivation of an acre of land in Koraput district was Rs. 299 in 1977, as per the Koraput survey by Dr. P.C. Mahapatro the net income accrued from cultivation of and acre land stood at Rs. 920 in 1987-88. Analysts argue for guaranteeing minimum prices for agricultural commodities before sowing operations to render agriculture remunerative. Mere fixation of procurement prices by public authorities is not enough. It is necessary to encourage direct purchase of paddy by F.C.I. to avoid manipulation of Prices by millers.

Section III

In social sector, the world development Report, 1990 has laid focussed attention on deprivation of education and limited educational opportunities, deprivation of health and poor access to health services; political deprivation entails a sense of voicelessness and powerlessness and deprivation in active participation to influence political decisions. The following diagram illustrates the point.

Poverty in Orissa

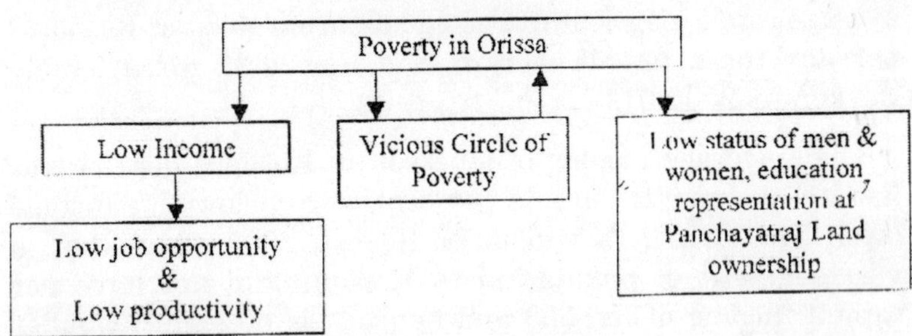

Source: Arundhati Chattopadhaya, Yojana 2006.

There is a general impression that Koraput district has very high percentage of depressed population, low literacy level, poor health facility, poor communication and transportation and poor rural electrification. The palpable deficiency of economic andsocial infrastructure retards earning capacity of workers.

The district has electrified nearly 66.74 per cent of villages. The industrially backward district has 0.54 medical centres per 10000 population and for 100 sq km area there are 0.71 medical centres. By contrast, the state of Orissa has 0.51 medical centres for 100 sq km area. The district has 72.06 km of roads for 10000 population but the road length per 100 sq km is merely 93.061, below the state average 140.41 km. The percentage of irrigation facilities is lamentably low that 29.84 per cent in the resource poor district. The per capita deposit of the present economy has to short up from the present low level of Rs. 2.53 to impressive level. The performance of Koraput in providing bank branches per lakh population is moderate i.e. 6.11. The railway route length per 1000 sq km has area has not yet reached the All Orissa average of 15.03 km.

Conclusion

To conclude "These tribals mostly are simple, truthful and freedom loving, honest and hospitable by nature. Wants and their deprivation do not stand on their way to express such precious values by the tribals living in remote rural area.

In the words of Verrier Elwin "Let us teach them that their own culture, their own arts are the precious things we respect and need. When they feel that they can make a contribution to the country, they will be part of it (integration).

The daunting task of plan exercises in Orissa is to enable tribal people to develop along the lines of their own genius without imposing anything on them, train up and build up a team of their own people to run administration and development, respect tribal rights in forests and lands, avoid over administration of these areas and judge results on the basis of of character of people and not money spent (Eswar Rao Patnaik).

The three fold strategy of education, health and employment has been rightly recognised by planners to raise the status of depressed population in the socio-economic ladder of society. Shifting cultivation may be rationalised by measures, like horticultural lines, terraced cultivation, growth of commercial crops, agro-silvy-culture, and sericulture. There is agreement among scholars that, tribal rights over land and minor forest produce like tamarind, lac, honey and herbs may be respected to dissuade migration of labour (S.N. Tripathy, 2005). The scale of public endeavour may be raised to enforce land alienation Act to prevent transfer of land to non-tribals. Strict enforcement of Minimum wages Act and Equal Remuneration Act, 1976 may enforce workers, entitlement to labour. To strengthen linkages between agriculture and industry, the focus of fruit processing, dairying, khandsari and pampad preparation and may be widened.

Mid-day meals may be introduced in tribals schools with supportive measures like introduction of music, dance, child to child learning and demonstration by tribal teachers.

As wage employment schemes like E.A.S. and J.R.Y. have failed to create more than 16.68 man days of employment for a poor family in a year, plan emphasis may be on transparency, honest and sensitive administration and responsive to tribal needs. In agriculture the lines of action should be on scientific agriculture, irrigation, dryland farming technology, extension work, timely supply of seeds to needy people, shifting cropping pattern from cultivation of food crops to growth of commercial crops like pulses, vegetables, horticulture and sugarcane.

Economic independence of tribal women may be accelerated by encouraging them to form themselves into self-help groups in activities like Palmgur, embroidery and food processing with the help of banks (Prof. Haridash). In health front, people's awareness to health aspects may be heightened by teachers, social workers and doctors by organisation of health camps and provision of sufficient medical personnel in hospitals in tribal areas.

All this calls for sensible administration, sympathetic people and honest officers in charge of implementing various schemes to wipe out tears from every eye.

Legislation is a wonderful thing but in the absence of implementation there is nothing to commend it.

REFERENCES

1. *District Statistical Handbook*, Koraput, 2001.

2. K. Mohanti, P.C. Mohapatra and J. Samal, "Tribes of Koraput" Hindustan Official, Jeypore-2006.

3. S.N. Tripathy, *Woman and Rural Development*, Sonali Publications, New Delhi, 2006.

4. Unpublished Thesis of Dr. B. Eswar Rao Patnaik, *Agricultural Development in Koraput District*, 1992.

5. Economic Survey, Government of Orissa, 2004-05.

6. B. Eswar Rao Patnaik, "Empowerment of Tribal Women in Orissa—A Case Study of Koraput District".

7. S.N. Tripathy, edited volume "Women and Rural Development" 2006.

8. Orissa Development Report-2002.

9. S.N. Tripathy, *Tribals in Transition*, 2006.

10. P.C. Mahapatra, *The Strategy of Tribal Development in India*, Asish Publishing House, New Delhi, 1987.

16

Rural Development through Genetic Engineering

*Miss Sumita Tripathy**
*Mr Dinesh Roshan Sahu***

Needless to mention that genetic engineering is the most dynamic branch of science which properly applied can bring about catalytic change in rural scenario. For rural development we can apply this branch of science for the development of human resources, agricultural development, bio-technology etc. This chapter makes an attempt to explain the concept, history, uses of genetic engineering and its future prospects. Every scientific advancement may not automatically make our life ore meaningful unless we apply it for social development and for the well-being of the society.

Photochemistry of Planetary Atmospheres and the Origins of Life—James P. Ferris

Photochemical reactions, driven by solar UV, are believed to be the principal source of complex molecules observed in most planetary and lunar atmospheres. For example, photochemical transformations of the simple components of

* Associated with Academy of Technocrats, Gajapatinagar, Berhampur, Orissa.

** Associated with Academy of Technocrats, Gajapatinagar, Berhampur, Orissa.

the atmospheres of Jupiter and Titan result in the formation of more complex organic molecules. It is proposed that knowledge of the photochemical routes by which organics are formed in other planetary atmospheres provides insight into photoproducts that were formed in the atmosphere of the primitive Earth.

The photochemical reaction pathways by which these complex organics and polymers are formed on Jupiter and Titan are under investigation. Since solar UV light is believed to have had a profound effect on altering the composition of the atmosphere of the primitive earth, knowledge of the photochemical pathways on Jupiter and Titan will provide important insight into how atmospheric photochemistry may have proceeded on the early earth.

If the atmosphere of the primitive earth contained methane and ammonia, then some of the photochemical reactions there were similar to those on Jupiter. But the methane and ammonia were present only for a short period of time because they are not regenerated as they are on Jupiter and because the solar UV flux was greater on the primitive Earth than on Jupiter. The continued presence of methane on Titan, after 4.5 billion years irradiation by solar UV, suggests that it is being slowly released from Titan's crust into its atmosphere. Methane may have also been slowly released into the primitive Earth's atmosphere so it may have been present there for a somewhat longer time than predicted by atmospheric modeling experiments.

Understanding Gene

Genes are composed of DNA and are located within the chromosomes. Each genes contains information coded in the form a specific sequence of porine and pyridine nucleotides within its DNA molecules. The unit of genetic information called coden, is a group of three adjacent nucleotides that specific a single amino and in a polypeptide chain. Thus the genetic code is a triplet code. Each code of gene signals a particular amino acis to be incorporated into a specific protein which contains a specific function in the body.

Chromosomes are the carriers of hereditary characters (traits) in all organism. In other word chromosomes are the carriers of genes. The term 'gene' was proposed by Johannsen in 1909. According to him, Gene is a unit of function, unit of mutation and unit of recombination. In other words gene is an independent hereditary unit that can control a function resulting into phenotic appearance of the concerned character trait. This concept was based on the assumption that a gene is just a locus on the chromosomes having no distinct shape on size.

DNA

Any discussion of genetics makes reference to DNA (deoxyribonucleic acid), a molecule that contains genetic codes for inheritance. DNA resides in chromosomes, threadlike structures found in the nucleus, or control center, of every cell in every living thing. Chromosomes themselves are made up of genes, which carry codes for the production of proteins. The latter, of which there are many thousands of different varieties, make up the majority of the human body's dry weight.

The double helix of DNA has these features:

- It contains two polynucleotide strands wound around each other.
- The backbone of each consists of alternating *deoxyribose* and *phosphate groups.*
- The phosphate group bonded to the 5' carbon atom of one deoxyribose is covalently bonded to the 3' carbon of the next.
- The two strands are "antiparallel"; that is, one strand runs 5' to 3' while the other runs 3' to 5'.
- The DNA strands are assembled in the 5' to 3' direction and, by convention, we "read" them the same way.
- The purine or *pyrimidine* attached to each deoxyribose projects in toward the axis of the helix.

- Each base forms *hydrogen bonds* with the one directly opposite it, forming *base pairs* (also called nucleotide pairs).

Discussion of Base Pairing in DNA

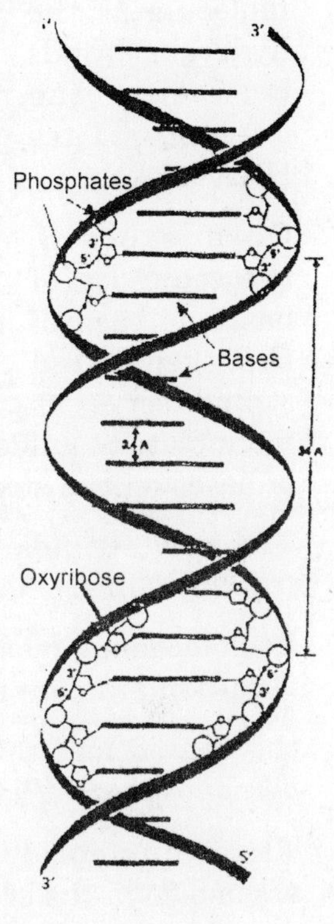

- 3.4 Å separate the planes in which adjacent base pairs are located.
- The double helix makes a complete turn in just over 10 nucleotide pairs, so each turn takes a little more (35.7 Å to be exact) than the 34 Å shown in the diagram.
- There is an average of 25 hydrogen bonds within each complete turn of the double helix providing a stability of binding about as strong as what a *covalent bond* would provide.
- The diametre of the helix is 20 Å.
- The helix can be virtually any length; when fully stretched, some DNA molecules are as much as 5 cm (2 inches!) long.
- The path taken by the two backbones forms a major (wider) groove (from "34 A" to the top of the arrow) and a minor (narrower) groove (the one below).

DNA Replication

Before a cell can divide, it must duplicate all its DNA. In eukaryotes, this occurs during S phase of the *cell cycle.*

The Biochemical Reactions

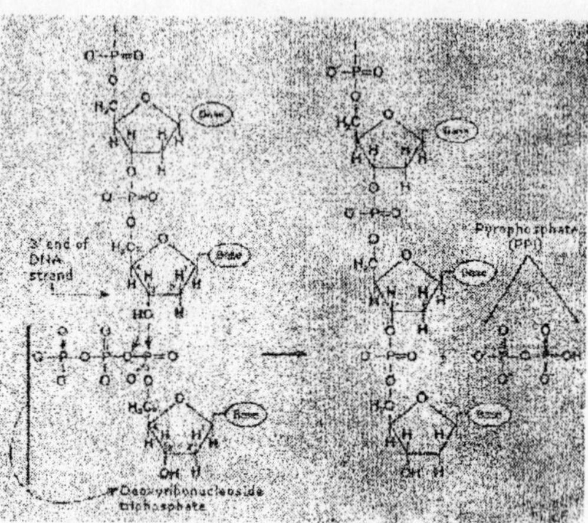

- DNA replication begins with the "unzipping" of the parent molecule as the hydrogen bonds between the *base pairs* are DNA broken.
- Once exposed, the sequence of bases on each of the separated strands serves as a template to guide the insertion of a complementary set of bases on the strand being synthesized.
- The new strands are assembled from *deoxynucleoside triphosphates.*
- Each incoming nucleotide is covalently linked to the "free" 3' carbon atom on the pentose (figure) as
- the second and third phosphates are removed together *pyrophosphate (PPi).*

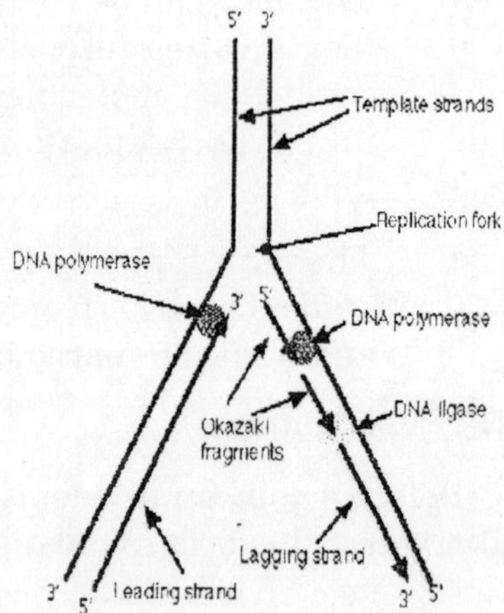

- The nucleotides are assembled in the order that complements the order of bases on the strand serving as the template.
- Thus each C on the template guides the insertion of a G on the new strand, each G a C, and so on.
- When the process is complete, two DNA

molecules have been formed identical to each other and to the parent molecule.

The Enzymes

- A portion of the double helix is unwound by a *helicase.*
- A molecule of a *DNA polymerase* binds to one strand of the DNA and begins moving along it in the 3' to 5' direction, using it as a template for assembling a *leading strand* of nucleotides and reforming a double helix. In eukaryotes, this molecule is called DNA polymerase delta (δ).
- Because DNA synthesis can only occur 5' to 3', a molecule of a second type of DNA polymerase (epsilon, ε, in eukaryotes) binds to the other template strand as the double helix opens. This molecule must synthesize discontinuous segments of polynucleotides (called Okazaki fragments). Another enzyme, *DNA ligase I* then stitches these together into the lagging strand.

Recombinant DNA Technology

Making Recombinant DNA (rDNA): An Overview

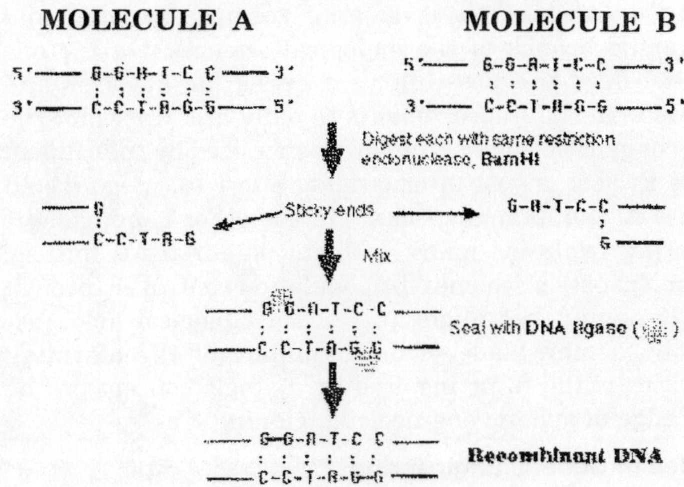

- Treat DNA from both sources with the same *restriction endonuclease* (BamHI in this case).

- BamHI cuts the same site on both molecules

  5' GGATCC 3'

  3' CCTAGG 5'
- The ends of the cut have an overhanging piece of single-stranded DNA.
- These are called "sticky ends" because they are able to base pair with any DNA molecule containing the complementary sticky end.
- In this case, both DNA preparations have complementary sticky ends and thus can pair with each other when mixed.
- DNA ligase covalently links the two into a molecule of *recombinant DNA.*

Genetic Engineering

Genetic engineering is the alteration of genetic material by direct intervention in genetic processes with the purpose of producing new substances or improving functions of existing organisms. It is a very young, exciting, and controversial branch of the biological sciences. On the one hand, it offers the possibility of cures for diseases and countless material improvements to daily life. Hopes for the benefits of genetic engineering are symbolized by the Human Genome Project, a vast international effort to categorize all the genes in the human species. On the other hand, genetic engineering frightens many with its potential for misuse, either in Nazi-style schemes for population control or through simple bungling that might produce a biological holocaust caused by a man-made virus. Symbolic of the alarming possibilities is the furor inspired by a single concept on the cutting edge of genetic engineering: cloning.

Principles of Genetic Engineering

Just as DNA is at the core of studies in genetics, recombinant DNA (rDNA)—that is, DNA that has been genetically altered through a process known as *gene splicing*—is the focal point of genetic engineering. In gene splicing, a DNA strand is cut in half lengthwise and joined with a strand from another organism or perhaps even another species. Use of gene splicing makes possible two other highly significant techniques. Gene transfer, or incorporation of new DNA into an organism's cells, usually is carried out with the help of a microorganism that serves as a vector, or carrier. Gene therapy is the introduction of normal or genetically altered genes to cells, generally to replace defective genes involved in genetic disorders.

DNA also can be cut into shorter fragments through the use of restriction enzymes. (An enzyme is a type of protein that speeds up chemical reactions.) The ends of these fragments have an affinity for complementary ends on other DNA fragments and will seek those out in the target DNA. By looking at the size of the fragment created by a restriction enzyme, investigators can determine whether the gene has the proper genetic code. This technique has been used to analyze genetic structures in fetal cells and to diagnose certain blood disorders, such as sickle cell anemia.

If you remove the two restriction enzymes and provide the conditions for *DNA ligase* to do its work, the pieces of these plasmids can rejoin (thanks to the complementarity of their sticky ends).

Mixing the pKAN and pAMP fragments provides several (at least 10) possibilities of rejoined molecules. Some of these will not produce functional plasmids (molecules with two or with no replication origin cannot function).

One interesting possibility is the joining of

- the 3755-bp pAMP fragment (with *amp*^{r} and a replication origin) with the
- 1875-bp pKAN fragment (with *kan*^{r})

Sealed with *DNA ligase,* these molecules are functioning plasmids that are capable of conferring resistance to *both* ampicillin and kanamycin. They are molecules of *recombinant DNA*.

Because the replication origin, which enables the molecule to function as a plasmid, was contributed by pAMP, pAMP is called the *vector*.

Gene Transfer

Suppose that a particular base-pair sequence carries the instruction "make insulin"; if a way could be found to insert that base sequence into the DNA of bacteria, for example, those bacteria would be capable of manufacturing insulin. This, in turn, would greatly improve the lives of people with type 1 diabetes, who depend on insulin shots to aid their bodies in processing blood sugar. (See Non-infectious Diseases for more about diabetes.)

Although the concept of gene transfer is relatively simple, its execution presents considerable technical obstacles. The first person to surmount these obstacles was the American biochemist Paul Berg (1926-), often referred to as the "father of genetic engineering." In 1973 Berg developed a method for joining the DNA from two different organisms, a monkey virus known as *SV40* and a virus called *lambda phage*. Although the accomplishment was clearly a breakthrough, Berg's method was difficult. Then, later that year, the American biochemists Stanley Cohen (1922-) at Stanford University, and Herbert Boyer (1936-) at the University of California at San Francisco discovered an enzyme that greatly increased the efficiency of the Berg procedure. The gene-transfer technique developed by Berg, Boyer, and Cohen formed the basis for much of the ensuing progress in genetic engineering.

Real-Life Applications

Big Business in DNA

Ever since the breakthrough discoveries of Watson, Crick, and others in the 1950s made genetic engineering a possibility, the new field has promised increasingly bigger payoffs. These payoffs take the form of improvements to human life and profits to those who facilitate those improvements. The possible applications of genetic engineering are virtually limitless—as are the profits to be made from genetic engineering as a business. As early as the 1970s, entrepreneurs (independent business people) recognized the commercial potential of genetically engineered products, which promised to revolutionize life, technology, and commerce as computers also were doing. Thus was born one of the great buzzwords of the late twentieth century: biotechnology, or the use of genetic engineering for commercial purposes.

Medicines and Cures

The use of rDNA allows scientists to produce many products that were previously available only in limited quantities: for example, insulin, which we referred to earlier. Until the 1980s the only source of insulin for people with diabetes came from animals slaughtered for meat and other purposes. The supply was never high enough to meet demand, and this drove up prices. Then, in 1982, the U.S. Food and Drug Administration (FDA) approved the sale of insulin produced by genetically altered organisms—the first such product to become available. Since 1982 several additional products, such as human growth hormone, have been made with rDNA techniques.

One of the most exciting potential applications of genetic engineering is the treatment of genetic disorders, which are discussed in Heredity, through the use of gene therapy. Among the more than 3,000 such disorders, quite a few of which are quite serious or even fatal, many are the result of relatively minor errors in DNA sequencing. Genetic engineering offers the potential to provide individuals with correct copies of a gene, which could make possible a cure for that condition. In the 1980s scientists began clinical trials of a procedure known as *human gene therapy* to replace defective genes. The technique, still very much in the developmental stage, offers the hope of cures for diseases that medicine has long been powerless to combat.

In 2001 scientists at the Weizmann Institute in Israel brought together two of the most exciting fields of research, biotechnology and computers, to produce the DNA-processing nanocomputer. It is an actual computer, but it is so small that a trillion of them would fit in a test tube. It consists of DNA and DNA-processing enzymes, both dissolved in liquid; thus its input, output, and software are all in the form of DNA molecules. The purpose of the nanocomputer is to analyze DNA, detecting abnormalities in the human body and creating remedies for them.

The Human Genome Project

At the center of genetic studies, with vast potential applications to genetic engineering, is the Human Genome Project (HGP), an international effort to analyze and map the DNA of humans and several other organisms. As discussed in the essay Genetics, the HGP began with efforts by the Atomic Energy Commission, a predecessor to the U.S. Department of Energy, to study the genetic effects of radioactive nuclear fallout. In 1990 the Department of Energy in cooperation with the National Institutes of Health (NIH), launched the project. At about the same time, the governments of the United Kingdom, Japan, Russia, France, and Italy initiated their own, similar undertakings, which are coordinated with American efforts.

The purpose of the project is to locate each human gene and determine its specific structure and function. Such knowledge will provide the framework for studies in health, disease, biology, and medicine during the twenty-first century and no doubt will make possible the cures for countless diseases.

Cloning

A clone is a cell, group of cells, or organism that contains genetic information identical to that of the parent cell or organism. It is a form of asexual reproduction (see Reproduction), and as such it is not as new as it seems; what is new, however, is humans' ability to manipulate cloning at the genetic level. The first clones produced by humans as long as 2,000 years ago were plants developed from grafts and stem cuttings. By cloning—a process that calls into play complex laboratory techniques and the use of DNA replication—people usually mean a relatively recent scientific advance. Among these techniques is the ability to isolate and copy (that is, to clone) individual genes that direct an organism's development.

The cloning of specific genes can provide large numbers of copies of that gene for use in genetic and taxonomic research as well as in the practical areas of medicine and farming. In the latter field, the goal is to clone plants with specific traits that make them superior to naturally occurring organisms. For example, in 1985 scientists conducted field tests using clones of plants whose genes had been altered in the laboratory to generate resistance to insects, viruses, and bacteria. New strains of plants resulting from cloning could produce crops that can grow in poor soil or even underwater and fruits and vegetables with improved nutritional qualities and longer shelf lives. A cloning technique known as twinning could induce livestock to give birth to twins or even triplets, and on the environmental front cloning might help save endangered species from extinction.

In the realm of medicine and health, cloning has been used to make vaccines and hormones. It has become possible, by combining two different kinds of cells (such as mouse and human cancer cells), to produce large quantities of specific antibodies, via the immune system, to fight off disease. When injected into the bloodstream, these cloned antibodies seek out and attack disease-causing cells anywhere in the body. By attaching a tracer element to the cloned antibodies, scientists can locate hidden cancers, and by attaching specific cancer-fighting drugs, the treatment dose can be transported directly to the cancer cells.

Experiments in Cloning

The first successful cloning of mammals occurred nearly

20 years later, when scientists in Switzerland and the United States successfully cloned mice using a method similar to Gurdon's approach. Their method required one extra step, however: after taking the nuclei from the embryos of one type of mouse, they transferred them into the embryos of another type of mouse. The latter served as a surrogate, or replacement, mother. The cloning of cattle livestock was tried first in 1988, when embryos from prize cows were transplanted to unfertilized cow eggs whose own nuclei had been removed. An even greater breakthrough transpired on February 24, 1997, with the birth of a lamb named Dolly in Edinburgh, Scotland. Dolly was no ordinary sheep: she was the first mammal born from the cloning of an adult cell. Thus, she had been produced by asexual reproduction in the form of genetically engineered cloning rather than by anything resembling a normal process. Nonetheless, she proved her own ability to reproduce the old-fashioned way when, on April 23, 1998, she gave birth to a daughter named Bonnie.

Though Dolly's and Bonnie's births excited hopes, they also inspired fears. If large mammals could be cloned, could humans? As early as 1993 an attempt had been made at cloning human embryos as part of studies on in vitro (out of the body) fertilization. The purpose was to develop fertilized eggs in test tubes and then to implant them into the wombs of women having difficulty becoming pregnant. These fertilized eggs, however, did not develop to a stage that was suitable for transplantation into a human uterus. Then, on October 13, 2001, scientists at Advanced Cell Technology in Worcester, Massachusetts, successfully cloned a human embryo. They had not created human life, as it might sound; what they had developed instead was a source for nerve and other tissues that could be harvested for use in medicine and research. Still, the news—overshadowed though it was in America, where people were still reeling from the September 11 terrorist attacks—was earth-shattering. Human cells had been reproduced, and once again it appeared that the production of human clones might be possible.

It is easy to understand how people might respond with alarm to such frightening news with alarm. Such fears have a great deal more to do with Hollywood than they do with science. In fact, the accomplishment of the Massachusetts firm, while impressive from a scientific standpoint, was fairly modest compared with the Frankenstein-like image presented by antigenetic engineering scaremongers. "Cloned an embryo" actually sounds a great deal more dramatic than what the Massachusetts scientists achieved, with just one embryo reaching the size of six cells before the cells stopped dividing. This is hardly the beginnings of a clone army.

Consequences of Genetic Engineering

What will it be like in a future world it where your life started with your parents designing your genes? In addition to screening for unwanted genetic diseases, they select for sex, height, eye-, hair-, and skin-colour. Pressured by the current social fads, they may also choose genes whose overall functions are not clearly understood but are rumored to be connected with temperament, intelligence, mindfulness, and perhaps sexual orientation. You may be genetically engineered to be an enhanced clone of one of your parents, or of a celebrity whose genetic heritage your parents have purchased at great price.

It will not be inappropriate to mention here about an early warning signaled as early as in 1976 when Prof. George Wald, nobel prize winner biologist remarked:

Recombinant DNA technology [genetic engineering] faces our society with problems unprecedented not only in the history of science, but of life on earth. It places in human hands the capacity to redesign living organisms, the products of some three billion years of evolution.... It presents probably the largest ethical problem that science has ever had to face. Our morality up to now has been to go ahead without restriction to learn all that we can about nature. Restructuring nature was not part of the bargain.... For going ahead in this direction may be not only unwise but dangerous.

Potentially, it could breed new animal and plant diseases, new sources of cancer, novel epidemics.

Conclusion

In conclusion we can note that for all the advantages claimed for genetic engineering, in the overwhelming number of cases the price seems too high to pay. In order to ensure megaprofits for multinational corporations well into the next century, we will have to mortgage the biosphere, seriously compromise life on the planet, and even risk losing what it means to be a human being. Genetic engineering poses serious risks to human health and to the environment. It raises serious ethical questions about the right of human beings to alter life on the planet for the benefit and curiosity of a few.

Index

❑❑❑